Analecta Biographica

Analecta Biographica

A HANDFUL OF
NEW ENGLAND
PORTRAITS

by

Walter Muir Whitehill

THE STEPHEN GREENE PRESS

BRATTLEBORO, VERMONT

79-605

TO
JAMES
MADISON
BARKER

CONTENTS

INTRODUCTION

LAST WINTER when Stephen Greene suggested that he would like a book of mine on his list, I recited a doleful litany of books that I already owed other presses. But since an alert publisher seldom takes No for an answer, he asked whether there were not some scattered writings of mine that might warrant reprinting. When I took stock of the past thirty years, I realized that I had indeed often written about good friends, living and dead, and that these unrelated sketches constituted a kind of personal New England portrait gallery. As James Madison Barker of Chicago, long an appreciative reader of any ephemera I have sent him, had several times urged me to make a collection of some of these memoirs, Stephen Greene's interest provided an admirable opportunity to carry out this suggestion.

Although Mr. Barker, born in Pittsfield, Massachusetts, eighty-two years ago, has been away from the region for nearly half a century, he retains a keen interest in New England and its people. A member of the Massachusetts Institute of Technology class of 1907, he taught structural engineering there from 1914 until 1919, when he joined the First National Bank of Boston. In 1920 he went to Buenos Aires to establish an Argentine branch of that bank. During the eight years in which he was in charge of the "Banco de Boston," its handsome building at the intersection of the Calle Florida and the Avenida Roque Saenz Peña was completed. Having joined Sears, Roebuck and Company in 1928 as regional manager in Philadelphia, he soon moved on to Chicago, where he became vice-president and treasurer of that firm. At the age when most men are retiring from business, he took on still another active career at the head of the Allstate Insurance Company.

A mutual interest in Elizabethan voyages brought us together, for he was a member of the Hakluyt Society, of which I have been for some years honorary secretary for the United States. After an exchange of letters, Jim Barker one day asked me to breakfast with him at the Ritz during a hurried visit he was making to Boston for a meeting of the M.I.T. Corporation. We have been good friends ever since. Few men that I have known have as wide-ranging interests, sound judgment, or inquiring mind as he, or more perceptive literary taste. His enthusiasm for these scattered memoirs having made me think them worth reprinting, I happily take the opportunity to dedicate the collection to him.

Because the sketches were written for various purposes, their length and their styles are by no means uniform. The only common element is that all the subjects were New Englanders or had early or late in life migrated to the region. Not all of them knew each other, but I knew them all, although with varying degrees of time and intimacy; admired them, and greatly enjoyed their company. Several of them were decisively responsible for the shaping of my life, tastes, and professional career. To link the eighteen sketches together, I have provided introductory notes explaining the circumstances of my association with the subject, where it is not self-evident in the text.

As all but two of my subjects were born in the nineteenth century, between the Presidencies of James Buchanan and Benjamin Harrison, only five are still living. Twelve professions are represented, for there are three Harvard professors (A. Kingsley Porter, Samuel Eliot Morison, and John Otis Brew); three lawyers (William Crowninshield Endicott, Roger Wolcott, and Willard Goodrich Cogswell); three practitioners of the graphic arts (Fred Anthoensen, Rudolph Ruzicka, and Rosamond Bowditch Loring); a Boston trustee (Augustus Peabody Loring, Jr.); a Boston banker (Allan Forbes); a Boston bookseller (Charles Eliot Goodspeed); a Boston restaurant keeper (Jacob Wirth); an historical editor (L. H. Butterfield); a librarian (George Parker Winship); a journalist (Lincoln Colcord); an admiral (Ernest J. King); and a great lady (Louise du Pont Crowninshield).

Although Admiral King is the only regular naval officer in the group, S. E. Morison, after a lifetime of cruising, achieved the rank of Rear Admiral in the United States Naval Reserve. Lincoln Colcord was born off Cape Horn in a Maine ship commanded by his father. Gus and Rose Loring and Louise Crowninshield were experienced cruising people, while Jacob Wirth was one of that resolute group who, being over-age for the Navy in World War II, in order to get to sea became boatswain's mates in the Coast Guard. So seven of my eighteen had more than respectable competence at sea.

There are eleven members of the Massachusetts Historical Society in the group: Winship, Endicott, A. P. Loring, Cogswell, Goodspeed, Forbes, Wolcott, Ruzicka, Butterfield, Brew, and Morison, and four trustees of the Peabody Museum of Salem—Endicott, both Lorings, and Mrs. Crowninshield. But the greatest similarities occur in the matter of collecting. Nine of the subjects had been members of the Club of Odd Volumes, for which collecting is a *sine qua non* of admission—Winship, A. P. Loring, Cogswell, Goodspeed, Anthoensen, Ruzicka, Butterfield, Brew, and Morison—while a tenth, Rose Loring, was the club's assistant librarian. Kingsley Porter collected early Italian paintings and furniture; William C. Endicott, almost everything that bore on the past of the Endicott and Peabody families; Louise du Pont Crowninshield, superlative examples of furniture and the decorative arts; Allan Forbes, whaling prints, furniture, and the Lord knows what not. Indeed the only complete noncollector of the group was Admiral King, who, it might be noted, had the slightest tie with New England of the eighteen.

Twelve of my subjects were born in New England—indeed thirteen, if one can consider the cabin of a Maine ship off Cape Horn as a wandering fragment of New England. Louise du Pont was born in Delaware but became a Bostonian by her marriage to Francis Boardman Crowninshield. Lyman Butterfield first saw the light in New York State, but came to Harvard College and for fourteen years has been settled at the Massachusetts Historical Society. Fred Anthoensen, although a Dane by birth, has been a resident of Maine for more than eighty years, while Rudolph Ruzicka, although born in Bohemia, has lived in New England for two decades. Admiral King only summered at the United States Naval Hospital, Portsmouth, New Hampshire, for the last eight years of his life, but as he often visited us in North Andover and as I was constantly working with him I regard him as a kind of honorary New Englander. Moreover, it was his admiration for Admiral Henry T. Mayo that first brought us into the northern Vermont valley where we have for thirteen years owned the house in which the greater part of this book was prepared.

The title of the collection I owe to the joint efforts of my friends David McCord and John Petersen Elder. It is an accurate description, for these random biographical sketches are indeed *analecta*—things gathered or picked up, scraps, crumbs, gleanings.

WALTER MUIR WHITEHILL

Starksboro, Vermont
North Andover, Massachusetts
June 1968

CHAPTER I

George Parker Winship

1871 – 1952

AS I WAS BORN in Cambridge on 28 September 1905, almost within sound of the Harvard Hall bell, two years and a quarter after my father had been graduated from Harvard College, my parents and I took it for granted that I would in due course follow in his steps. In those simpler and less competitive days one applied for admission, and if one appeared on registration day clean and sober, having passed entrance examinations, one was amiably welcomed as a member of the freshman class without further ado. So in September 1922, a few days before my seventeenth birthday, I found myself a member of Harvard College.

Having already haunted the Boston Public Library and the bookshops of Cornhill during my school days, I headed as rapidly as possible for the Widener Memorial Library—then new, resplendent and uncrowded, with room for everyone in the University to use books under ideal conditions. In the Widener Room I encountered George Parker Winship, with momentous consequences not only for my personal enthusiasm but for my career. Through him I entered the world of printers, calligraphers, printmakers, collectors, and bibliographers, where I have had many valued friends. What is more important, through one of Winship's seemingly casual inspirations, I came to know Professor A. Kingsley Porter, who led me into the Spanish Middle Ages, where I spent the first decade following my graduation from Harvard in 1926.

Analecta Biographica

The memoir that follows was written for the Massachusetts Historical Society—one of the learned bodies that I first heard of through Winship—and was published in their Proceedings, LXXI *(1953–57) 366–375. The photograph of Winship at his desk shows the Widener Room as I first knew it in the early Twenties. I am grateful to his daughter, Mrs. Ann Winship Davis of Concord, Massachusetts, for lending me this picture.*

GPW

GEORGE PARKER WINSHIP was born in Bridgewater, Massachusetts, on 29 July 1871. He went from the Somerville High School to Harvard College, where he received an A.B. *cum laude* in 1893 and an A.M. in 1894. After two years as an assistant in history at Harvard, he went to Providence in 1895 as librarian of the great private collection of Americana formed by John Carter Brown, which was then owned by his widow. In 1898 Mrs. Brown gave the library to her son, John Nicholas Brown, who immediately made plans for its safekeeping and use by scholars as a public trust. Although the new owner died before his generous intentions could be carried out, he left the books, with an endowment, to trustees who in 1901 gave them to Brown University. In accordance with John Nicholas Brown's instructions, his father's collection was to be housed in a separate building with its own staff, and administered by a committee of management appointed by the Corporation of Brown University. Thus the John Carter Brown Library, as a semiautonomous institution under the wing of the university, was opened for scholarly use on 17 May 1904. Thus also George Winship, who had gone to Providence as a private librarian, was drawn into the Brown faculty.

Working in one of the great collections of Americana, Winship was early fascinated by the literature of discovery and exploration. *The Coronado Expedition*, which he published in 1896 in the fourteenth annual report of the United States Bureau of Ethnology, and his *Cabot Bibliography*, which appeared in 1900, established his reputation as a working bibliographer in the field. Soon after his election to the American Antiquarian Society at the precocious age of twenty-eight, he read a paper there on "Some Facts about John and Sebastian Cabot." His appreciation of the contents and of the beauty of language of some of the books committed to his care was shown in his edition of *Sailors' Narratives of Voyages along the New England Coast, 1524–1624*, published in 1905 by Houghton Mifflin Company. Four hundred and forty copies, handsomely set in large Caslon type, were printed from a design by Bruce Rogers, who was then at the height of his career at the Riverside Press.

Winship's interest in contemporary fine printing was to some extent connected with the Club of Odd Volumes in Boston, of which he became a nonresident member in 1898. This little knot of bibliophiles and collectors, founded in 1887, was still an itinerant dining club without premises of its own. Its earliest publications had been expensive rather than discriminating: witness two pretentious volumes of Imbert de Saint-Amand concerning the mistresses of Louis XV, rather stupidly printed by the University Press, Cambridge, but with luxurious color plates done by Goupil in Paris. The paper that Winship read at the club in 1900 on the five-hundredth anniversary of Chaucer's death was converted, with equal lack of inspiration, by the University Press into a little book chiefly distinguished as to form by the excellence of its handmade paper and the limited size of its edition.

Within a very few years someone in the club—and I strongly suspect it was Winship—woke up to the fact that, with Bruce Rogers at the Riverside Press and D. B. Updike at the Merrymount Press producing some of the handsomest books of the day, the club had an opportunity and an obligation to place itself in the advance guard of the revival of fine typography. Thus in 1906 Mr. Updike printed for the club the *Historie of The Life and Death of Sir William Kirkaldie of Grange, Knight* and the next year Bruce Rogers designed the publication of Percival Merritt's *Horace Walpole, Printer*. Once embarked on this experiment of using the best available designers and printers, the club even crossed the Atlantic. Winship's paper *William Caxton*, read at the January 1908 meeting, was superbly printed the following year in London by T. J. Cobden-Sanderson at the Doves Press.

Although George Winship remained in Providence for twenty years, he was intimately involved in things that were going on in Boston. In 1899 he was elected a corresponding member of the Colonial Society of Massachusetts, and in 1905 to the same status in the Massachusetts Historical Society. From 1904 to 1915 his name appeared in the Harvard catalogue in the honorary capacity of Curator of Mexican History in the Harvard College Library. Of his two decades in the John Carter Brown Library, his successor, Lawrence C. Wroth, has observed that Winship's "bold and intelligent collecting had more than doubled the size of the library and had added to its resources a considerable number of books and maps of the highest individual importance." He wrote a history of the library, a great number of articles, and edited an extraordinary variety of early documents.

Partly because of these widely scattered enterprises, and partly because he had the temperament of an intellectual gadfly, Winship never became a second Justin Winsor, as his earliest work might have suggested. Some unkind observers of methodical temperament might have been inclined to call him lazy, although he was usually buzzing about in a variety of directions. He viewed the constituted order of New England with a curious mixture of veneration and disrespect; although his manner verged on the obsequious under certain circumstances, he had a sharp and whimsical wit that he could turn in any direction. As C. K. Shipton observed: "He was never happier than when reprinting some account of isolated ancestral misbehavior in such a way as to cloud the reputation of a whole generation." Paradoxes enchanted him; so did succulent bits of gossip, old and new. They filled his conversation and often crept into his writing, as in the Foreword to *An Odd Lot of New England Puritan Personalities*, where he wrote:

"Some of the statements made or implied on the following pages cannot be substantiated by documentary evidence because it never occurred to anybody to write anything about them. They were matters of very commonplace ordinary human experience which were general knowledge in the community, circulating as daily gossip. . . . The truth regarding them cannot be proven, and it might be even harder to prove that they do not state correctly what actually took place. The only people who really knew, whose

accounts of the events might have been contradictory, are no longer living. . . . A few of the statements, on the other hand, are authenticated by documents that are supported by sworn depositions that have been preserved in the archives of the criminal court of Middlesex County in the State of

Massachusetts. Some of these sworn statements are demonstrably untrue."

It can be seen from this passage that Winship was a lively and unpredictable adversary in a serious argument.

When Mrs. George D. Widener of Philadelphia offered Harvard University an immense library to replace the long outgrown Gore Hall, in memory of her son, Harry Elkins Widener (A.B. 1907), provision was made for the handsome accommodation of Harry Widener's own library. In the short years preceding his death in the *Titanic*, he had given himself with fervor to collecting. When the new library was opened in 1915, Harry Widener's collection was behind tall glass doors in a high-ceilinged room entered from the landing halfway up the monumental staircase.

Luther S. Livingston, a New York bookseller-bibliographer-horticulturist who had been Harry Widener's mentor in collecting, had been asked by Mrs. Widener to become librarian of the Harry Elkins Widener Collection when it was installed in its new home. The Harvard Corporation appointed him to that post on 30 November 1914, but he died within the month before taking up his duties. George Winship was then induced to leave Providence and become librarian of the Widener Collection, with Mrs. Livingston as his assistant. Thus after twenty years he was back at Harvard, with an additional faculty appointment as Lecturer on the History of Printing.

So far as obligations were concerned, the Widener Collection librarianship was a dignified sinecure. The shelves were filled; nothing was to be added; a guard did the dusting, and Mrs. Livingston did what small amount of work there was. A man of another temperament might have used it as the means of completing some major historical or bibliographical enterprise. Winship's solution of what he described in his twenty-fifth anniversary class report as "the interesting problem of making a somewhat ornamental fifth wheel carry its share of the load in an institution which is not accustomed to such luxuries" was different. He outlined his theory in the following terms: "The Harvard Library has been, in the opinion of many who use it, the best students' library in the world. It is also a very great collection of rare and valuable books, which have never had the care and attention that they deserve. If this can now be given to them, and an increasing number of owners of precious volumes realize that their treasures will be appreciated, intelligently preserved for the delight of future book-lovers, and made available under proper restrictions and oversight for the use of investigators, the Harvard Library can confidently anticipate rivaling some day even the Bodleian at Oxford. Laying the foundations for such a future is what my present job calls for."

The Harvard College Library, like the Boston Athenæum, had during the nineteenth century acquired books for their scholarly content and usefulness, without any particular regard for bibliographical rarity, association interest, or the whims that entrance private collectors. The extraordinary additions to its resources made after Professor Archibald Cary Coolidge became director of the University Library in 1910 were similarly designed to help the faculty's research. The architects who planned the Widener Library provided on the main floor a modest Treasure Room for exhibition purposes that, it was hoped, would also accommodate the books that had been segregated in Gore Hall because of their rarity. Since this provision proved inadequate from the beginning, a door was cut through to the adjoining stack, a few bays of which were enclosed with wire grilles for the Treasure Room overflow. When I first saw this Treasure Room in 1922 it was presided over by a Miss Moulton, who used in her lunch hours to go home to bathe her canary. It was a place where one went rather unwillingly to consult specific books whose call numbers one had found in the catalogue, in contrast to the Widener Room which George Winship made a welcoming center for members of the university who cared for fine books in a broader sense.

Winship gave much thought to means of attracting his fellow members of the Club of Odd Volumes and other private collectors to the Harvard library, and of securing their continued interest in its growth and welfare. In the pages of *Harvard Library Notes*, an unofficial occasional publication that first appeared in June 1920, one sees numerous instances of the attempt to convey the idea that the library welcomed the collaboration of private collectors. In the June 1921 issue, for example, is reported the gift by Dr. William Norton Bullard '75, of "71 volumes to the Library's store of 'collector's books,' which will be cared for in the Treasure Room with a proper regard for the condition in which each volume has been preserved by its previous owners." This unsigned article, which is fairly clearly Winship's work, notes that among the Dickens and Thackeray first editions in parts are some titles already in the library, "but the Bullard copies contain 'points,' dear to the book collector's heart, which the others lacked." The February 1923 issue contains a piece on "Specimens of Typography" which indicates the "increasing realization that certain books were more important for what they are, than for what they contain."

While George Winship was always anxious to attract collectors from outside the university, he was perhaps even more interested in proselytizing from within, for he was keenly aware that the undergraduate body included many actual and potential lovers of books. My own life and career were so extraordinarily shaped through the chance accident of knowing him that I owe his memory a sincere tribute to his quite uncanny genius for reading the mind of youth and tossing out offhand suggestions that proved of lasting influence and value.

I met him sometime during my freshman year, 1922–1923, through having entered the Widener Room out of casual curiosity. The marble-domed anteroom, whose great niches still after four decades cry out for baroque sculpture, is a somewhat forbidding approach, but the cheerful log fire that could be seen blazing under Harry Widener's portrait emboldened me to cross it and penetrate the inner library. There, installed on the left behind a vast desk whose recesses contained the makings of tea, was Winship, while on the right Mrs. Livingston industriously typed away at a long table.

To my freshman's eyes he was a curious figure—a little man with a billy-goat beard and piercing, roving eyes behind rimless spectacles. He was dressed in tweeds that were reminiscent of his Charles River farm, and would move disconcertingly about the room at lightning speed on unexplained errands. The exhibition cases under the four windows gave me a convenient excuse for lingering to appraise the scene. In the course of my examination, I noted with delight on the steps of a movable platform ladder a great pile of current English booksellers' catalogues. As soon as he observed the effect of this discovery upon me, George Winship engaged me in conversation and explained that this treasure trove was there for the benefit of anyone who might care to use it. Thus I fell into the way of returning to the Widener Room to explore the latest catalogues. On all these visits Winship and Mrs. Livingston made me welcome, passing along hints about dealers, prices, and much else that was invaluable to an inexperienced undergraduate who had to stretch his pennies to the utmost.

A collected Oxford edition had given me an enthusiasm for the poems of Robert Bridges; through George Winship I found the means of assembling a considerable number of that poet's works, including some of those privately printed by the Daniel Press at Oxford. Thus when Bridges came to Harvard in June 1924 to receive an honorary degree, Winship asked me to install my belongings in the four cases in the Widener Room. These were duly shown off by Mr. Lowell during a tour of the library, with the result that I was summoned to 17 Quincy Street to meet the Poet Laureate. Bridges had little patience with collectors as such. As he and I walked back and forth along the sidewalk opposite the president's house, he lectured me severely on the foolishness of wasting my money on bibliographical trivialities before asking me what particular titles I lacked. In consequence of this encounter, Bridges subsequently sent me copy Number 1 of the large paper edition of the *Yattendon Hymnal* in parts, as well as several of his earliest and rarest pamphlets.

There are doubtless many similar unrecorded instances of George Winship's helpfulness to individual undergraduates. It was, however, through a highly individualistic course titled Fine Arts 5e, History of the Printed Book, that his influence was most widely exercised. This course, which had been established by William Coolidge Lane before World War I, was taken over by Winship in 1915. It had all the earmarks of a "snap." It met on Tuesday and Thursday afternoons at three o'clock in the Widener Room, and was conducted with extreme informality. Winship would bring up from the Treasure Room armfuls of incunabula, Aldines, French illustrated books of the eighteenth century, products of the Kelmscott, Doves, and Ashendene presses, and simply talk about them in the most off-hand manner. If there were any examinations I cannot recall them. The standard grade was a gentleman's C, which was quite automatically bestowed unless the student showed cogent cause why he needed something else. If a gentleman firmly wished, for his own reasons, to flunk out of Harvard College and needed an E to accomplish this, Winship would oblige. When I took the course in 1924–1925 I was in process of achieving a somewhat rapid transition from Groups VI to II of the rank list, and felt that an A would improve my morale and consolidate my position. I got it, and, incidentally, stayed in Group II and received an A.B. *cum laude* in 1926 in spite of accidented and unpromising beginnings.

The enrollment was limited, because of the number of chairs possible around a table. The students were chosen entirely on Winship's hunches. All were well washed, but not all were gilded, like Lucius Beebe; for Winship, although he had a healthy respect for property, was quite capable of gathering in impecunious products of parsonages like myself. Despite the air of seeming frivolity about the course, or perhaps more truly because of it, Winship gave his students an intimate insight into the history of printing from the fifteenth to the twentieth centuries that could not have been acquired in any other way. His *Gutenberg to Plantin, An Outline of the Early History of Printing* that appeared in 1926 indicated only a part of the ground covered, for he made us quite as familiar with contemporary work as with the beginnings.

In addition he had an oblique way of bringing in all kinds of things that had nothing to do with printing at all. I first heard of both Increase Mather and Kenneth Murdock in conversation with Winship, and also, to my lasting gratitude, of A. Kingsley Porter. In January 1925 as Fine Arts 5e was drawing to a close, I was in search of a substitute course for the spring term. Winship asked if I knew Kingsley Porter, who had recently been brought to Harvard as Professor of Fine Arts. I did not. Winship then explained that he was not only an eminent medieval archaeologist but an extraordinary person, and one that he thought I would like. I was urged to take whatever course Porter might be offering, as he was abroad every other term and gave but one course when in Cambridge.

Upon consulting the catalogue, I found that Fine Arts 14c, Romanesque Architecture, was being offered in the 1925 spring term. As it was listed in the "Primarily for Graduates" group, and as I was a junior only recently retrieved from probation, it was clearly necessary to seek the permission of the instructor. Thus I first went to see Kingsley Porter, with whom I enjoyed until his death eight years later as happy a relationship as can have ever existed between student and teacher in the long centuries during which there have been universities. For me Kingsley Porter was the ideal master. The years spent in his company shaped everything that I have done in the years since his death or may do in whatever time I have left. Without George Winship's offhand suggestion, it is unlikely that I would have encountered him at the right moment. The ability to make such intuitive suggestions is a gift that cannot be too highly valued in a community of scholars; because

Winship possessed it to a remarkable degree he merits happy remembrance, not only as a bibliographer and librarian, but as an inspired teacher.

Not only my scholarly interests but my personal life have been dependent upon the happy accident that first led me into the Widener Room. On May Day of 1926 I attended a dance at Professor Herbert Weir Smyth's house on Elmwood Avenue. As was the general habit during the Prohibition drought, I took gin whenever I found it lest I not meet it again when wanted. Consequently I arrived at the dance regrettably disguised in drink. Although I first met my wife on this occasion, a second chance meeting with her in the Widener Room a few days later proved more fortunate.

In 1926 Winship ceased to be librarian of the Harry Elkins Widener Collection and moved downstairs as assistant librarian in charge of the Treasure Room. The following year he organized the John Barnard Associates, a characteristically Winship-ian group designed to honor an eighteenth-century Marblehead divine "who loved books and did what he could for Harvard." The means of honoring this long-forgotten worthy were to hold exhibitions, print occasional books, and to dine handsomely every now and then at the Club of Odd Volumes. The first publication, *John Barnard and his Associates*, designed by Bruce Rogers, contained a sketch of Barnard, the articles of association, and the current roster. Such senior alumni as George Herbert Palmer '64, Percival Merritt '82, Francis Randall Appleton '75, William Augustus White '63, and Grenville Howland Norcross '75, were honorary members. So were the less venerable Edgar H. Wells '97, and James B. Munn '12, who were both valued friends of the library. Bruce Rogers was included, but Daniel Berkeley Updike was not, even though Winship admired Updike's work. The resident members ranged in age from Francis Greenwood Peabody '69, to thirteen undergraduates, including Carl Pforzheimer, Lincoln Kirstein, Paul Herzog, and Arthur Houghton. Winship, Kenneth Murdock, Ed Whitney, Paul Sachs, André Morize, Nathan Starr, and David M. Little represented the faculty, and there were a few graduate students like Douglas Gordon, Eric Sexton, and myself. Henry Moriarty, the presiding genius of the Harvard Coop's book department, appeared as typographer.

I recall a Barnard dinner on an arctic night when George Herbert Palmer, high in his eighties, appeared at 50 Mount Vernon Street, bowler-hatted but without an overcoat, as was his wont. When he wished to go home in mid-evening, he was bent on walking to the Park Street subway and only with the greatest urging could be persuaded to accept a lift. Perhaps in view of the convivial nature of the Associates he thought the subway safer.

The company was extraordinarily pleasant, and the dinners gave Winship the excuse to print elegant labels to dignify our bootleg-brew, and to write heroic couplets in retrospect. *The Historiographer's Recollections of the Annual Dinner To Welcome into Honorary Membership Alfred Claghorn Potter and Augustin Hamilton Parker*, held at the C.O.V. on 10 February 1928 contains the quatrain:

> *Reports, 'tis said, were made, and things were read.*
> *(One hears of incidents e'en now not dead)*
> *Of how a Member's glass ('till all grew dim)*
> *By miracle stayed fill'd to the brim.*

Such miracles were frequent, and to Winship's way of thinking indispensable. It was therefore somewhat dashing, when he organized a Barnard picnic at his farm in Charles River for Eric Millar, Keeper of Manuscripts in the British Museum, to discover that the guest of honor did not drink.

The John Barnard Associates published in 1928 *A Leaf of Grass from Shady Hill*, which contained a poem by Charles Eliot Norton, inspired, surprisingly enough, by Walt Whitman. The following year they became more ambitious by issuing *The Shelley Notebook in the Harvard College Library*, with a facsimile of the manuscript and notes by George Edward Woodberry. This was an unfortunately ambitious undertaking on the eve of a depression. In 1930 I went off to Spain, and when I returned six years later the Associates had vanished into space. I have a copy of verses printed for a picnic in Wenham in May 1932, but no evidence of later jollifications.

In 1936 George Winship reached the Harvard retirement age. In the years that have followed, William A. Jackson's Houghton Library and Philip Hofer's Department of Printing and Graphic Arts have been built upon foundations that he began to lay upon his return to Cambridge in 1915. From 1932 Winship's health was never robust, and he spent most of his time on his Charles River farm or in North Sandwich, New Hampshire. He rarely appeared at the societies in which he had been active during his earlier years, although in 1941 he gave the Rosenbach Lectures at the

University of Pennsylvania, which were published four years later as *The Cambridge Press, 1638–1692*. By the time of his death, which occurred on 22 June 1952, he was an unfamiliar figure in his old haunts, but some of us have cause to keep his memory with extraordinary gratitude.

CHAPTER II

Arthur Kingsley Porter

1883 – 1933

ALTHOUGH he had become an almost legendary figure in medieval archae-ology, Kingsley Porter, when I first met him in 1925, was only forty-two. He was tall and slender, shy and reticent although immensely thoughtful and con-siderate, withdrawn from his surroundings, living in a world of his own that he had created to shut out the bustle of contemporary American life. Born in Stam-ford, Connecticut, on 6 February 1883, he was graduated from Yale in 1904. From his parents, who died when he was young, he inherited property that gave him complete freedom of action. Once he had proved to his elder brother—a conventional New York lawyer—that he was not wasting his time in Europe, he devoted himself single-mindedly, with New England conscientiousness, to the pursuit of medieval architecture and art.

On 1 June 1912 he married Lucy Bryant Wallace, a Connecticut teacher who was seven years his senior and, superficially, his exact opposite. He was tall and she short; he was withdrawn and sparing of words and she sociable and talkative. With greater breadth of sympathy than her husband and a more ebullient down-to-earth view of life, Lucy Porter had disciplined these qualities. From the first she set herself to compress and direct the often erratic energies of her mind and body in the path she perceived he would be taking. The point to be noted was that her intuition matched his. That her short quick steps kept pace with his strides happened because she intensely willed it so. As I came to know them I grew to feel that with all the obvious differences they moved as perfectly in step as any couple I have ever known. As they had no children, their lives became the pursuit of Kingsley's work; thus they were much of the time in Europe, traveling, studying, and photographing medieval monuments.

During the first World War, Kingsley Porter was in France with the Services des Oeuvres d'Art dans la Zone des Armées as the only foreigner asked by the Commission des Monuments Historiques to assist in the protection and salvage of the Gothic churches that he knew and loved so well. After the war they thought of settling in Florence, but in 1921 Kingsley Porter was asked to become Professor of Fine Arts at Harvard. Thus they rented, and eventually bought, Elmwood in Cambridge, long the home of James Russell Lowell. To this four-square wooden Palladian house of 1767 they brought not only their very Florentine lares and penates, but four Italian servants who cooked admirably and made wine that relieved the drought of Prohibition. Here there was space and peace in a crowded city, with ample room for Kingsley's library and immense collection of photographs. Here too Lucy could mix Harvard and Boston at Sunday teas and occasional handsome dinner parties, which Kingsley endured, with an air of absent-minded detachment, because he loved his wife.

After all they were only in Elmwood part of each year; the other months were usually spent in highly uncomfortable corners of Europe, where Romanesque and Byzantine monuments had survived. The Porters kept in Milan a Fiat town car, with which their devoted chauffeur Niccolo Anfossi would meet them at their port of disembarkation. Thereafter they would be on the road for months, photographing by day and developing their negatives by night in hotel bathrooms to be sure that the necessary evidence had been collected before moving on.

I was seldom asked to large parties at Elmwood, for as Kingsley did not enjoy them he assumed that I would not either. But I often lunched with the Porters à trois in more monastic circumstances. One summer in the Twenties I lunched there daily as we explored Thoreau's journals, one of us reading aloud as the others ate, with frequent exchanges of the book.

In the summer of 1927, when I first went to Spain, I met the Porters and Anfossi at Lugo, and drove with them to Santiago de Compostela and along the north coast of Spain. The next year they went to Ireland, and fell so in love with the country that they eventually bought Glenveagh Castle in the wilds of Donegal. A month after I was married in 1930, my wife and I went to the Porters' in Donegal, and in the summer of 1931 and 1932 we drove from Spain to Ireland for quiet weeks at Glenveagh, during which the poet Æ was often the only other guest. In the summer of 1933 we were to meet the Porters in Stockholm and return with them to Ireland. But Kingsley was drowned on 8 July, and as Lucy had to return soon after to the United States, we went alone to Glenveagh and kept the flag flying there until November.

Soon after his death I wrote a few paragraphs about him that were published in the Harvard Alumni Bulletin *for 17 November 1933. Several years later I contributed an article, "Changes in the Study of Spanish Romanesque Art," to the two-volume* Medieval Studies in Memory of A. Kingsley Porter *(Cambridge: Harvard University Press, 1939), edited by Wilhelm R. W. Koehler, and in 1952 wrote a Foreword for the posthumous private first printing of Kingsley Porter's* Three Plays: Pope Joan, Conchobar's House, Columcille Goes. *This chapter is a mosaic, containing elements from all three pieces.*

WITH THE PUBLICATION in 1909 of *Medieval Architecture*, Kingsley Porter began the series of studies in medieval architecture which developed so widely until his death in the summer of 1933. One day in the summer of 1904, soon after graduation from Yale, he had stood in front of the cathedral of Coutances. Suddenly, as in a vision, a great light dawned and he knew that his way to salvation lay through art and not the law. No longer had he any doubt about the road to choose, but to convince his family, and himself, of the sincerity of his purpose, he wrote his two great volumes on *Medieval Architecture*. Chapters of sensitive and intuitive appreciation of the medieval spirit were followed by extensive lists of monuments, bibliographies, and all the apparatus of exact description—a characteristic combination—which gave a still unsurpassed view of French Gothic architecture, the real subject of the book. Completed when he was only twenty-five, *Medieval Architecture* was on a scale that suggested a last rather than a first book, but in reality it was only the point of departure for his later works.

Its publication set in motion a chain of circumstances that were to govern his life. As a New Englander, with a strict conscience and a high sense of intellectual integrity, Kingsley Porter could never escape the consequences of this first adventure in scholarship, for what he undertook he did with all his might. Examination of rib-vault construction drew him to Lombardy, where his energetic quests led him into an even more monumental study of Lombard Romanesque architecture. A monograph on *The Construction of Lombard and Gothic Vaults* appeared in 1911 and four volumes on *Lombard Architecture* in 1917. Problems in the Romanesque sculpture of Lombardy turned his attention to the style elsewhere in Europe, and seizing upon the idea of the pilgrimage to Santiago as a motivating principle, he followed the roads through Italy, France, and Spain.

Kingsley Porter brought with him to Spain the most extensive firsthand knowledge of Romanesque sculpture of other countries of any scholar who had come to the peninsula, and, struck by the beauty and originality of much of the Spanish Romanesque work, spent a number of years studying and photographing it. In 1923 he published his *Romanesque Sculpture of the Pilgrimage Roads*, in which, for the first time, Spanish medieval art was related, on a wide basis of personal experience, to similar phenomena in other countries. In the 1,500 plates that illustrated this ten-volume work, he presented the nearest approach that has been made to a corpus of Romanesque sculpture, while the text of the book represented his own personal views upon certain fundamental problems of the art. The book, by the very audacity of its conception, aroused both interest and controversy. The controversial publications that it provoked are chiefly valuable for having

Arthur Kingsley Porter

induced further study on the part of other scholars and having brought to wide attention new or little-known material.

Five years later in *Spanish Romanesque Sculpture* he described the Spanish monuments in even greater detail, prefixing to the book a survey of pre-Romanesque sculpture throughout Europe. This inevitably spelled Ireland, where he spent much of the last six years of his life. The lectures on *The Crosses and Culture of Ireland*, given in 1930 at the Metropolitan Museum, expressed his first vision of Irish art rather than his final judgment. So the road went from Paris and Chartres to Kells and Monasterboice, as straight spiritually as it was winding geographically.

An earnest seeker after truth, Kingsley Porter took nothing at second hand for granted, and as he acquired knowledge he felt the obligation to share it. Often his firsthand experience set him at variance with apparently established theories, and involved him in controversies that interested him not at all, save for the obligation that he felt to maintain the truth as he saw it. He never sought conventional rewards, but neither would he shrink from anything that seemed to him a serious duty. So when he was asked to become Professor of Fine Arts at Harvard College, he could not in conscience refuse, and for a dozen years, with singular generosity, diffidently shared his thoughts and knowledge with any students who cared for the things that he loved. Thus, by an inexorable sequence of events that he had never consciously sought to bring about, he became a teacher and the author of a series of monumental and highly acclaimed works on medieval art, in which archaeological considerations often outweighed the aesthetic.

Having the freedom to travel, he visited innumerable monuments over a period of thirty years, studying each with the greatest thoroughness. To him no clue was too insignificant to follow, and rightly so, for one of the discoveries that gave him the greatest pleasure—the Aragonese church of Iguácel—came from a clue so slight that normally one would have passed it by unnoticed. Traveling constantly, and photographing as he went, he acquired a unique experience of Romanesque architecture and sculpture. When he published it was from firsthand knowledge, although the monuments visited far outnumbered those which appeared in his books. The fresh viewpoint given him by actual contact with the art of widely separated regions spontaneously produced new theories, often unorthodox but always stimulating. However valuable the theories, they were not the end in view, for he was drawn to medieval art not by its controversial possibilities but by its beauty.

Kingsley Porter's life was an endless search for truth, and to him, as to Keats, beauty and truth were synonymous. Even when enmeshed in archaeological controversy he never lost sight of his early vision, as may be seen from a passage in *Beyond Architecture*, published in 1928, where he endeavored to explain the relation between scholarly consideration of minutiae and aesthetic experience:

"By infinitely patient study we may perhaps determine whether the doors of Hildesheim were executed in 1015 or 1022. What we have gained is not so much the acquisition of an after all barren historical fact, but that we have come to know a great work of art deeply and intimately, to feel its harmonics and let them sink into our consciousness. Our study forces us to return time and time again, notice each detail and impress it in our memory. Thus we gradually come to change passive enjoyment into creative activity; we approach the source; we taste aesthetic emotion with a freshness, a clarity, and a purpose unknown to the mere spectator. If we historians of art were honest, we should, I think, confess that we are historians of art because we are irresistibly attracted by the beauty of ancient monuments, and that we study them because by that means our artistic enjoyment is increased. . . . The purpose of a telescope is not a telescope but the stars."

During Kingsley Porter's years as a professor at Harvard his time was divided between teaching and his own research, and therein lay his power as a teacher. A lecture was never given twice, for he brought to his students the problems upon which he was working at the time. Frequently his lectures came from the manuscript or the proofs of a forthcoming book; frequently they were used to try out as yet uncrystallized ideas; but always they were open to the questioning of the student. The same spirit that in Spain led to the finding of Iguácel, in the classroom made him consider every point raised, however trivial. Whenever a suggestion seemed to him good it was immediately acknowledged in a way which pushed the student on to further investigation. His library, his great collection of photographs, and his own time were more than generously placed at the disposition of his students. So personal a method was made for small numbers, but as more and more came to him each year he carried it on without stint. What he received was in no way comparable to what he gave, but his feeling was summed up in the dedication of his last book: "To my teachers—my Harvard students."

Even more remarkable than his writing or his teaching was the life that produced them both. Such a chapter as "The Pilgrimage to Compostela" in *Romanesque Sculpture of the Pilgrimage Roads*—an artistic creation in itself quite apart from its context—shows how deeply he lived into the Middle Ages, and the same sensitiveness which gave him such insight made him rebel against the mechanized organization of modern life. His plays and essays were the means by which he poked fun, with a light and epigrammatic maliciousness, at his pet detestations. With singular consistency he carried his beliefs into practice, for at Elmwood there was a measured quality to his life reminiscent of the nineteenth-century New England which he loved. He lived even more deeply into Ireland, going beyond its art into its history, language, and literature, with a feeling for the country which made it his own to the end, for his death in a storm on the island of Inishbofin is strangely in the tradition of the Irish saints who sailed west in that very sea in search of the Land of Promise.

In the Foreword to *Spanish Romanesque Sculpture* Kingsley Porter wrote: "For in archaeology, as in other things, it is not to arrive, but the journeying that is valuable. Not the pragmatic result of fact demonstrated, but the by-products of aesthetic enjoyment, justify archaeological research." His volumes of "fact demonstrated" fill a substantial shelf. These are the monuments of a scholar, but they tell little of the man, beyond his absorption in medieval art and his integrity. Those who shared his friendship and confidence in Elmwood, in Ireland, or on the Continent, felt that the man was greater than the scholar, and that his most characteristic thoughts were far removed from conventional archaeology. His gods were not those of the twentieth century. The American craving for bigger and better elephants he acutely disliked, and to this and related detestations he applied a penetrating and critical mind. When he was drowned at Inishbofin on 8 July 1933 many of the by-products of his journeying were lost with him. Those that survived are hidden in the plays, through which from time to time he chose to express in parables the thoughts that to him had especial value. Others remain in the memories of the friends who walked with him by the Charles, through Irish bogs, or in a Spanish *plaza mayor*. To their possessors these are even more precious than the impressive shelf of "fact demonstrated."

CHAPTER III

William Crowninshield Endicott

1860 – 1936

WHEN Kingsley Porter introduced me to the cathedral of Santiago de Com-postela in the summer of 1927, he started me on an investigation of Spanish eleventh-century architecture that was to be my principal interest during the next nine years. I returned to Spain during the academic year 1928–1929, and in the autumn of 1930, after visiting the Porters in Donegal, my wife and I settled in an apartment in the Calle Balmes in Barcelona. That was our home until 1936.

When the Courtauld Institute in the University of London opened in the autumn of 1932, I became, at Kingsley Porter's suggestion, a candidate for a Ph.D. there, for it was not difficult to combine terms of residence in London with our normal migrations between Donegal and Barcelona, and my study of Spanish eleventh-century architecture was acceptable as a thesis subject. When Kingsley died in the summer of 1933, I was halfway through my degree requirements. With his death my chief link with Harvard was broken. American universities in the depth of the Depression showed little interest in hiring anyone, and, as we could live in Europe on a shoestring pleasantly enough while continuing medieval research, we kept our apartment in Barcelona until the spring of 1936, when the political chaos of Spain indicated that it was time for us to go home to New England. I received my London degree in 1934, although it was 1941 before the Oxford University Press *published my* Spanish Romanesque Architecture of the Eleventh Century. *Appearing in wartime in a small edition, the book soon went out of print; now in 1968 it is about to be reissued in the Oxford Reprints.*

Our frequent stays in London during the early Thirties were made pleasant by visits to 17 Dean's Yard, Westminster, where Mrs. William Hartley Carnegie, wife of the rector of St. Margaret's, Westminster, canon and subdean of the abbey, presided gracefully in a charming Georgian house. Born in Salem, Massachusetts, in 1864, Mary Crowninshield Endicott (a second cousin of my wife's father, Julian Lowell Coolidge) had lived in England since 1888 when she married the British statesman Joseph Chamberlain. In 1916, two years after Chamberlain's death, she married Canon Carnegie. Although childless, she was beloved by numbers of Chamberlain and Carnegie stepchildren, and was hospitable to all New England cousins who appeared in London, ourselves included. As my daughter, Diana Whitehill Laing—born in London in 1934 and baptized by Canon Carnegie at St. Margaret's—has written her biography, titled Mistress of Herself *(Barre: Barre Publishers, 1965), I need say no more about this remarkable lady.*

When we returned to the United States with two young daughters, and settled in North Andover in the spring of 1936, Mrs. Carnegie's only brother, William Crowninshield Endicott, played a brief but decisive role in our lives. I had agreed, before leaving Spain, to lecture at the University of Pennsylvania Summer School in 1936. I did so, leaving my family in New England for the six weeks of the season. Philadelphia in summer was hot and uninspiring. Since I wanted, short of being in Europe, to stay in Massachusetts, I began looking for a job that would keep me there until the Spanish Civil War was over. I was delighted when, in the autumn of 1936, William Sumner Appleton, founder of the Society for the Preservation of New England Antiquities, in Boston, wished to hire me. My pleasure in this prospect was short-lived, for at 8:00 A.M. the morning after agreement was reached, William Crowninshield Endicott, president of the society, telephoned me in a rage. Growling like a bear, he informed me that he would not put up with this "damned nonsense." If I wanted a job, I was to go to the Peabody Museum, of which he was vice-president, and of which I knew nothing. In this autocratic manner he was wont to dispose the affairs of many institutions and people in and about Boston. The next day I went to lunch with him in Danvers, where he was as kind and delightful as his sister had been in Dean's Yard, and on 1 November 1936 I joined the staff of the Peabody Museum of Salem as assistant director. Four weeks later, Cousin William died.

During the past thirty-two years, as an officer or trustee of the Peabody Museum of Salem I have constantly been grateful for the brief moment when the kindly autocracy of William Crowninshield Endicott shaped the second stage of my professional life as decisively as Kingsley Porter had directed the first. His methods were arbitrary, but his instincts were intuitive and benevolent. Sumner Appleton and I would doubtless have driven each other crazy in a short time, whereas I loved the Peabody Museum, and through it became so attached to New England that I have not yet returned to Spain.

Soon after William Crowninshield Endicott's death I wrote a brief memoir of him for the Essex Institute Historical Collection, LXXIV *(1938) 205–210, which was separately reprinted in 1938 by the Peabody Museum of Salem. Eventually I edited and the Peabody Museum published in 1962 a volume titled* Captain Joseph Peabody, East India Merchant of Salem, *which contained the record of his ships and family compiled by William Crowninshield Endicott, with a sketch of Joseph Peabody's life that I wrote from scratch. The pages that follow are chiefly derived from my Introduction to this volume and from the Essex Institute memoir.*

The photograph here reproduced shows him standing by the pear tree at the Orchard Farm, Danversport, Massachusetts, in the Twenties. The tree, whose history went back farther than that of any cultivated tree in New England, was planted by Governor John Endecott (1588–1665/66) on a property granted to him in 1632. Although shattered by gales in 1815 and 1837, the persistence of its original strain was shown by the suckers which long bore the same fruit as that of the branches of the main trunk. When this photograph was taken, the original trunk had entirely disappeared, but two tall suckers were valiantly blossoming. Although William Crowninshield Endicott gave the ancient pear tree every possible care, it did not long outlive him.

WCE

WHEN WILLIAM CROWNINSHIELD ENDICOTT died it was remarked that the list of official positions that he occupied in connection with the arts or historical tradition read like Homer's catalogue of ships. President of the Massachusetts Historical Society, of the Society for the Preservation of New England Antiquities, of the Essex Institute, of the Isabella Stewart Gardner Museum, former president of the Massachusetts Horticultural Society, vice-president of the Peabody Museum of Salem, of the Humane Society of the Commonwealth of Massachusetts, of the Massachusetts Society for Promoting Agriculture, treasurer of the Museum of Fine Arts, and so on at length. He was a lawyer, chiefly concerned with the care of estates, who had, by temperament and interest, become the residuary legatee of the history and traditions of the Endicott and Peabody families. He and his wife were childless; so was his only sister. Thus his eyes were cast toward the past rather than the future. The Salem of his boyhood had changed beyond recognition. Essex County and Boston were going the same way, albeit more slowly. Thus he gathered around him, with the acquisitiveness of a New England collector, all the vestiges of the more engaging past that his ample energies and means could compass.

Over the years it came to be widely assumed in Boston that certain kinds of family possessions—"luxurious bric-a-brac found in garrets, treasures left at the death of old people, furniture whose history had not been preserved," as Bishop Lawrence described them—should be given to him as the best means of assuring their preservation. Amid these accumulations he lived handsomely and expansively, for he loved good company as dearly as he loved possessions. The family farm in Danvers, enlarged through the architectural imagination of his friend Herbert Browne, had more bay trees in tubs, garden statuary, French silver-gilt ornaments, Aubusson rugs, and Chinese export porcelain than its original builder could have imagined. His wife's assertion, "This is just a farm—we only have plated silver here," was as sincere and as innocent as her reply to my wife, who, when we were invited to dinner, asked whether to dress for the occasion: "Oh, no, dear; just black tie." The Boston house at the corner of Marlborough and Dartmouth streets to which they migrated for the winter—now, alas, a lodginghouse but described and illustrated by my daughter, Diana Whitehill Laing, in the 1960 *Proceedings* of the Bostonian Society—represented the Back Bay at its handsomest.

William Crowninshield Endicott died at 163 Marlborough Street on 28 November 1936. The first day of December his funeral was held at Grace Church, Salem, a stone's throw away from the house at 365 Essex Street where he had been born on 28 September 1860. This burial service, unlike any other in the experience of Salem, is best described in the words of a participant and old friend, Bishop Lawrence: "A company, unique in its variety of interests and personalities, filled the church; each one had his or her own personal reason for their presence there. The dominant note was affection and a pride in their friendship with one who in himself gathered up the memories of generations, and represented in himself the end of an era." In the weeks which followed, certain friends gave words to the feelings shared by a multitude of others, and in the *Boston Evening Transcript* of 11 December the following tribute by Ellery Sedgwick was published:

> For many citizens Boston will be a sadder place to live in now that William Crowninshield Endicott is gone. There are few in our generation remotely like him, and to many of us he was the most definite living link with the era of our fathers. It was not merely that he believed in the old ways and the old standards: he was the embodiment of them. The inheritor of a great New England tradition, he felt a personal responsibility that tradition should

not die. He represented a society which had its obligations as well as its pleasures, and of that society he knew that manners are not an ornament but the essential core. The most social of human beings, his doors were wide open to strangers, and for his friends there was no hospitality like his. The Farm at Danvers, where the long windows of the parlor looked out on the loveliness of an ancient garden, and the Victorian drawing room at 163 Marlborough Street, with its old-fashioned elegance, seemed alike always full of friends, friends in troops, friends in legion; and if friendship is the test of life, I cannot name a happier life than his. For fifty years he had known everybody in the great world, and in the little world —which, after all, he loved best—his affections were hoops of steel. His interests ranged widely—art, history, biography, politics, the changing order. But it was his gusto for living which made him so necessary to our well-being. There were within him infinite layers of anecdote and reminiscence, one leading to another, and as he unrolled them, that deep, reverberant laugh of his always met its instantaneous response. A large-hearted, obstinate, charitable, enthusiastic, delightful man: his business was to give pleasure and rich was his success.

Both through his father, Judge William Crowninshield Endicott—a descendant in the eighth generation from Governor John Endecott—and through his mother, Ellen Peabody, William Crowinshield Endicott the Younger inherited a great New England tradition. Surrounded by witnesses to that tradition he passed his childhood, remaining in Salem until 1879, when, as good New Englanders should, he entered Harvard College. He was graduated in 1883, and after a few months of European travel went into the Salem law office of Tuckerman, Huntington and Fitz. In the autumn of 1884 he entered the Harvard Law School, but the following year returned to the Salem law firm, and in 1886 was admitted to the the Essex County Bar. From July 1886 to May 1889 he was in Washington, mostly in the office of the Attorney General of the United States, but for a time as private secretary to his father, who was Secretary of War under the first Cleveland administration. On 30 October 1889, he married, at Lenox, Marie Louise, daughter of Joseph and Anna Barker Ward Thoron.

William Crowninshield Endicott

In the same year he began the practice of law in Boston, and continued until March 1893, when he returned to Washington as private secretary to the Honorable Richard Olney, then Attorney General. In May 1894 William Crowninshield Endicott was appointed Pardon Attorney in the Attorney General's office, and held that post until the end of the second Cleveland administration, when he returned to the practice of law in Boston, with offices in the Ames Building. His interest lay in the care of estates, and for the last forty years of his life he carried on that profession for which he was by temperament and inheritance so well fitted.

William Crowninshield Endicott realized fully that the New England which he had known in his boyhood was rapidly disappearing, and that his relatives and friends of older generations possessed something which would soon be lost in the changing world—"The inheritor of a great New England tradition, he felt a personal responsibility that tradition should not die." Having boundless energy and enthusiasm, and the capacity for obstinately accomplishing the impossible when he knew that he was right, he soon translated this feeling of responsibility into action and, both through his private life and his service in innumerable public institutions, preserved for the future much that was good in the past of New England.

As early as his first period in Washington, during the Eighties, he was copying documents relating to his great-grandfather, Jacob Crowninshield, who had been named Secretary of the Navy by Thomas Jefferson; and as the years passed it came to be assumed by a variety of people that family papers, portraits, and heirlooms in general should be turned over to him for study and preservation. These responsibilities he assumed with the spirit and technique of an historian, for he recognized that much concerning the history of New England was to be found among the possessions of the families which had helped to make the region. This material he studied with the greatest care. When he caught an oral tradition he wrote it down, and when he heard of a possible source of information he pursued it immediately and thoroughly. Thus he secured from the descendants of P. and A. Filicchi, Joseph Peabody's correspondents in Leghorn, first a transcript of and finally the original letter book covering the Italian firm's dealings with Salem over the period from 1823 to 1842, which supplied some at least of the information that was lost when the Peabody countinghouse records were destroyed. At the beginning of the search he knew only that his great-grandfather had maintained business relations with the Leghorn firm a century before. Eventually he located the Filicchi descendants, and at last, after several years of persistence, obtained what he wanted.

While "there were within him infinite layers of anecdote and reminiscence" which added immeasurably to the gaiety of his conversation, he had in his library quantities of files and loose-leaf binders full of documented information, systematically arranged, which allowed him to quote chapter and verse for all that he remembered, and more too. In his semiannual moves between Danvers and Marlborough Street, he was accompanied by several hundred of these binders and leather-labeled filing boxes. No detail was too insignificant to arouse his enthusiasm, but like many an amateur historian he enjoyed the assembling of sources far more than their reduction to narrative. He had an immense talent for collecting information, delighted in its elegant arrangement, remembered good stories when he met them, and told them with gusto: but composition came hard to him.

In 1924, with the aid of George Francis Dow, William Crowninshield Endicott privately printed, in an edition of one hundred and twenty-five copies, a *Memoir of Samuel Endicott with a Genealogy of His Descendants*. This account of his shipmaster-grandfather, liberally illustrated with photogravure reproductions of portraits and houses, was followed in 1929 by a companion volume, *Family Gatherings relating to the Smith and Blanchard Families with a Memoir of the Rev. Elias Smith, Pastor of Middleton, Massachusetts, By his Grandson George Peabody*, which dealt with one branch of his mother's family. A similar book on the life of his great-grandfather, Joseph Peabody, was a constant preoccupation. Time and again he drafted title pages, chiseled a dedication to his admired grandfather—in its final form: "To the Memory of GEORGE PEABODY, ESQUIRE of Salem, Massachusetts, A True Gentleman, To Whose Wisdom, Cultivation in Art, Music, and Literature, as Well as Business Acumen, His Descendants Owe a Debt of Lasting Gratitude"—wrote a Preface, and bogged down in the immensity of material that he had collected. So matters stood upon his death in 1936.

Almost until her death on 12 March 1958, I was intermittently involved in helping Mrs. Endicott transfer to appropriate libraries and museums the vast accumulation of material that her husband had assembled. Both 163 Marlborough Street and the Danvers farm resembled the widow's cruse of oil. No matter how much one removed they were always full! The material concerning Joseph Peabody went appropriately to the Peabody Museum of Salem, where I was then based. Although I offered at the time to edit some parts of it for publication, the museum's funds—and Mrs. Endicott's—were then committed in other directions. The war intervened. In 1954 when G. Peabody Gardner persuaded some twenty other descendants of Joseph Peabody to make a gift to the Peabody Museum toward the publication of some part of William Crowninshield Endicott's material on Joseph Peabody, I renewed my offer to prepare the manuscript.

The list of Peabody ships that he had compiled was clearly of interest to the museum and to maritime historians. The genealogy of Joseph Peabody's descendants was another matter, for at first sight it appeared to be of value only to a few people within the family. It was, however, an absolutely complete record down to 1936 of a close and extraordinarily homogeneous corporation that had wandered very little as modern American life goes. William Crowninshield Endicott had cared intensely about it, and, by making the Peabody Museum of Salem the residuary legatee of his estate, had become its most generous single benefactor, not excluding its founder, George Peabody of London. It therefore seemed only decent to include the genealogy. If it were to be printed, it would obviously be more useful if brought down to date. At this point I made a serious error in judgment by ignoring the "population explosion." As of 1 November 1936 there were less than three hundred entries. I bravely began sending questionnaires to living descendants to bring births, marriages, and deaths down to date. After more than six years of nagging correspondence, I had 602 entries! It therefore in 1962 seemed essential to get the manuscript into print before any more children were born, for I had added five grandchildren to the list while attempting to complete the record of others. So in 1962 the Peabody Museum of Salem published a volume with the lengthy but accurate title *Captain Joseph Peabody East India Merchant of Salem (1757–1844) A Record of His Ships and of His Family compiled by William Crowninshield Endicott (1860–1936) edited and completed with a Sketch of Joseph Peabody's Life by Walter Muir Whitehill.*

Some men can be reasonably judged and warmly appreciated long after death through their writings; William Crowninshield Endicott cannot. The three books that bear his name convey only a very incomplete picture of the man, for when he took pen in hand he froze into the icy monumentality of nineteenth-century New England filiopietism. In human relations he was very different. Being himself the ripened and mellow fruit of the tradition which he loved, there was nothing of rusty antiquarianism in his daily life. His limitless capacity for friendship and his genius for giving pleasure to his friends caused the Danvers farm and 163 Marlborough Street to be eagerly frequented, for an instinctive ability to enter fully into a situation and a complete lack of self-consciousness made him the best of hosts.

The innumerable offices that he held were in no sense empty honors, for William Crowninshield Endicott made an institution a living force by his own part in it. Each one represented a genuine interest, and as his interests were many, so were his activities. His usefulness increased with his responsibilities, for, as his connections multiplied, he was more and more able to override petty parochial difficulties, and to direct the work of each institution along lines which were to the advantage of all of them. On occasion he might enforce his convictions by methods not wholly compatible with the democratic process. If, for example, he disliked a painting approved for purchase by his committee colleagues at the Museum of Fine Arts, he was capable of exercising a treasurer's pocket veto by failing to pay for it; thus the seller would eventually carry it away. But at his best he was capable of flights of generous intuition and benevolent autocracy like the one that sent me to the Peabody Museum of Salem in 1936. I am sorry that I did not have the fun of working with him there for more than four weeks.

CHAPTER IV

Rosamond Bowditch Loring

1889 – 1950

IN 1942 the Department of Printing and Graphic Arts of the Harvard Library published Rosamond Bowditch Loring's Decorated Book Papers. *As it was illustrated by specimens of original papers, the edition was limited to two hundred and fifty copies, which were sold within a few months. Ten years later the Harvard University Press published a memorial second edition, to which Dard Hunter contributed an essay on "Rosamond Loring's Place in the Study and Making of Decorated Papers," Veronica Ruzicka a piece titled "Rosamond Loring as a Teacher and an Artist," and I the memoir that follows. It is reprinted by permission of the Harvard University Press and the Department of Printing and Graphic Arts, Harvard College Library. The photograph shows Rosamond Loring demonstrating the making of marbled papers to a group of service men and women during World War II.*

RBL

I N T H E W I N T E R of 1936–1937 I went to 2 Gloucester Street, Boston, in search of memorabilia of Nathaniel Bowditch for a special exhibition to be held at the Peabody Museum of Salem. A few weeks before, I had joined the museum staff—supposedly only to sit out the civil war that had interrupted some years of medieval studies in Spain—and I knew little enough of the history of my native Massachusetts. The figure of Nathaniel Bowditch attracted me, and I can never be sufficiently grateful for his posthumous kindness in bringing me to the house of his great-granddaughter, Mrs. Augustus Peabody Loring, Jr. On that visit I found what I sought—including a bust of the Navigator, consigned character-istically to the wood closet because its owner was tired of having her children's friends inquire if it were Julius Caesar—and came to know a rare person whose friendship brightened the next fourteen years.

The dining room and library windows of 2 Gloucester Street overlooked the Charles River Basin from the Harvard to the Longfellow bridge, for the house, in spite of the deceptive numbering that has ensnared and plagued so many cab drivers, stood on the water side of Beacon Street. It was a vast house, built for Judge William Caleb Loring in the period when a somewhat overornate revival of Georgian decoration had tempered the original brownstone character of the Back Bay, with a tremendous central hall, in which a broad staircase easily led the visitor past a tapestry bristling with Gothic dragons to the second-floor library. There bookcases extending from floor to ceiling framed the river views, except on the interior wall where their height was reduced to allow space for two Stuart portraits and a Copley. An enormous table occupying the center of this huge apartment was usually loaded with piles of books, papers, letters, gadgets, and children's toys. Ample window seats were available for anyone who did not wish to risk sinking into the deep red-plush sofas and armchairs.

In other hands, the library at 2 Gloucester Street might have become portentous and somber, but with Gus and Rose Loring as its occupants it was easily the most delightful and comfortable room in Boston. Rowlandson and Gillray cartoons came out of print boxes, Strawberry Hill imprints off the shelves, and bottles and cigars never remained long in their cupboards. Good talk flourished early and late, with a freedom and wit reminiscent of the eighteenth century, and laughter abounded. Even the papers of the acid and austere Nathaniel Bowditch took on a lively and delightful character when Rose Loring pulled them out of a battered leather trunk in that room. Sometimes in New England traditions, houses and possessions come to dominate their heirs and in the end own their owners. In 2 Gloucester Street, however, there lived a warm, generous and rotund pair of New Englanders, marvelously suited to each other in tastes and temperament, who, while inheriting all the good qualities of the past, had added thereunto a great variety of original and unanticipated interests and talents, and who were always the masters of themselves and of their surroundings.

The combined gaiety and serenity that characterized Rose Loring came from a happy childhood in Jamaica Plain, by turns admonished or petted by nurses and elder sisters, in a house that had plenty of fireplaces, and corners to play in, with pastures and woodland close by. In 1854, Jonathan Ingersoll Bowditch—son of Nathaniel the Navigator—had bought Moss Hill, on the western side of Jamaica Pond, five miles from Boston. On this two-hundred-acre property houses were subsequently built for his sons, Henry Ingersoll, Charles Pickering, and Alfred. Alfred, the youngest son, married Mary Louise Rice in January 1880 and had two daughters, Margaret (Mrs. N. Penrose Hallowell) and Mary Orne, born before the family moved to Moss Hill in 1885. There Rosamond Bowditch was born on 2 May 1889.

Moss Hill in the Eighties and Nineties combined the merits of city and country. It was near enough Boston to allow Alfred Bowditch to go regularly to his trustee's office without the sorrows of modern commuting,

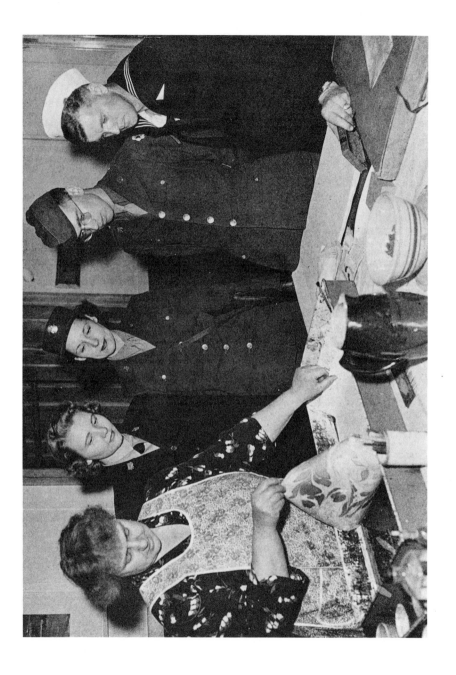

and sufficiently rural to permit his wife unbroken enjoyment of the peace of her garden. Miss Mary Orne Bowditch's reminiscences of the place, written in 1950 for her sisters, make it seem an ideal scene for childhood, and Rose, as the baby of the family, was particularly cherished by her elder sisters. She was both wise and gay, full of whimsical pranks, and on occasion would from the pure joy of living emit long, shrill and clear ecstatic cries, called by her sisters "piercers." One of her early delights was a collection of broken bits of colored glass and china that she kept under a pine tree at the foot of the driveway, whose colors, shining in the sun on their bed of pine needles, gave her endless delight. Balfour, the coachman, who tended the children's pony named Poppy, taught little Rose to sing "Sweet Rosie O'Grady" with style and spirit. She loved the garden, and, with her tan-and-white Boston terrier, Jury, would spend long hours there, helping her mother by carrying tools. One of her great pets was Jimmy, a crow that she had tamed so thoroughly that, when the mail arrived by bicycle, Jimmy would frequently be seen riding on the postman's hat.

In 1896 the Bowditches moved to Boston for the winters and the Jamaica Plain house was occupied only in spring and autumn. Summers were spent in North Haven, Maine. Rose attended the Haskell School. On 22 June 1911—when twenty-two—she was married to Augustus Peabody Loring, Jr., of the Harvard class of 1908. For the first eight years of their married life Gus and Rose Loring lived summer and winter at Prides Crossing. In 1920 they bought 81 Marlborough Street, and spent the winters there until 1931, when, after the death of Gus's uncle, they moved to 2 Gloucester Street. Their original house at Prides Crossing they continued to use in summer until 1945, when they took over Burnside, the house built by Gus's grandfather, Caleb William Loring, in 1852. In these houses an active family of five daughters and two sons—Mary Bowditch (Mrs. Nathaniel D. Clapp), Rose (Mrs. Townsend Heard), Augustus Peabody, III, Ellen Gardner (who died at four), Elizabeth Smith Peabody (Mrs. Augustus H. Fiske), William Caleb, and Jane Gray (Mrs. Ralph G. Straight)—were brought up and endless friends were made welcome.

Although she had a full-time career as a wife and mother, Rose Loring somehow found the leisure to take up bookbinding. The practice of this craft in a fifth-floor studio at 81 Marlborough Street led to the discovery that good decorated papers were not easy to come by, and so she experimented with making both marble and paste papers. Presently she gave up bookbinding, for the beauty and originality of her end-paper designs caused her work to be sought after by the Merrymount Press, the Club of Odd Volumes, and publishers concerned with fine bookmaking. Dard Hunter and Veronica Ruzicka will explain in detail what this craft involved, but it is significant to remember that, in spite of a full and busy life, Rose Loring not only created designs of extraordinary beauty and originality, but produced them in quantity as professionally as if she had not another obligation in the world.

The search for examples of decorated papers led her to form a unique collection. If a fine paper appeared on the binding of Benjamin Franklin's edition of Cato Major, she bought it with no less enthusiasm than she would acquire a French children's book or a German Lutheran sermon. This collection, together with her Kate Greenaways and children's books, was housed in a tall little room on the third floor of 2 Gloucester Street, and the librarians and collectors who found their way there to see the papers marveled no less at the books that they enclosed. Although the most modest of scholars, she was unsurpassed in her field, and her books, *Marbled Papers*, published by the Club of Odd Volumes in 1933, and *Decorated Book Papers*, originally published by the Department of Printing and Graphic Arts of the Harvard College Library in 1942, are unique sources in regard to the craft that she practiced with such skill.

Although Gus Loring's business responsibilities were varied and exacting, he began in the 1930's to take an active part in many of the learned societies, institutions, and clubs of Boston. In 1932 he joined the Club of Odd Volumes; the following year he was elected its clerk and continued until 1942 when he became president. In the fall of 1936 his wife was appointed assistant librarian, and until 1949 she made herself responsible for the library, and quietly did all the hard work in connection with the club's exhibitions. Similarly in 1942, when the staff of the Peabody Museum of Salem (of which Gus had become a trustee in 1939 and president in 1942) was depleted, Rose Loring was appointed honorary curator of exhibitions, and ably and unobtrusively filled the places of those absent upon military service. Anyone privileged to see her arranging an exhibition marveled both at the sure taste of her choices and the ease and skill with which she executed plans. While it was fitting that the first woman to serve as a trustee of the Peabody Museum of Salem should be a great-granddaughter of Nathaniel Bowditch, it was entirely for her own out-standing qualifications that Rose Loring was elected to the board in 1946. Although a graceful and very feminine person, with devoted women friends, Rose Loring had unusual skill in working on an equal basis with men. Every summer she cruised with Gus along the Maine coast, and from this understood the terms upon which men enjoy one another's company. Consequently at Salem one thought of her not as the "first woman" but as a valued and well-nigh indispensable worker, and as a warmhearted, sympathetic and outspoken friend.

Her work at the Peabody Museum and the Club of Odd Volumes indeed showed her ability to share her husband's interests with enthusiasm matched by intelligence, but it was in her own home that the capacity was supremely demonstrated. With Gus's genial but shrewd appreciation of other men went an instinct for abundant hospitality. He was the host at innumerable men's dinners (and famous dinners they were); but when he was not, as the moment came for the company to separate, he found it natural to ask some of them to go home with him afterward. And there in the library would be Rose. If it was like most of her days, this day might have been crowded with obligations and activities, yet, however late the hour, she managed to greet the new arrivals with an air of tranquil enjoyment. If Gus brought old friends she met them with delight; if they were strangers she conveyed in her greeting some air of sympathetic expectation. Then while some of the guests converged on the fire in the big hearth, Gus would bring out crackers and cheese and a thoughtful choice of bottles, and Rose with unobtrusive skill would set the entire group at ease. She had as quick an intuition as he, perhaps an even wider imagination; if the talk was running easily she was content to listen, only filling the occasional pauses with an interjection. If, as now and again happened, the guests were awkward and Gus faltered for a remark, that was the moment when Rose appeared to be feeling, "Here is what I have been waiting for!" and she forthwith gathered them to her, her audience of friends, to whom she told whatever story came into her head. Very soon her spontaneity would kindle theirs. On such occasions her behavior always seemed prompted by her own kindly ingenuity, never by preconceived formula, and the dignity she achieved sprang from adapting her actions to the particular circumstances. The same spontaneous ingenuity solved many problems of daily life, as it did on 15 February 1940, when Sam Morison was to give the Colonial Society his first account of the Harvard Columbus Expedition at the Club of Odd Volumes. The Peabody punch that Gus had brewed for the occasion was still at 2 Gloucester Street, and because of the St. Valentine's Day blizzard no cabs dared to venture up Beacon Hill. Consequently Rose perfectly simply trudged up to Mount Vernon Street, dragging the jug of punch behind her on a child's sled.

From the summer of 1949 Rose Loring had not been well, but her death on 17 September 1950 surprised her friends quite as much as it grieved them. A few weeks later Gus remarked to me that forty years earlier Dr. George Minot had given her not more than ten years to live. She characteristically told Dr. Minot that she had consulted him as a physician and not as an undertaker; changed doctors, and outlived him.

In January 1951 an exhibition of Rose Loring's book papers and the tools used in their production was held at the Boston Athenæum, and in February it was shown at the library of Boston University. Her collection has a permanent place in the Harvard College Library. It was her husband's wish that her *Decorated Book Papers* might be made available to the students and craftsmen who would care for it, and the plans for this edition were completed before his death on 1 October 1951. Neither this nor any other memorial could adequately recall the many facets of the woman who was at once the ideal wife, the selflessly loyal, energetic, humorous, and sympathetic mother of a numerous family, a highly successful working craftsman, a distinguished and original collector, a valuable museum curator and trustee, and a warm and generous friend. There was singular appropriateness in the seventeenth-century verse chosen by M. A. DeWolfe Howe for the broadside announcing her death to the Club of Odd Volumes:

> *Death! ere thou hast slain another*
> *Fair and learn'd and good as she*
> *Time shall throw a dart at thee.*

CHAPTER V

Augustus Peabody Loring

1885–1951

AUGUSTUS PEABODY LORING, JR., was a second and third cousin of my wife, but we first came to know him and his wife through the search for Bowditch memorabilia for a Peabody Museum exhibition in 1936. Although we were in age midway between them and their children, we soon came to regard them as close and valued friends. Gus became a trustee of the Peabody Museum of Salem in 1939 and its president in 1942, and I saw him often in the line of duty; as he brought me into the Club of Odd Volumes, of which he was clerk, in 1940, and passed that office on to me when he became president of the club in 1942, I saw him even oftener under genial and frivolous conditions. Like William Crowninshield Endicott, his offices were too numerous to count, but he was forever passing them on to younger friends whom he trusted. Without ever being didactic, he taught me as much of how Boston, its institutions, and its people worked, as Kingsley Porter had taught me of scholarly method, and was the best of company into the bargain. From 1942 to 1946, when I was on duty at the Navy Department in Washington, the Lorings made 2 Gloucester Street a second home whenever I returned to Boston on leave.

In January 1946 when I formally notified Gus Loring that I would be ordered to inactive duty in July and proposed to return to the assistant directorship of the Peabody Museum, which I had left on military leave in November 1942, Gus, as president, suggested to his fellow trustees that the time had come for the director—then well past seventy—to retire. They temporized, and Gus was annoyed. Soon afterward, at a meeting of the trustees of the Boston Athenæum, of which Gus was vice-president, the librarian resigned. Gus blandly and success- fully put my name in nomination, explaining to me by letter that he thought it was a more appropriate base of operations. He was, as usual, right. So since 1946 I have been director and librarian of the Boston Athenæum, while keeping in touch with Salem first as historian, and then as trustee and secretary of the Peabody Museum.

The memoir that follows was published by the museum in 1952. The photo- graph shows him in his office at 35 Congress Street, Boston, surrounded by papers, prints, books, and samples of cordage. As an administrator, he never suffered from the "clean desk" fallacy.

O N   T H E   E V E N I N G of 14 October 1949 delegates from more than seventy institutions, museums, and learned societies met in East India Marine Hall. Settling their knees under a long dining table decorated with ship models, birds of paradise, and East Indian booty, they made ready to celebrate the one-hundred-and-fiftieth anniversary of the foundation of the museum of the Salem East India Marine Society. At the center, elegantly flanked by a pair of great Chinese porcelain soup tureens in the form of geese, given to the East India Marine Society in 1803, sat Augustus Peabody Loring, Jr., president of the Peabody Museum of Salem. The rum punch he dispensed had been made by his own hands from a recipe brought from the West Indies by his great-great-grandfather, Captain Joseph Peabody (1757–1844). At the end of dinner, when the glasses had been replenished, Gus, as presiding officer, rose and proposed the toast, "The Mariners of Essex—and their tributes in peace and war, to the glory of their country," originally offered by President John Quincy Adams at the dedication of the hall one hundred and twenty-four years earlier. Meanwhile a rustic orchestra sawed out "Hail Columbia."

Although the toasts on the later occasion were prudently reduced from fifty-one to twelve in number, the pattern of the evening closely followed that of the early dinners of the East India Marine Society, and certainly the presiding officer strikingly resembled an eighteenth-century gentleman who had temporarily mislaid his wig. The following day, when Samuel Eliot Morison, the delegate from Harvard College, offered the visitors' thanks for the entertainment provided, he lamented, with feeling, that the delegates had been deprived of the pleasure of seeing Mr. Loring dressed in the costume of a Chinese mandarin, reclining in the Indian palanquin that occupied so prominent a place in the East India Marine Society processions, borne upon the shoulders of the director and assistant director of the museum and the brothers James Duncan and Stephen W. Phillips. The picture conjured up made the audience laugh till they cried, but the suggestion had this appropriateness—even without a procession the president was the center and heart of the entire celebration.

By temperament, historical interest, inheritance, and business acumen Gus Loring was uniquely fitted to guide the affairs of this ancient Essex County institution concerned with the sea and the distant lands visited by seafaring men.

He was, first of all, a skillful sailor with a competence in seamanship that would have enabled him to be spectacular, if it had not always been repugnant to him to act solely for the sake of making an effect. As a boy at Prides Crossing, where his great-grandfather and grandfather had been among the earliest summer residents, he had mastered the ways of boats. In fact, before he was in his teens, Gus, with a boy of similar age, had put to sea one day and—without having warned their families of any such intention—cruised to the eastward until they reached Pemaquid. This was the beginning of a lifelong pleasure. For over forty years he regularly ranged the Maine coast, and in the month spent afloat each summer renewed his strength for the varied and onerous occupations that filled every waking hour of the remainder of the year. He chose his boats rather as he

chose his clothes, for quality, serviceability, and comfort. He cruised comfortably too, and noncompetitively, without preconceived ideas of course or speed, planning from day to day as wind and weather indicated. By the end of the afternoon he would be in a sheltered anchorage, happily at work preparing a monumental dinner that would be preceded by a swizzle and accompanied by a bottle of wine. The very magnitude of his person suggested the pleasures of the table, although anyone who saw him rowing an overloaded boat in a rough sea knew that much of it was muscle. Not only did he know and like good food, he could cook also it. His knack with pressure cookers allowed him to produce in a tiny galley, with neat and rapid dexterity, a dinner that would have done credit to a French cook. He rarely went ashore, except for ice and provisions or to see an old friend, but when he did he knew how to behave in Maine. His father had owned much of Bartlett's Island in Blue Hill Bay and the Lorings understood Maine people.

The sea was in Gus Loring's blood. His great-great-grandfather, Joseph Peabody, had gone to sea as a boy, and on his death in 1844 as the richest merchant of the day in Salem, had built and owned eighty-three ships that he freighted himself. His great-grandfather, John Lowell Gardner, was a Boston shipowner and merchant in the East India and Russia trades. Another great-great-grandfather, Caleb Loring, had been a founder of the Plymouth Cordage Company in 1824, and his grandfather and father were successively its presidents from 1890 to 1936. Gus himself became a director of that company in 1913 and its president in 1939. In 1941 upon retiring as president he became the first chairman of the board of directors. Neither at Plymouth, nor anywhere else, was he shackled by the past. Although a firm upholder of traditions when they were good and still useful, he was constantly looking ahead and seeing around corners. In 1920, at his insistence, the Plymouth Cordage Company established the first laboratory in the cordage industry; the experiments with synthetic fibers that began about 1936 proved their worth when the great fiber-producing areas were cut off in World War II. Plymouth's nylon rope—used extensively by the United States Navy and Air Corps—gave him particular satisfaction.

In 1911 Gus Loring married Rosamond Bowditch, a great-granddaughter of Nathaniel Bowditch. The following year he entered the business of managing trusts and estates with his father-in-law, Alfred Bowditch. In that capacity he was responsible for the management of innumerable personal and business properties, continuing with probity and brilliance the tradition of the private trustee that had begun in Boston more than a century earlier with Nathaniel Bowditch. Outside his office he participated in many business enterprises, being a director—among other companies—of the

Boston and Maine Railroad, Houghton Mifflin Company, Massachusetts Hospital Life Insurance Company, New England Trust Company, and, as far away as Texas, president and director of the Galveston-Houston Company.

In the 1930's Gus Loring began to take an active rôle in historical and antiquarian matters, and usually, soon after becoming a member of an organization, he found himself doing most of its hard work. In 1931 he was elected a resident member of the Colonial Society of Massachusetts, in 1934 its recording secretary and in 1946 its president. In 1932 he joined the Club of Odd Volumes, became its clerk in 1933 and its president in 1942. In 1936 he was elected to the American Antiquarian Society, and from 1941 was a valued member of its council. Having become a resident member of the Massachusetts Historical Society in 1937, he served as its treasurer—and a particularly thankless job it was—from 1943 onward. So, in a familiar pattern, it was in no way surprising that, having been elected a trustee of the Peabody Museum of Salem in 1939, he was the obvious person to become its president in 1942. Many Boston institutions work together harmoniously, with singularly little time wasted in lengthy committee meetings, because in them the same people do business with each other in different capacities, but Gus Loring was the "puller-to-gether" extraordinary. It would be a considerable undertaking to attempt to list his activities, but it should be noted that in 1946 he became vice-president of the Boston Athenæum and in 1951 president of the Bostonian Society. One might well consider whether any other member of the Somer-set Tavern and Union clubs also belonged to the Masons, Elks, Odd Fellows and Grange, or whether another Boston corporation executive also was a member of the Fabian Society!

In the breadth of his acquaintance and sympathies lay the secret of his usefulness to all of these groups. He had packed an extraordinary number of experiences into his years. As a not overly promising Harvard under-graduate in the class of 1908, he had surprised his professors by running for the Beverly city council, and getting elected, defeating the senior local politician in the process. During his first trip abroad, he and Starling Burgess, with whom he was traveling, had been summoned by King Edward VII to a luncheon *à trois* at the Royal Yacht Squadron at Cowes. He flew with Burgess in the early days of aviation. Although his wife prudently made him quit flying when they were married, he hung onto a steamboat engineer's license for some years. Strawberry Hill imprints always attracted him, and he collected Rowlandson and Gillray with zest. His knowledge of wine was encyclopedic; so too was his knowledge of and sympathy for people.

As he lumbered down the street—pockets bulging with papers and carrying a great leather bag that might contain anything under the sun from incunabula to fish, from plumber's tools to Peabody punch—judges and police officers, lawyers and cab drivers, were equally delighted to see him. He accomplished almost as much business on the sidewalk as an ancient Athenian might have in the market place. To his office at 35 Congress Street—crowded with old prints of Boston, samples of rope, an incredible clutter of papers, and usually a few rare books that he had ordered as a surprise addition to his wife's collection—came the business and troubles of a great variety of institutions and individuals. He had a sympathetic ear for all, and the ability to seem unhurried, no matter how pressed he might be. He accomplished more than most men, partly because he picked his helpers skillfully and trusted them fully, but mostly because he thought faster and more incisively. Gus Loring's physical appearance and the difficulty with which he sometimes found words had less than no relation to the subtlety of his mind. If provided with a red coat and a wig he would have made a convincing eighteenth-century portrait. When digging in his garden, running a clambake, or climbing over his boat he more than occasionally suggested Atlas, Silenus, or Father Neptune. His realistic appraisal of his own beauty is shown by his delight in recalling that when a bee stung him on the end of the nose he reflected that if he could only keep the swelling permanently he might make a fortune as Cyrano on the vaudeville stage.

Time and again he might come into a meeting, and when some controversial matter was leading to wordy discussion, fold his hands over his stomach and go to sleep. But at the crucial moment he would stir, and suddenly introduce an apparently innocent and simple remark that solved the problem, frequently not only to the advantage of that meeting but of other institutions as well. When something needed to be done he had uncanny skill in suggesting someone, often known only to himself, who could not only do it well but would enjoy doing it. Thus he broadened the horizons of many groups and furthered the happiness of many individuals.

He was generous in both great and small matters. Many a New Englander will be posthumously generous on a large scale, but uncommonly mean where small sums of money are concerned. Gus made up for these by his ready perception of what was needed to oil the machinery of human relations. He made large gifts, but he also made an extraordinary number of small ones, so promptly and unhesitatingly that their value was trebled.

At the Peabody Museum of Salem his first accomplishment was restoring to its original appearance East India Marine Hall, built in 1825. This magnificent room, one hundred by thirty-five feet in size, had been sadly defaced in 1867, when it was, in a period of zoölogical enthusiasm, rammed full of exhibition cases and galleries that entirely destroyed its architectural quality. Under Gus Loring's urging the late Thomas Barbour, a trustee from 1940 to 1946, undertook the Herculean task of separating rubbish from valuable specimens, installing the latter elsewhere, and clearing the hall so that it might be restored. Its rededication on 4 November 1943 for the exhibition of objects pertaining to maritime history marked both the resurrection of one of the noblest rooms in New England and a milestone in the museum's progress.

Equally valuable for the future of the institution was the painstaking thought, based upon wide experience, that he gave to the museum's investments and business affairs. Although the casual observer might have expected the bearer of so many responsibilities to confine himself to attendance at stated meetings, there was nothing perfunctory about Gus Loring's manner of discharging his duties. On the contrary, he was constantly in and out of the museum, bubbling with ideas and friendly assistance; and, incidentally but characteristically, through serving on the council of the Essex Institute he was able to strengthen the ties between two neighboring institutions.

Gus Loring was generous to the museum both in gifts of objects and of funds, but perhaps his greatest service was in bringing the institution into a more intimate relation with the community by enlarging its parish boundaries to coincide with the breadth of his own enthusiasms and acquaintance. It was his idea to establish the Friends and Fellows of the Peabody Museum in the spring of 1951, and the gratifying response to the invitations to join these groups is evidence of the manner in which he and the museum had become identified with one another. Without disrespect to his warmth of feeling and willingness to help other institutions, it seemed clear to his friends that the Peabody Museum of Salem and the Club of Odd Volumes were the closest to his heart, and the places where he was most at home.

He did much to encourage and assist the museum staff, and from 1942 his wife, as honorary curator of exhibitions, quietly and unerringly filled the place of members absent on wartime service. Her election as a trustee in 1946, in recognition of what she had already done for the museum, gave him singular pleasure.

Rose Loring was a unique complement to Gus. They had the same warmth and generosity of spirit, the same catholic friendliness, and they always laughed at the same things. I can never think of her without recalling Anne Bradstreet's lines "To my dear and loving husband":

> *If ever two were one, then surely we.*
> *If ever man were lov'd by wife, then thee;*
> *If ever wife was happy in a man,*
> *Compare with me ye women if you can.*

In the great house at 2 Gloucester Street in Boston and at Prides Crossing she presided with apparently effortless skill, abetting Gus's instinct for abundant hospitality. People streamed in and out of both houses; old friends were greeted with delight, and strangers rapidly became friends. For good company, talk, food and drink there was nothing like the Loring houses, but then there has never been anything quite like their owners. Then on 17 September 1950, Rose died. Gus resumed his customary duties without faltering, but one could not help remembering the word of the Lord to the prophet Ezekiel:

> Behold, I take away from thee the desire of thine eyes with a stroke; yet neither shalt thou mourn or weep, neither shall thy tears run down. Forbear to cry, make no mourning for the dead. . . . So spake I unto the people in the morning; and at even my wife died; and I did in the morning as I was commanded.

In January 1951 I arranged an exhibition of Rose's decorated book papers at the Athenæum. Gus brought a group of her tools, and it was touching to see how completely he remembered the use of each one and how precisely he knew the technique of her craft. In late March, on returning from his annual trip to Texas, he fell into the hands of the doctors for a brain operation. After long weeks in the Phillips House, outside which the piledrivers were hammering on a new highway, he was able to go home to Prides late in June. There with the sea, and the sight of his boat, surrounded by children and grandchildren, he passed a relatively happy July and August. Friends came to see him; he talked of the future, and one day toward the close of this Indian summer of his life he drove to Salem to see the improvements that his fellow trustee, Mrs. Francis B. Crowninshield, was making in the exhibition rooms at the Peabody Museum. But his illness was too devastating even for his rugged strength to overcome, and on 1 October 1951 he died. During these weeks a paraphrase of Sir Henry Wotton's lines frequently ran through my head:

> *She first deceased; he for a little tried*
> *To live without her, liked it not, and died.*

Without him the climate is colder and the sky less bright around here.

CHAPTER VI

Lincoln Colcord

1883–1847

SOON AFTER I joined the staff of the Peabody Museum of Salem in 1936, Lincoln Colcord turned up there. In due course I went to Searsport, Maine, to see the new Penobscot Marine Museum which he and his kinsman, Clifford Nickels Carver, had just founded. Although Link was then only in his early fifties, he had several careers already behind him, and, married to his third wife, had retired from the great world to the quiet coastal town that was the home of his shipmaster father. Like his elder sister, Joanna Carver Colcord, he had been born at sea in the bark Charlotte A. Littlefield, *commanded by their father, Captain Lincoln Alden Colcord.*

Brother and sister grew up at sea, as the children of some New England shipmasters did, until they came ashore to attend the University of Maine. Although Joanna Colcord spent most of her adult life in New York City as a social worker, her books Roll and Go, Songs of American Sailormen *(1924, enlarged and reissued in 1938) and* Sea Language Comes Ashore *(1945) are precise records of the shanties and language that she heard during her childhood at sea. Lincoln Colcord's three volumes of sea stories,* The Drifting Diamond *(1912),* The Game of Life and Death *(1914), and* An Instrument of the Gods *(1922) similarly sprang from firsthand experience. To this man of unique vigor, his boyhood years at sea remained the supreme experience of his life. Tiring of journalism in New York, he early retreated to his parents' old house in Searsport, from whose back porch one looked out into Penobscot Bay.*

Lincoln Colcord

To this house there came an extraordinary diversity of people, among them journalists, seamen, historians, actors, poets, and painters. In his back yard you might find almost anyone. Similarly there were few limits to the range of his ideas. He dearly loved to talk. His friends wished he would write as he had spoken, but in later years he seldom did, save in book reviews in the New York Herald Tribune and exuberant letters that still remain uncollected and unprinted.

In 1932 a 225-page "Record of Vessels Built on Penobscot River and Bay" that he and his wife, Frances Brooks, had compiled from Custom House records, was published as an appendix to George S. Wasson's Sailing Days on the Penobscot, The River and Bay as they were in the Old Days *(Salem: Marine Research Society, 1932). When the Penobscot Marine Museum was founded four years later, the Colcords were much involved in gathering paintings, models, and logs of local ships for it. As they did not personally cope with automobiles, we would often on visits to Searsport drive Link to places around Penobscot Bay where, thirty years ago, one still occasionally found retired shipmasters or widows who knew Singapore and Hong Kong better than Bangor. Although Link's head was crammed with detailed information about maritime history, it was next to impossible to persuade him to reduce it to paper. But as the undisputed "Sage of Searsport" he stirred others to action. The piece that follows recounts his decisive role in creating* The American Neptune, A Quarterly Journal of Maritime History, *that I edited from 1941 to 1950 and that Ernest S. Dodge, director of the Peabody Museum of Salem, has carried on since. This appeared as an editorial in the January 1948 issue (VIII, 3–6).*

In the years that I knew him, Lincoln Colcord stuck close to Searsport. In the winter of 1937–1938 he, his wife, and young son, Brooks, accompanied Samuel Eliot Morison in a reconnaissance of the Windward and Leeward islands in the yawl Ptarmigan *that was the first step in Morison's retracing of the voyages of Columbus. Now and then Link would turn up in the Augustus Lorings' hospitable house at 2 Gloucester Street, or pay us a visit in North Andover. I remember too seeing him once in Washington during the war. But mostly he stayed in Searsport and the world came to him. Although he has been dead for twenty-one years, I keep stumbling across traces of his earlier and more active life that he never spoke of in the years when I knew him.*

In May 1963 when I was addressing the triennial meeting of the Norwegian-American Historical Association in Minneapolis, a chance mention of Lincoln Colcord's name in connection with The American Neptune *revealed to me how warmly he was remembered from having lived there a third of a century earlier. The Governor of Minnesota, Karl F. Rölvaag (now United States Ambassador to Iceland), at once told me of the help that Link had given his father, the novelist O. E. Rölvaag, in creating the English text of his* Giants in the Earth, A Saga of the Prairie, *first published in 1927. Link had never mentioned to me that he had written an Introduction to* Giants in the Earth, *or that O. E. Rölvaag had stated in the Foreword that without his "inimitable willingness to help, this novel would most likely never have seen the light of day in an English translation," for he "unified and literally rewrote the English text."*

Still another aspect of his earlier life I first knew of through Christopher Lasch's The New Radicalism in America 1889–1963, The Intellectual as a Social Type *(New York: Alfred A. Knopf, 1965), where Chapter 7 is titled "Lincoln Colcord and Colonel House: Dreams of Terror and Utopia." Here is the record of his friendship with Colonel E. M. House during the years 1916–1918 when he was on the staffs of the* Philadelphia Public Ledger *and* The Nation. *But here too is a revealing letter that Link wrote Colonel House in 1916 about his affection for Searsport:*

"It's not a bad place, much as many others, but the secret of our love for it lies in what I have just said—we know it intimately. This is the lesson I got from Thoreau. Love your own pond. All are beautiful. Be contented where you are. Content! —a lost word in our America. This restless ambition—I cannot feel the truth of it. I cannot follow there. I am quite willing to be out of touch with my times. I would live as if the times were out of touch with me." Kingsley Porter would have subscribed to the last two sentences, had he ever seen them.

LC

FOR SEVEN YEARS the editorial comment on this page has been written in the name of the editors of *The American Neptune*. It is now necessary, in one instance at least, to depart from this collective anonymity, because the death of Lincoln Colcord on 16 November 1947 has broken, for the first time, the small group of friends who have been responsible for the editing of this journal. It consequently seems appropriate to give some account of the part that he played in its foundation.

In February 1939 the Peabody Museum Marine Associates were organized at the Peabody Museum of Salem. This group consisted of men interested in various aspects of maritime history, who agreed, without formal organization of any kind or without the ceremonies of electing officers and bickering over bylaws, to meet at the museum on the fourth Monday of each month to hear a paper and discuss matters of mutual interest. It was natural that Lincoln Colcord, during one of his visits to me at North Andover, should wish to foregather with the Marine Associates, and I therefore asked him to read a paper titled "The Last Forty Years of American Sail—1865–1905" at the meeting of 23 October 1939. This was a subject that he knew at first hand, for he had been born off Cape Horn, aboard his father's ship, on 14 August 1883, and had grown up at sea in the characteristic manner of a Maine shipmaster's son. The gifts of literary expression that were added to this firsthand experience made him the spokesman for many less articulate seamen. To his house at Searsport there came a great variety of people of all kinds and experiences who shared their enthusiasms with him. Consequently he was uniquely at the center of maritime knowledge in New England and aware of what was passing through the minds of many people who cared for the history of New England seafaring. In the course of the 23rd of October while at Salem, Link became more and more emphatic about the necessity of a journal where scattered accounts of American maritime history could be brought together. By eight o'clock, when the hour for the Marine Associates' meeting had arrived, he had forgotten all about his announced subject and had only the new journal in mind. In completely characteristic fashion he spoke extemporaneously upon that theme, and with such conviction and fervor that by the end of the evening there was no longer any doubt in anyone's mind that something of the sort should be attempted by the Marine Associates.

Various conversations followed during the winter, and on 5 May 1940 a group of friends who formed the nucleus of the editorial and editorial advisory boards assembled in my barn in North Andover for a day's discussion. To the New Englanders present it seemed fine and balmy spring weather, although Alec Brown and Vernon Tate, coming respectively from Newport News and Washington, sat shivering in their overcoats. With Link, as always, in the center of the discussions, the final plans for the publication of *The American Neptune* were laid at that time. The name had been supplied by Phil Cranwell, with a considerable basis of historical analogy. The Society for Nautical Research in England had called its journal *The Mariner's Mirror* after the great sixteenth-century collection of nautical charts. For an American counterpart of *The Mariner's Mirror* it seemed appropriate to adapt to American use the name of the principal eighteenth-century compilation, *The Atlantic Neptune.*

To give a sound basis for the business side of the venture, and to avoid a suggestion of regionalism which might have been imputed had the journal been published by the Peabody Museum Marine Associates, the group applied for incorporation, and The American Neptune, Incorporated, received its charter from the Commonwealth of Massachusetts in the autumn of 1940. Publication began in January 1941, and the rest of the story is already familiar to readers. It seems very unlikely, however, that without the enthusiasm and drive furnished by Lincoln Colcord it would have been possible, in a matter of fourteen months, to bring together a group of people from widely scattered parts of the country and gain their support in such an enterprise.

Throughout the past seven years Link Colcord constantly aided the

Neptune by advice and criticism of manuscripts. His own contributions were fewer than I could have wished, for the extent of his correspondence, and the remarkable number of friends who appeared in person in the back yard at Searsport, left him little time for writing. I was one of the many

callers who at all seasons were likely to distract him. Whenever I have drawn up beside his gaunt old yellow house, and paused momentarily to look out to a sea whose intense blue was matched by that of the delphiniums in the grass, I have always been visited by a sense of anticipation—an anticipation that each time was unfailingly rewarded. Since Link's death I have reflected often on that feeling, and have wondered whether it has not been shared by many of his friends.

To meet him was to be aware of the vitality of the man. Gusto is the only word for it. He met life eagerly, equally alert for the savor of a situation, a dish of food, a bottle of rum, an anecdote, or a stretch of landscape. Whatever ills Link had gallantly encountered—and he had stood up to his fair share—boredom was not one of them.

As one's friendship with him grew, to that first impression of unique vigor there was added a second. This was that his boyhood years at sea had been all-significant for him. Through them he had established, somehow, a private quarter-deck of the mind, from which he passed judgment on men and things. With characteristic fairness, though, he was more than willing to allow each of his fellow men a similar retreat. Many a time I have heard him express apparent approval of behavior which I knew must have been distasteful to him. But stronger in him than any distaste was his respect for the rights of the individual. Much that was strange or perverse he would tolerate, provided only it arose from wholehearted conviction; contrariwise, his scorn for affectation and pettiness was blistering. I think it was really this all-engrossing concern for the independence of the individual that led him to decry our contemporary processes of regimentation, and to exalt the past, particularly the seafaring past of New England, which, to his imagination, had fostered the hardihood of man.

And lastly, all who knew Link must have recognized as an adjunct of his fervent and independent spirit, his love of talk. Thoughts and fancies we wished he would take time to write brimmed over in conversation, such conversation as we shall not hear again. He dearly loved an argument. Consistency being no vice of his, it did not disconcert him in the slightest to make a rightabout-face with no warning and absolutely no apology. That was all part of the game. I have said that many of us wished he would write as he had spoken. A natural feeling, no doubt, but perhaps a mistaken one. For all of us, his friends, he by his manner of talking fulfilled the function of breathing life into a faltering idea, of renewing our courage in ourselves, and heartening us for action.

During my last visit in September 1947 we drove to Mount Desert Island for a glorious day's sail in Sam Morison's *Emily Marshall*, and when we returned to Searsport for more talk, in which Waldo Peirce joined, there was no thought that the plans we discussed would not be brought to completion. Link's death in the hospital at Belfast, very early Sunday morning, 16 November, was entirely unexpected. His funeral took place Wednesday afternoon in the Congregational Church at Searsport. Sam Morison and I took the morning train trom Boston to Rockland. It was late in arriving, and when we reached Rockland the sun was already low. As we drove along the shore of Penobscot Bay the setting sun, reflected from the water, cast a radiant purple mantle over the hills and the islands. This sad but triumphant autumn afternoon was one that Link would have loved, and as we reached the church in Searsport in the twilight we felt that it was such a day as he would have chosen to show his own country at its best. "So he passed over, and all the trumpets sounded for him on the other side."

A few days later Storer B. Lunt and I arranged for Fred Anthoensen to print as a broadside the following verses by Lincoln Colcord originally published in his long poem *Vision of War* (New York, 1915), which were read at the funeral.

I went out into the night of quiet stars;
I looked up at the wheeling heavens, at the mysterious firmament;
I thought of the awful distances out there, of the incredible magnitudes, of
*   space and silence and eternity;*
I thought of man, his life, his love, his dream;
I thought of his body, how it is born and grows, and of his spirit that
*   cannot be explained.*

All about me slept the land in peace, and nature slept in deep serenity;
An off-shore wind had died at sunset, the bay was calm and golden as twi-
*   light fell;*
Not a cloud broke the clear and tender blue of the evening sky;
Then the quiet stars came out, the air grew cool with the breath of night;
A land-breeze flurried, wafting the odor of damp woods and late hay-fields;
A gentle breeze, that scarcely turned the sleeping leaves.

I walked on through the village, I saw the lights go out in houses as men
    and women prepared for bed;
Safe and secure, the homes of my neighbors rested in the shadow of tall trees,
    that had been growing there peacefully a long time;
I passed on into the country, crickets were singing in the fields, fireflies were
    glimmering in the pastures among low growths of spruce and pine;
I mounted a hill; high overhead brooded the majestic and silent heavens;
On the eastern horizon a great bright star arose, casting a track across the
    bay.

I have never seen the world so calm, the air so clear and still;
I have never known an hour so full of quietness.

CHAPTER VII

Willard Goodrich Cogswell

1881–1955

THE FRIENDSHIP of Willard Cogswell of Haverhill, Massachusetts, was one of the most agreeable fringe benefits of our having settled near by in North Andover in 1936. We saw each other often in Essex County, but even oftener in the train going to and from meetings of the Club of Odd Volumes, or some related organization in Boston. Zorn's etching "The Toast," which hung in the Cogswells' dining room, has now come to the walls of ours in North Andover through a characteristically thoughtful provision in the will of Willard's widow.

The memoir that follows was written for the Massachusetts Historical Society. It appeared in their Proceedings, LXXI *(1953–1957) 402–409, and was afterward reprinted in* Willard Goodrich Cogswell 1881–1955, A Selection of his Writings *(Haverhill, 1960) 3–10.*

WGC

A TYPE OF MIND common in eighteenth-century New England that has all but disappeared has been recalled by Professors Harry J. Carman and Rexford G. Tugwell in their edition of Jared Eliot's *Essay upon Field Husbandry in New England*. "There used to be a kind of man," they wrote, "found rather often in earlier generations, who stood to a whole countryside as the representative there of learning. He might be a doctor or a lawyer; sometimes he was a craftsman; at any rate his ubiquitous interest in things of the mind made him notable. Men of this sort have a tendency now to flock together and, having done that, they specialize and develop a fantastic exclusiveness. This spoils the unique quality of the village philosopher."

Such a man was Willard Goodrich Cogswell, who was born in Haverhill on 21 December 1881 and died there on 20 May 1955. From the Haverhill public schools he entered Harvard College with the class of 1904. Receiving the A.B. degree in 1903, not only in three rather than four years but also *cum laude*, he studied law, for a year at the Harvard Law School and then in the Haverhill office of Nichols and Brewster. He was admitted to the Massachusetts Bar in 1907. The following year he went West. In 1908 he was admitted to the California Bar, where he practiced for about a year before returning to Haverhill for good. Once at home again, he thereafter moved only to the eastward. For the next forty-six years he remained in his native city, practicing law but also enlarging his mind and cultivating the arts in a manner more suggestive of the eighteenth than the twentieth century.

When the *Haverhill Gazette* announced his death, it had an extended list of local accomplishments to catalogue. He was at the time the senior member of the law firm of Cogswell, Davis and Soroka, vice-president and director of the Merrimack National Bank, a director of the Haverhill Cooperative Bank, a trustee of the Pentucket Five Cents Savings Bank, a director and clerk of the Hoyt and Worthen Tanning Corporation, a director and treasurer of the Dole and Childs Funeral Home, a trustee of the Haverhill Public Library and of Atkinson Academy, and president of the trustees of the John Greenleaf Whittier Homestead. For thirteen years he had served on the Haverhill Planning Board. He had been president of the Haverhill Civic Music Association, and had over the years taken part in a great variety of other local enterprises.

What such a list fails to reveal is Willard Cogswell's intense concern with the individuality of Haverhill as a place, his detailed affection for its past, and his desire to preserve whatever was distinctive in its character. It completely overlooks the extraordinary variety of subjects that he explored solely because they intrigued and fascinated him. This is not surprising, for he was a shy man, who by nature concealed the breadth and diversity of his interests. To the end of his life he alleged, and more than half believed, that he was a simple countryman, drawing wills in a northern Essex County industrial city, a man whose opinions and tastes could be of no conceivable interest to anyone except himself.

I came first to know Willard Cogswell through plants and trees. In 1936 we settled in North Andover—the next town to Haverhill—in a house whose rear windows looked out upon a somewhat senile orchard and a great number of weedbound perennial beds. In the attempt to bring some pattern and order into this garden I found my way to the nursery of Gray and Cole in Ward Hill. Paul Gray and Harry Cole, whom I first visited by accident, soon became valued friends, for in addition to being the best nurserymen in the region, they are opposite-minded Thoreauvians whose tastes in books, music, landscape, and conversation rival their skill with plants. As we fell into the way of exchanging visits in the summer twilight, I began to hear of their friend Cogswell, who, it appeared, had around his house in Haverhill some spreading Japanese yews of magnificent proportions, as well as a remarkable planting of azaleas. So it eventually came about that I met the yews and their owner.

Willard Cogswell had settled, immediately after his marriage in June

1912 to Julia Hayes, in a high-shouldered wooden house of the Eighties on Winona Avenue, a shady suburban street at the northern extremity of Haverhill. From the fields behind the house one looked across the state line to the low hills of Plaistow, New Hampshire. The house in itself had no particular architectural distinction, although its rooms were high and tolerably convenient. The Cogswells might well have gone elsewhere, for they both loved eighteenth-century houses, had they not irrevocably planted themselves into 119 Winona Avenue. The man who sets out trees for the future cannot lightly shift his abode when his planting is reaching maturity. Willard had placed around a normal enough side lawn a number of small specimens of *Taxus cuspidata nana*, bought from Paul Gray. Now, the Japanese yew is a versatile and accommodating tree: if clipped systematically it will resign itself to becoming part of a hedge, or even an example of topiary fantasy, but if left to its own devices, and given room, its branches will spread into extraordinary and picturesque shapes. Willard had given the yews their head. Over the years they had grown to such dimensions that they rivaled the best specimens in the Arnold Arboretum. They had encroached upon the grass and finally obliterated it, so that from the windows of the house one looked into a rich sea of evergreen branches, of unparalleled beauty and fascination.

Time and the Lord had made the yews what they were, but in Willard Cogswell's "back yard," as he consistently called it, he had helped the Lord a good deal. It was originally a back yard and nothing more, but, as he loved New England forests, he planned and planted one behind his house, setting out evergreens in quantity, moving boulders to spots where they might well have cropped out naturally, and, as the trees grew to sufficient height, transplanting to the shady ground below them a rich profusion of ferns and the delicate wild plants that ordinarily resist cultivation. Beyond the wood one emerged into an open space, bordered by masses of azaleas, laurel, and rhododendrons. Willard had an uncanny gift for reproducing nature so skillfully that plants recognized their natural habitats and responded to his persuasion. The only bit of formality in the place was a pair of stiff beds of rather fearful petunias and zinnias, known as "Catherine's garden," where the Cogswells characteristically allowed a devoted cook to indulge *her* theories of horticulture.

The azaleas, which were in their season the bravest show of the place,

Willard Goodrich Cogswell

once marked the extreme limit of the "back yard," but as years passed Willard extended his operations further and further afield, creating an additional herb garden here, a birch grove there. All these points of interest were connected by woodland paths, along which he installed highly comfortable stone armchairs, in which one boulder formed the seat, another the back, and two more the arms. He had a Japanese appreciation of the natural beauty of stones and a Cornish quarryman's skill in moving great boulders with seeming ease. Thus he would pick stones that were attractive in themselves and by some legerdemain set them at angles accommodating to the human posterior. As a result of this gift, six or eight friends might find themselves of a summer evening, seated on Mycenaean thrones, happily consuming noble mutton chops that Willard had brought out from Dole and Bailey in Faneuil Hall and grilled over a nearby open fire.

When darkness came and the company migrated indoors there was as much to admire there as in the "back yard." The walls were crowded with Audubon birds, Hogarths, English county maps, Zorns, Seymour Hadens, and Whistlers. The genial bearded professor, glass in hand, of Zorn's "The Toast" who presided over the dining room was an appropriate tutelary figure for a house in which a cocktail would always be taken out to the kitchen for Catherine Mahoney. The cocktails, the wine, and the dishes in that dining room had been planned with imagination and prepared precisely, only to be presented to guests with a beguiling offhanded modesty. Willard and his wife were the kind of artful hosts who succeed in pressing delicacies upon their friends and at the same time leaving the impression that it is the hosts who have received a favor.

The heart of the house was the second-floor library, whose walls were crowded with as carefully selected a choice of books as I have ever seen. Their owner clearly subscribed to Thomas Fuller's opinion: "It is excellent for one to have a library of scholars, especially *if they be plain to be read*. I mean of a communicative nature, whose discourses are as full as fluent, and their judgments as right as their tongues ready." This "library of scholars" was clearly assembled for reading rather than rarity; it was a collection of pure literature, with few books about subjects and none about how to do things. Lamb and Hazlitt held the place of honor, but the shelves were rich in English writing of all kinds, for Willard turned readily from Wordsworth to Chaucer, from Walton to Sterne, ranging through the centuries with a fine disregard for current critical fads. At one end of the library was a grand piano on which he played when alone or with his wife; the music available to guests came from a superb phonograph that anticipated the excellences of the "hi-fi" era.

On the magazine table *Punch, The Countryman, John o' London's Weekly,* and other importations were always to be found, for Willard loved the English countryside as passionately as he did New England. Three times he visited England, where he readily fell in with like-minded persons, such as the retired naval captain at Cheltenham who called his hens by name, as though they were puppies, while feeding them, and who competed with his gardener in raising onions in separate beds, to see which should gain first prize at the country fairs. On the outbreak of World War II he supported projects of the English Speaking Union, and had a particular interest in the welfare of H.M.S. *Bradford*, one of the United States destroyers turned over to the Royal Navy under lend-lease. On 26 June 1941 he represented the people of Haverhill, Massachusetts, in a short-wave broadcast to Haverhill, England, over station WRUL.

As Willard Cogswell never drove a car, his minute explorations of northern New England were made on foot. With his friend George Carter he tramped over most of the unsettled parts of southern New Hampshire. Every year he and his wife would spend some days at the hotel on the top of Mount Mansfield, whose trails he knew as if they were the paths in his "back yard." He knew the White Mountains intimately, and when approaching seventy was capable of climbs and tramps that exhausted supposedly hardy undergraduates who had been so rash as to accompany him.

On the backs of Appalachian Mountain Club maps he would transcribe, in a minute hand, passages of prose and verse that delighted him, on the theory that, if he should find himself stormbound at Guyot Shelter, these old friends would solace him in his imagined loneliness. When the fifty-fourth map was completed he compiled an index, which begins thus: Henry Adams, Addison, Arnold, Roger Ascham, Austen, Francis Bacon, Walter Bagehot, Baring-Gould, William Barnes, Richard Barnfield, Barrie, Clifford Bax, Francis Beaumont, Beerbohm, Belloc, A. C. Benson, Bernard Berenson, Bible, Blake, Borrow, etc. Horace, Homer, Logan Pearsall Smith, Pope, Ronsard, Santayana, Seneca, Charles M. Doughty, Osbert Sitwell, Emerson, Thomas More, and André L. Simon appear in new juxtapositions on the maps. The Book of Job and Brillat-Savarin jostle one another; so do Dante and Gilbert White. From Gilbert Murray's *The Stoic Philosophy* comes the quotation: "You remember the eighteenth century lady's epitaph which ends: 'Blond, passionate, and deeply religious, she was second cousin to the Earl of Leitrim, and of such are the kingdom of heaven.' One doubts whether when the critical moment came, her relationships would really prove as important as her executors hoped." I hope that some day a publisher will have the imagination to permit David McCord and me to turn these quotations into an anthology, for they are an endless delight.

A man of this turn of mind, however many useful functions he may have fulfilled there, and however great his feeling for the place, can hardly have been entirely at home in a twentieth-century industrial city. Willard Cogswell had intimate friends in Haverhill, but it was in Boston in the later years of his life that he found a greater number of like-minded companions. He and his wife had for years gone to Boston every Friday for the Symphony. They had a share in the Athenæum, and Willard in 1942 joined the St. Botolph Club. In the same year, after rebutting repeated protestations of his imagined lack of qualifications, I wheedled him into becoming a member of the Club of Odd Volumes, where he found himself thoroughly at home. In 1950 he succeeded his dear friend Charles Goodspeed as librarian of the club. When his 1952 report was presented in the form of two sonnets, the club promptly printed them as a broadside. In 1943 he was elected a resident member of the Colonial Society of Massachusetts.

Had Willard Cogswell lived in Haverhill in 1791 he would inevitably have been one of the close friends and correspondents of the Rev. Jeremy Belknap, and so one of the founders of the Massachusetts Historical Society. His election to the society in 1951 was a recognition that in northern Essex County he was the outstanding example of the type of broadly cultivated amateur, with a serious interest in history, that had for one hundred and sixty years been one of the society's strengths. When one looked north from Boston, he stood beyond a doubt in Haverhill as the conspicuous representative of learning. One could wish that he had written as profusely about his region as his British counterpart, Reginald L. Hine, did in *Confessions of an Un-common Attorney*, and other books about Hitchin in Hertfordshire. This "un-common attorney" of Essex County in New England was too much of a stylist to write rapidly. He chose his words with deliberation for their music and their sense, as in the final sentence of a tribute to one of his close friends, which began, "This then was George Carter who died in the spring." He was, moreover, too reticent to rush into print. Most of what he was induced to publish was in ephemeral form, as in the case of his perceptive "Notes on the Growth of Haverhill" that were sandwiched between advertisements in the program of a tercentenary pageant. The following extract from that piece is typical of his skill in synthesis, description, and evocation:

> Life here [from 1890 to 1915] may have been insular, but it was vibrant and various. Its atmosphere was a compounding of the inflowing of foreign peoples, the building of miles of new streets and row after row of new houses; the characteristic hum of steam-driven shoe-machinery along Washington Street, and the smell of leather being worked on there; the great piles of goods shipped each night across country and over-seas; the sequence of horse-cars, trolley-cars and buses, of driving-horses, bicycles, and motor-cars; toboggan-shutes, roller skating rinks, the Pines; troupes of repertory players at the Academy of Music, band concerts at City Hall Park; Merrimack Street crowded on Saturday evenings; the Haverhill baseball team in the New England League. People learned to use telephones without self-consciousness. Most streets were deeply muddy in early spring, but nobody really minded. They coasted down Main Street after snowstorms, held amateur horse-racing on the frozen river and professional trotting meets at the track on the Newton Road.

For an anniversary in 1939 of one of the banks of which he was an officer he prepared an historical sketch that was published in *One Hundred Twenty-Five Years of the Merrimack National Bank of Haverhill*, and in 1953 he wrote a sonnet in commemoration of the sesquicentennial of Bradford Junior College. The one paper that he gave to the Massachusetts Historical Society, "Highways and Low Ways in Haverhill from Grant to McKinley," is printed in the society's *Proceedings*, LXXI. During its presentation no one was asleep in the Dowse Library, although one literal-minded member loudly denounced the paper as frivolous. In consequence, the denouncer, when proposed for the Club of Odd Volumes, was resoundingly blackballed on the theory that any one capable of such stupidity would be no addition to the club.

Willard Cogswell cared deeply for history, literature, nature, and the arts; he was not only one of the most cultivated men of his day but to the relatively limited number of friends who knew him well the most engaging of companions. Whether on the top of Mount Mansfield or in a late train to Andover and Haverhill his conversation was a delight. I once attended a particularly dreary Haverhill funeral in his company. It was in winter and I drove him long miles over icy roads to a country cemetery. When it was over, back we went to his library and finished the day with *The Beggar's Opera* and a bottle of Irish whiskey. It was a delight to examine wildflowers with him, and equally pleasant to go to Dudley Street after a lunch at the C.O.V. to buy a phonograph record of "Paddy McGinty's Goat."

The only touch of bitterness that I ever noted in his conversation was in connection with Harvard College, where as an undergraduate he had led the lonely existence of many a country boy in the days when students lived wherever they could find lodging. At the Odd Volumes he was devoted to John Livingston Lowes, F. N. Robinson, George Lyman Kittredge, J. D. M. Ford, and David McCord as individuals, although his doubts about Harvard as an institution remained. In 1954 he was reluctantly persuaded to go to his fiftieth reunion, during which he was, to his equal pleasure and surprise, elected an honorary member of Phi Beta Kappa.

He was a man of upright character and religious conviction, intimately familiar with the King James Bible and the Anglicanism of the seventeenth century, yet tormented by his inability to accept without reservation the organized manifestation of any Christian body. He was happy in his family life and often accompanied his wife to mass, reverently envying her the comfort of her faith. On his deathbed he accepted the counsel of a wise and sympathetic priest, who, recognizing him as *anima naturaliter Christiana*, made it possible for him to be buried with a requiem high mass from St. James Church in Haverhill, which he had so often attended with his wife. In following him to his grave, many of us shared David McCord's feeling, expressed to her, "Willard has gone on a long walk but we shall overtake him." Those who have not yet done so rejoice that the birthplace of a man who cared so passionately for books has recently become the Cogswell Branch of the Haverhill Public Library.

CHAPTER VIII

Charles Eliot Goodspeed

1867–1950

FREQUENT CONVERSATIONS with Charles Goodspeed brightened my first four years at the Boston Athenæum. Although he lived to be eighty-three, he died too soon. This memoir appeared in Massachusetts Historical Society Proceedings, LXXI *(1953–57) 362–365, a volume in which I had to record the deaths of too many good friends. The photograph reproduced here was taken in his office in 1948 when Goodspeed's Book Shop had completed its first half-century.*

CEG

C
HARLES ELIOT GOODSPEED, who was born at Cotuit, Massachusetts, on 2 May 1867, went to work at the age of fourteen. After fourteen years as a traveling salesman in farm machinery and three in the New York office of the firm that he had represented on the road, he found himself out of a job in consequence of the

business depression following the Panic of 1893. He converted this misfortune into the opportunity to do what he most cared for, and became a bookseller. The shop that he opened in the basement at 5A Park Street, Boston, on 1 December 1898 started on a shoestring; it soon became a valued Boston institution, and in time one of the best known and respected antiquarian bookshops in the United States. In 1937 Charles Goodspeed told the story of Goodspeed's Book Shop and the more impersonal aspects of his first seventy years in a delightful autobiography, *Yankee Bookseller*. What I write here has to do with his thirteen last years and is a tribute to an example of old age in its ideal manifestation.

It is not surprising that, with a Cape Cod background, he should have made his mark in his chosen profession in the old New England way, but those who knew him well came to discover that he possessed qualities but rarely found in the successful New Englander. A devout disciple of Izaak Walton, he had much of Walton's simplicity and sweetness of character. After reaching the age of seventy he made his permanent home on a hillside at Shirley, where he had formerly summered. There, with a magnificent view across a valley toward Wachusett, he gardened, collected minerals, and read the seventeenth-century writers that he loved. Leaving the routine cares of business to younger members of his family, he experimented with the latest evolutions of iris in his perennial beds, and lovingly nurtured the wild things of the New England countryside in his woodland. It seemed entirely natural that Scotch heather grew readily for him, or that the rarer ferns responded to his wishes.

In 1941 his house in Shirley burned, completely destroying the personal library that he had assembled with care over the previous half-century. There can be no greater tragedy for a bookman than this, but his response was typical. On the same site he built a convenient modern house, the main portion of which was to be occupied by his son-in-law and daughter, Mr. and Mrs. Gordon T. Banks, while a secluded wing, with its own access to the garden, accommodated Mrs. Goodspeed and himself. At seventy-five he had no desire to attempt to re-create the library he had lost. Instead, he built only a few bookshelves, on which he placed the authors who gave him particular pleasure at the time. When space ran short he would give something to an appreciative friend to make room for a new enthusiasm.

Charles Eliot Goodspeed

I remember vividly coming back to my desk in the Athenæum in the summer of 1950 after three days in the Pentagon and a rocky night in the Federal Express. During my absence Charles Goodspeed had quietly left there three seventeenth-century editions of Launcelot Andrewes's writings, with a note suggesting that as his library shelves in Shirley were becoming overcrowded I might find room for these books on mine in North Andover. The enjoyment that these three volumes give me whenever I see them makes me particularly conscious of the tragedy of the Shirley fire when books conveying a lifetime's association were swept away.

In this new library in Shirley I first came to know the essays of William C. Prime, which have since given me much pleasure, and there I first encountered the unpublished correspondence—now in the Boston Athenæum—between the president of Rollins College and Will Rogers regarding an honorary degree, which Charles Goodspeed loved to share with his friends as an instance of the absurdity of academic scalp-hunting.

One day a dozen years ago, after dividing and resetting his finest iris, Charles intimated that Willard Cogswell and I might help him out by carrying away some of the corms for which he had no space. When we arrived at Shirley we were conducted to a shed where a great variety of roots was neatly arranged on a trestle table. As he wished some to go in my garden in North Andover, some in Willard's in Haverhill, and some in the front yard of the Club of Odd Volumes, he had prepared three sets of neatly lettered tags for each variety, on which were indicated not only the name but the height and color. We were then furnished with a great pile of fresh paper bags, a ball of string, and a pair of scissors, and invited to help ourselves. Thanks to Charles's meticulous preparations, the iris were soon divided three ways and ready to be carried home in the neatest and most convenient manner. We next walked through the woods—where we found at every turn wild plants looking completely at home, although in most cases transplanted by him—and finally settled down in his living room to admire the view of the western hills and talk about books.

In these last years when Charles Goodspeed came to Boston he was more likely to be found in my place of business at 10½ Beacon Street than in his own at Number 18. It was an unfailing delight to see him at a fourth-floor Athenæum table behind a pile of books, for he would look up with a singularly winning smile and convey, ever so briefly, some diverting bit of historical or bibliographical information that he had just uncovered. Early in his retirement he published his *Angling in America*, and in 1946 compiled *A Treasury of Fishing Stories*, which furnishes agreeable reading even for a nonfisherman like myself.

Charles Goodspeed became a member of the Club of Odd Volumes in 1914. From 1944 to 1951 he served as its librarian, occupying the high-ceilinged little second-floor room over the front door at 77 Mount Vernon Street. Mrs. Augustus Peabody Loring, the assistant librarian, would laughingly complain that she served no useful purpose in the club, for Charles could never bear to see her climb a ladder or carry an armful of books. In 1946 the club published his *Nathaniel Hawthorne and the Marine Museum of the Salem East India Marine Society or The Gathering of a Virtuoso's Collection*, which was an amusing piece of literary detective work.

In 1921 he was elected to the American Antiquarian Society, of which he was a devoted and generous member. He became a member of the Colonial Society of Massachusetts in 1926, and was its president in 1945–1946. The Massachusetts Historical Society elected him to resident membership in 1938; he served on the council from 1943 to 1945, and from 1943 was chairman of the library committee. Upon his death, Stewart Mitchell wrote: "Long before he became a Member, Mr. Goodspeed had served this Society with constant good will, in finding books and manuscripts which he always gave us the first chance to buy. His service as Chairman of the Library Committee terminated with his successful descent into the basement of this building, out of which he persuaded the Council to remove many precious books to the Special Libraries Room."

C. K. Shipton, his friend and neighbor in Shirley, described Charles Goodspeed as the best-educated man whom he, personally, had ever known. The appreciation of his scholarly qualities was however not confined to his friends and to the Massachusetts learned societies, for Brown University in 1935 made him an honorary Master of Arts, and in 1946 the Harvard chapter of Phi Beta Kappa elected him to honorary membership.

Charles Goodspeed was a deeply but unobtrusively religious man. He had in his day served as a Baptist deacon. His most fervent convictions were expressed in five verses—Romans vi. 23; John iii. 16–17; Romans

viii. 38–39—that he copied in his Bible and repeated as he died on 31 October 1950.

In attempting to describe him, I cannot do better than to repeat C. K. Shipton's appraisal: "Never in life or in history have I known any one in whom were combined to such a degree the qualities of gentle goodness, modesty, wisdom, knowledge, and practical ability."

CHAPTER IX

Allan Forbes

1874–1955

ALLAN FORBES I knew less intimately than most of the men and women described in this volume. He was an old friend of the Peabody Museum of Salem, and early in my years there he asked me to explore the collection of whaling prints that crowded his house at 70 Beacon Street. In 1940, before he made public announcement of the gift of this collection to the Francis Russell Hart Nautical Museum at the Massachusetts Institute of Technology, he was thoughtful enough to tell me that he would have given the prints to the Peabody Museum had there been space there to exhibit them. I used this intelligence to stir the trustees of the museum to the remodeling of East India Marine Hall, lest other desirable acquisitions be similarly lost. Thus Allan Forbes was indirectly the instigator of building campaigns that are still going on. After the war, I often saw him at council meetings of the Massachusetts Historical Society, of which he was treasurer.

An abbreviated form of this memoir was published in a limited edition by the Second Bank-State Street Trust Company in 1956; this chapter is reprinted from Massachusetts Historical Society Proceedings, LXXI (1953–57) 412–422.

AF

ON Tuesday noon, 12 July 1955, Salem Street in Boston was so abnormally congested by crowds pouring out of the Old North Church that an Italian fruit vendor hailed an out-of-region passer-by to inquire: "What's going on in the North End today?" His curiosity was well founded, for Allan Forbes's funeral had brought numbers from the rest of Boston to the normally crowded streets of the North End. The variety of people who filled every available pew and gallery bench in the old church—whose restored steeple had been raised into place only the week before—proved quite as much the affection in which this quiet and unassuming man was held as the place that his abilities had won for him in the community. The Vicar of Christ Church and the Rector of St. Paul's Church, Dedham, read—from the clerk's desk below the high pulpit—the Order for the Burial of the Dead from the Book of Common Prayer. The congregation sang John Bunyan's "He who would valiant be 'gainst all disaster" and James Russell Lowell's "Once to every man and nation." As the coffin was carried out of the church—during the singing of "For all the saints" to Vaughan Williams's confident and noble tune—many of us felt poignantly the extent to which Boston was lessened by the death of this good man.

When he died on 9 July 1955 Allan Forbes was in his eighty-first year, for he had been born in Boston on 20 November 1874. His father, James Murray Forbes, had been in China with Russell and Company in the

Sixties, and his mother was a granddaughter of Nathaniel Bowditch, compiler of the *New American Practical Navigator*. The Murray Forbes house on Milton Hill, built about 1830 by Allan's grandfather, Captain Robert Bennet Forbes (1804–1889)—the most imaginative and versatile of nineteenth-century New England shipmasters and merchants—brought the color and scent of China to Massachusetts. Llewellyn Howland, who visited there in the Nineties, recalls that "to arrive there late in the afternoon after a day of work perched on a high stool in a stuffy, noisy office, was for me as if I had become a guest of the famous Chinese merchant, Houqua, in his charmingly precise and peaceful country house, as it was depicted in an old painting by a Chinese painter I had lived with as a child. For within doors, here in Milton, there was the subtle and pervasive odor of camphor wood and teak, the muted splendor of blues, greens, golds and red of Canton pottery and of lacquer work; the inimitably correct portraits of vessels of all rigs by Chinese artists, and much else suggestive of traffic with the Far East. While as for the house itself, there were details both in its plan and construction which proclaimed the calling—shipmaster and China merchant—of its builder, and the influence this profession had exercised upon his character, tastes and occupation."

Had Allan Forbes been born into such a family and grown up in such surroundings a generation earlier, he might well have gone to sea as a supercargo or to Canton as a clerk. As it was, he attended Milton Academy and Noble and Greenough's, but he also haunted the workshop where his grandfather Forbes amused himself in old age making sailing-boat models for young relatives and friends. Allan's cousin, Mrs. Edward Cunningham, recalls how he once proudly took a completed model of his own to their grandfather, attempting to pass it off as a boat that the old gentleman had formerly given him. The deception was soon unmasked, for Captain Forbes, although he showed pleasure over his young grandson's interest in boatbuilding, at once pointed out various defects in workmanship.

After graduating in 1897 from Harvard College—where he had been more absorbed by polo than by academic subjects—Allan Forbes became a clerk in the banking firm of Blodget Merritt and Co., before going into the employ of Maynard and Child, commission merchants. During the winter of 1898–1899, after the weather became too inclement to exercise his string of polo ponies, he and his friend Llewellyn Howland hived up in the carriage house of his parents' home on Milton Hill and built a twenty-foot boat—appropriately named the *Wonderhow*—that won a race for them on the Neponset River on 19 April 1899.

When Allan Forbes became assistant treasurer of the State Street Trust Company early in 1899, it was a small bank then only eight years old. Its total force consisted of eight persons, and its deposits were less than two million dollars. From the carefree beginning of his banking career, pedestrian-minded prophets might not have foreseen that in a dozen years Allan Forbes would be president of a bank more than six times that size.

On 3 February 1899, when he was very new indeed at his job, came the ball given by the Myopia and Norfolk hunt clubs. As he recalled it forty-three years later in reminiscences of Myopia: "It was my first hunt ball and I had a gorgeous evening—in fact night. Half an hour at home was all that I had for rest and a change of clothes, before starting for the office. My eyes were more than three-quarters closed, but I tried to find the combination to the safe. Presently, after a few ineffective attempts, I saw my boss, Charles Lowell, peering over my shoulder. 'I think you ought to go home,' he said softly, and I accepted his advice promptly and it wasn't five minutes before I was on my way to bed."

This unpromising start was soon forgotten when the officers of the bank began to observe Allan Forbes's almost uncanny skill in discovering what was going on in Boston, while maintaining a drily humorous air of friendly unconcern and quizzical detachment. In the third and fourth reports of his Harvard class, the chief fact that he chose to record, beyond his connection with the bank, was the ownership of a dog that had reached the patriarchal age of twenty-one years, three months, and thirteen days at its death on 1 April 1909. With this disarming talent for the irrelevant went a singular ability to steer much needed new business to the State Street Trust Company. The latter gift was particularly welcome, for Charles Lowell, the bank's first actuary, was not skilled in human relations. Samuel H. Wolcott, after forty years of close association, observed that Allan Forbes had a keener nose for business than a bird dog has for game; that he would figure out where it was and instantly go after it. This talent led to prompt advancement, for in 1900 Allan Forbes was elected treasurer of the State Street Trust Company, and in 1901 he became secretary. When a branch office was opened in 1905 at the corner of Massachusetts Avenue and

Boylston Street—a pioneer banking effort in that area—he went up there
for six months to scour the region for new business. One of his few failures
occurred when Dr. Samuel A. Green, the formidable librarian of the

Massachusetts Historical Society, summarily ejected him from the society's
new building at 1154 Boylston Street. The recollection of this initial rebuff
always amused him during his subsequent service as the society's treasurer
from 1921 to 1928 and from 1951 to 1955.

Upon Charles Lowell's death in 1906, Allan Forbes became vice-president of the State Street Trust Company. Five years later, in 1911, he was promoted to the presidency, which he held until 1950, when he became chairman of the board.

Very early in his career, Allan Forbes began to develop his natural tastes for history and collecting in directions that gave him pleasure, and, simultaneously, brought the bank to the attention of a vast number of potential customers. It had begun business in the basement of the Exchange Building on State Street, which occupied the site of the granite colonnaded Merchants' Exchange of 1842. Late in 1900 it had moved across to a building (now demolished) at 38 State Street, on the corner of Exchange Street. Having grown up in Milton among the relics of the China Trade, Allan Forbes was particularly sensitive to the historical implications of the surroundings in which he did business. From the settlement of Boston, State—originally King—Street had been the center of the town, for it led from the Town House (subsequently replaced by what we know as the Old State House) to the Long Wharf that extended far into the harbor. Here sailors, townspeople, and visiting Indians had jostled each other for decades; here British troops had been landed in 1768; here the Boston Massacre had taken place in 1770; here, in the early days of the Republic, Federalist merchants had met (on the sidewalk in fair weather, in a tavern in foul) to trade views on ships, business, and politics.

Immediately upon becoming vice-president and actuary of the bank in 1906, Allan Forbes began the publication of a series of illustrated historical booklets that attracted the attention of a wide group of readers. From a 1906 booklet on State Street, the series had by 1955, with its thirty-ninth volume, reached an audience far beyond New England, for Allan Forbes, as early as 1913, very shrewdly sensed a growing interest in the maritime history of New England. Such booklets as *Old Shipping Days in Boston* (1918) and *Merchants and Sea Captains of Old Boston* (two parts: 1918 and 1919)—drawn largely from little-known sources still in private hands— gave New Englanders a foretaste of the material that was to be so brilliantly treated by Samuel Eliot Morison in his *Maritime History of Massachusetts* in 1921. To commemorate the tercentenary of the Landing of the Pilgrims, the State Street Trust Company published in 1920, as the sixteenth in the series, *Towns of New England and Old England, Ireland and Scotland, Part I*. This work, in a larger format than its predecessors, presented in 225 copiously illustrated pages brief accounts of the relations of British towns and their New England namesakes. A second volume, of equal dimensions, that appeared in 1921, attracted so much interest that, to meet the public demand for copies, Messrs. G. P. Putnam's Sons undertook to publish the books commercially in New York and London. Although Allan Forbes was personally almost entirely responsible for the collecting of material and the writing of the texts, he characteristically kept his name out of sight until 1921, when he reluctantly signed the Foreword to *Towns of New England and Old England, Part II.*

The 1925 centenary of Lafayette's visit to Boston led to the beginning of a three-volume series on *France and New England* (1925, 1927, 1929) dealing not only with the Revolutionary figures of Lafayette, Rochambeau, and Franklin, but with Champlain and early French exploration and settlement. For this series, Paul F. Cadman made extensive researches in France that continued over a number of years, and led in 1938 to the publication of *Boston and Some Noted Émigrés.* This last booklet made an important contribution to our knowledge of Paul Revere's French ancestry, as well as reviving the memories of Peter Faneuil, Bishop Cheverus, Pierre Baudouin, and other French émigrés to New England. Both the British and French series were notable for their richness of illustration of European scenes of interest to Americans. A typical example is the photograph of the Whitehall boat, presented to Lafayette by New York watermen in 1825, that is still preserved in a barn at the Château Lagrange—a craft whose existence is known to few students of American boatbuilding.

New England industries, Indian events, Boston statues, lithographed ship-sailing advertising cards, Massachusetts town and city seals, New England taverns and stagecoaches, and Benjamin Russell's paintings of whaleships, all in their turn became the subjects of State Street Trust Company booklets. The variety of subject represented the catholicity of Allan Forbes's curiosity. Although the material is presented simply for popular interest, each booklet contains a fair deal of information not readily available elsewhere. Allan Forbes, who already knew the obvious facts of New England history, constantly asked questions that were not easy to answer. When anyone in a library or museum received a letter from him, two things were certain before the envelope was opened. The letter would be pleasant, and, equally certainly, it would contain a request for some bit of information that was nearly impossible to provide. Yet he amiably persisted, inquiring in likely and unlikely places, and in the end often unearthed curious nuggets of information that would have eluded a less determined curiosity. All assistance received, he acknowledged with such genuine gratitude that the preparation of the booklets—as well as their distribution—enlarged the circle of his and the bank's friends considerably. These thirty-nine volumes maintained over nearly half a century a singularly high degree of quality and consistency for bank advertising, for, however much they were due to Allan Forbes's personal predilections, they were also an uncommonly shrewd bit of business that kept the State Street Trust Company in the minds of New Englanders, and made its name known to lovers of the sea throughout the United States.

The same might be said of the banking rooms, whose decoration was due to this same combined fondness for the past and canny eye to the present and future. While living as a bachelor at Westwood, in the company of his venerable dog, Mike, Allan Forbes had collected good polo ponies, but his interests presently grew to include old furniture and whaling prints. A collector of his enthusiasm could hardly be expected to pass his business hours in surroundings of functional severity. In his 1917 Harvard class report, Allan Forbes said: "When I have any spare time I go down to the State Street Trust Company where I meet picture and furniture dealers from nine-thirty A.M. to four P.M. After these hours I visit them." This report characteristically failed to mention that he had been collecting accounts with a like energy. By 1911, the State Street Trust Company was obliged to move diagonally across the street to the Worthington Building, to accommodate not only its increased business but the models and ship pictures with which its president was beginning to fill the banking rooms.

The new quarters proved inadequate almost as soon as they were occupied. When the bank moved into them in 1911, its deposits totaled $13,000,000; after fourteen crowded years the figure had risen to $57,-000,000. The assets and good will of the Paul Revere Trust Company, purchased in 1916, brought the State Street Trust Company not only a number of desirable customers and valued directors, but the Copley Square office, occupying the street floor of the Wesleyan Building at 581 Boylston Street. In 1925, soon after the move to the bank's present location at the corner of State and Congress streets, the National Union Bank—founded in 1792—was merged with the State Street Trust Company.

In the planning and decoration of the present banking rooms, Allan Forbes's tastes found their most complete expression. A new building, with a severe granite façade reminiscent of the early nineteenth century, was built on the narrow slice of land at the southeast corner of State and Congress streets. Behind this dignified and apparently self-contained façade lay the vast recesses of the Exchange Building into which the bank could, and did, expand as necessary during the course of the next thirty years. In the banking rooms flagstone paving, granite counters, oak and pine paneling, antique lanterns, ship models hanging above the tellers' cages like votive offerings in a Basque fishermen's church, innumerable prints and ship portraits, tavern chairs, trestle tables, and pewter inkwells combined to create an atmosphere unique in Boston business. These new counting-rooms, occupied on Labor Day 1925, were in no sense a reconstruction of the surroundings in which business had formerly been transacted in Boston. Although they evoked the past they did not reproduce it archaeologically, for they were rather an original creation of Allan Forbes's imagination, basically intended for up-to-date banking, but built around the multiplicity of relics, antiques, pictures, and models that he and the bank were constantly collecting. The words of B. Nason Hamlin's "State Street Trust Chanty"—sung at a dinner on 1 February 1949 commemorating Allan Forbes's fiftieth anniversary with the bank—sum matters up concisely.

> *In this banking life,*
> *With its stress and strife,*
> *There's only one way to the top.*
> *Let the public gaze*
> *On whaling days,*
> *And give 'em an antique shop.*
> *Let the harpoon men*
> *Wield a wicked pen,*
> *Safe from all mammal harm.*
> *No blubber—no smell,*
> *While the ink in the well*
> *Is brown like genuine sparm!*

Chorus

Yo ho! My lads, yo ho!
Keep her east of the State House so.
Oh! a banker's life
On the ocean wave,
When the sea runs high
On the old stone pave.
Heave away, my hearties!
And so we'll yell "Let's go"
And deposit our slip
'Neath the model of a ship!
Yo ho, my lads, Yo ho!

All this was at once good fun and good business, for many times those who first came to see the models returned to deposit their slips beneath them.

When one had business with Allan Forbes, he was quickly found, with none of the normal ceremony by which less busy men often endeavor to convey an illusion of their own importance. He would be ensconced in a low-studded room of seventeenth-century inspiration, with heavy beams, and a great kitchen fireplace, suggesting that he might be about to roast a haunch of venison or cook a mess of succotash. Seated in a Carver-Brewster chair, originally from the taproom of the Wayside Inn, surrounded by ship models and prints, with fire buckets for waste baskets and a sea chest serving as a woodbox, Allan Forbes would deal with an extraordinary variety of twentieth-century business in the course of a day.

Although never a "joiner" in the usual American sense, he had from the beginning of World War I become accustomed to doing the work of many charitable enterprises and relief committees. In 1916 he had been one of the leaders in raising money for a flying school for Harvard undergraduates, known as the Undergraduates' Flying Corps. In December of the same year he was involved in the Boston National Allied Bazaar, which turned over $465,000 to the Allied countries that were then at war, and before the 1918 Armistice he had served on thirteen foreign war charities, as well as acting as treasurer for one of the Red Cross campaigns, the War Camp Community Service, and other such enterprises. With the approach of World War II, he was one of the organizers, and Massachusetts chairman, of the

Committee to Defend America by Aiding the Allies, and later became secretary of the United Nations Relief Fund. He was treasurer of Bundles for America, Inc., Bundles for Britain, Inc., American Aid to France, Massachusetts National War Fund, Massachusetts Branch U.S.O., and American Bureau for Medical Aid to China. His war services were recognized by the award of Chinese, Danish, Belgian, and Dutch decorations, as well as by his appointment as an Officer of the Legion of Honor and as an Honorary Commander of Civil Division of the Order of the British Empire.

In the years between the wars, Allan Forbes constantly sought to stimulate and preserve friendly contacts between New England towns and cities, and the communities in Great Britain from which they take their names. He had collected over two hundred and fifty prints of such English towns, with particular emphasis on views of Boston, England. This interest, to which the State Street Trust Company publications bear evidence, was shown even more tangibly in 1930 when he was instrumental in raising here more than $50,000 for the restoration of the tower of St. Botolph's Church in Boston, England. In recognition of this effort, he was awarded the Freedom of the Borough of Boston. From its foundation after World War I, he was a stanch supporter of the English Speaking Union.

In the normal course of events, he was active in the charitable work of the Salvation Army, the American Red Cross, the Community Fund, as well as serving as president of the Boston and Albany Railroad, and as a director or trustee of such organizations as the New England Mutual Life Insurance Company, the Boston Consolidated Gas Company, Franklin Savings Bank, Boston Insurance Company, and the Boston Woven Hose and Rubber Company.

Allan Forbes was president of the State Street Trust Company for thirty-nine years. In 1936, when the Union Trust Company was merged with the State Street Trust Company, Charles Francis Adams became chairman of the board of the combined banks. The Union Trust Company office at 24 Federal Street, which was retained as a second banking office in the downtown district, was soon, through Allan Forbes's incorrigible enthusiasm as a collector, decorated with a series of prints and models depicting the development of aviation from the eighteenth-century balloon to the present-day airplane. In May 1950, on the retirement of Charles Francis Adams, Allan Forbes became chairman of the board of the State

Street Trust Company. Five years later—when the bank's deposits exceeded $187,000,000 and its employees numbered 799 persons—it merged with the Second National Bank to form the Second Bank-State Street Trust Company. In the new organization Allan Forbes became, on 18 February 1955, co-chairman of the advisory committee. Although designations might alter, he and his familiar surroundings remained unchanged. At the time of his death, he had spent more than fifty-six of his eighty years in the bank—thirty-nine of them as president and five as chairman of the board. The deposits of $318,856,509.94 shown in the 30 June 1955 statement of condition of the Second Bank-State Street Trust Company are a far cry from the $2,000,000 that existed when he joined the staff in 1899. As a touch of New England frugality, the 1,232 employees of June 1955 represent a *smaller* number of persons in relation to the size of deposits than the eight that composed the staff of the State Street Trust Company fifty-six years earlier. When one considers the present flowering of bureaucracy in American life—even with due allowance for the marvels of business machines—this simple statistic is worth noting.

For all his record of business and charitable accomplishment, Allan Forbes had an equally full private life. In 1913 he married Josephine M. A. Crosby of New York City. Three years later they bought the spacious granite-fronted house at 70 Beacon Street—facing the Public Garden—that, with his country place at Westwood, remained his home for the rest of his life. In his 1917 Harvard class report he wrote that "after discarding mourning [for the aged dog, Mike], I took up polo again as before, and my chief motive then was to see how many good polo ponies I could collect. Since my marriage, four years ago, I have made more of a specialty of children, and prefer the latter. We have two children, the older being called Phyllis, for no one in particular, and the younger named Robert Bennet Forbes, for my grandfather." Shortly before the birth of his second child, he called on his aunt, Mrs. Charles E. Perkins, at 223 Commonwealth Avenue, who soon after wrote one of her sons in the following vein: "Allan tied the tiny oars into the little rowboat that my father made so many years ago, and which has always been on the mantelpiece in the Red Parlor. We agreed that it was wonderful that it had never warped and was in such perfect condition. I said, 'Allan, if your baby is a boy, that boat is his!' and the very next evening I received this note, 'Send round the rowboat!! Allan.' Then came another note—'R.B.F. sends you his love. All well. Allan.' " Three other sons, born after World War I—Allan, Jr., James Murray, and Henry Ashton Crosby—completed the family. All four, and their brother-in-law, S. Tudor Leland, were in the service during World War II. The eldest, named for his grandfather, died in 1944 as a lieutenant in the United States Naval Reserve.

Although of a frail physique as a child, Allan Forbes' early love for horses led to a varied career as a sportsman. He was on the winning Dedham Polo Team in the 1900 National Club Championships held at Brooklyn, New York, and eventually gathered in over 225 cups and prize ribbons won in sporting events that included sailing, polo, bicycle polo, horse shows, and model yachting. As a young man, he wrote the rules for bicycle polo, a game that was later to be revived by his eldest son, R. B. Forbes, with whom he collaborated on a combined history and rulebook that was published in 1942. In 1917 he wrote: "The last few years I have taken up golf in a way to replace polo, but have found it consistently more expensive for the beginner than the latter sport. I prefer golf to tennis because of the lack of spectators." In historical monographs on *Sport in Norfolk County* and *Early Myopia* he preserved numerous details of Massachusetts sporting history that would otherwise have been forgotten.

In addition to outfitting the State Street Trust Company with objects that evoked the maritime and aeronautical past of Boston, Allan Forbes assembled a great collection of whaling prints, which included two hundred and fifty versions of Jonah's misadventure with the whale. In 1940, when these prints had invaded even the bathrooms and back stairs of 70 Beacon Street, he gave the collection to the Francis Russell Hart Nautical Museum at the Massachusetts Institute of Technology. His comprehensive collection of military currency he gave in 1952 to the Massachusetts Historical Society.

Such a summary as this may suggest the manner in which a sensitive nose for game, combined with unobtrusive energy, dry humor, and quiet friendliness, led to remarkable accomplishments both in work and play. It cannot begin to express the extent to which those who made their way to Christ Church, Salem Street, on 12 July 1955 felt that Boston was poorer for the death of Allan Forbes.

CHAPTER X

Roger Wolcott

1877 – 1965

ROGER WOLCOTT I knew only from 1946, when I came to the Boston Athenæum, and thereafter on a somewhat formal basis there and at the Massachusetts Historical Society. Nevertheless I became fond of him because of his remarkable understanding of the proper relationship of the trustees and staff of such an institution. As a member of too many boards, I have always tried to pattern my behavior on his.

This memoir appeared in Massachusetts Historical Society Proceedings, LXVII (1965) 145–150.

ROGER WOLCOTT, who died at Milton, Massachusetts, on 21 April 1965, was elected a resident member of the Massachusetts Historical Society on 14 April 1927, and served as corresponding secretary from 1940 until failing health caused his retirement in 1957. A tall, straight, handsome man, he was an ornament to that undemanding office, which he assumed a year before my own election to the society. At monthly meetings in the Dowse Library, he would rise from his seat on the president's left and, with immense dignity, announce the names of gentlemen from whom letters had been received accepting election to membership, and, if elections were to take place, join his colleague Frank Grinnell in passing the mahogany ballot boxes with their moth-eaten supplies of Indian corn and black beans. And, as soon as the formal business was completed and the paper about to be given, Roger Wolcott would, with equal dignity, march out of the Dowse Library, square-shouldered, looking neither to right nor left, with the air of a Guards officer crossing a palace courtyard after the arrival of his relief. He had done his duty for the month, and was now free to return to his wife in Milton.

I saw Roger Wolcott in that ceremonious manifestation only a few times before I disappeared to Washington for four years in naval uniform. When I returned in the summer of 1946 to become director and librarian of the Boston Athenæum, I found, with slight misgiving, that Roger Wolcott had become my boss. He had been elected a trustee of the Athenæum in 1927. Six years later he became chairman of its library committee, and in 1936 vice-president. Following the death on 18 April 1946 of George Edward Cabot, who had made all the arrangements about my coming there upon my release from active duty, Roger Wolcott became president of the Boston Athenæum. Almost immediately I found that he was a completely congenial man to work for, as well as an admirable administrator. Like Fleet Admiral Ernest J. King, whose papers I had pushed and whom I greatly admired, Roger Wolcott told his subordinates *what* to do, and *when*, but never *how*. His manner invariably remained formal; his words were few but always relevant. He explained to me in the most general way the policies of the library, told me what money I had to work with, and turned me loose. He appeared at the Athenæum each Monday afternoon at two o'clock, following a class luncheon at the Union Club, coming and going with the same military precision that marked his progresses through the Dowse Library. On other days of the week I knew when and where he could be found, whether at a somewhat dusty rolltop desk in his law office at 60 State Street or at home in Milton, for his habits were unchanging. In the ten years that I worked with him he never once tinkered with routine details or offered irrelevant advice, yet he was unfailingly helpful in every respect whenever I sought him out, as I often did. When presiding at a meeting, he wasted neither time nor words. The annual meetings of the proprietors of the Boston Athenæum seldom lasted more than ten minutes, for the reports had been previously printed and distributed by mail, and his manner discouraged needless chatter or featherheaded inquiry.

Roger Wolcott's contributions to the Massachusetts Historical Society were, as with the Boston Athenæum, by no means limited to parade-ground appearances, for he had deposited there a huge collection of the correspondence, manuscripts, and notes of his historian great-grandfather, from which he had selected, transcribed, and edited a workmanlike volume of nearly seven hundred pages, *The Correspondence of William Hickling Prescott, 1833–1847*, printed at the Riverside Press for the society in 1925. This he dedicated to his mother, Edith Prescott Wolcott, "like her grandfather in her stoical refusal to allow bodily infirmity to interfere with a life of gracious service to her fellow-men."

In 1939 he distributed within his family a 120-page volume, *Family*

Jottings, privately printed by the Merrymount Press. This little book, although ostensibly genealogical, is full of accurate reminiscence and humorous observation which preserve nuggets of information useful to anyone who cares for the history of Boston. He describes George Ticknor's *Life of William Hickling Prescott* as "a great treasury of information, but errs on the side of glossing over the Historian's gay and irresponsible youth and making him out a far more sober-minded person than he actually was." He characterizes Rollo Ogden's biography thus: "A good short life, but stating to Mother's great amusement that Prescott always kept licorice tablets in his pocket as a treat for his young friends. They were for his own constipation." He describes his own childhood misfortune, when lunching with Mrs. George Ticknor in Park Street, of biting a piece out of one of the very thin tumblers that were then fashionable, cutting his lips and making a rather bloody scene. "Aunt Ticknor immediately sent for what she considered the proper remedies to stop bleeding. It was impossible to find a cobweb in the house (I suppose the cobweb would have been applied to the cuts) and so a cold door key was put down the back of my neck instead." He recalls his Grandmother Wolcott's disgust with his father's joining the Somerset Club as "entering a gang of wanton sybarites," and describes his mother's first cousin, Joseph Peabody (1824–1905), thus—"of the three wigs of different lengths, according to the time between his supposed haircuts, the Imperial and the surtouts in the style of Napoleon III." Finally in a postscript he tells the story of the teacher who, when his brother Oliver was seven or eight, asked the class who was Governor of Massachusetts. "Nobody answered, and she told Oliver to ask his father and tell the class the next day. Again when the question was repeated nobody answered, and she asked Oliver if he had forgotten to put the question to his father. He replied, 'Oh no—Papa said he was, but he's such a joker you can't believe anything he says.'"

The ideal of service came to Roger Wolcott from both sides of his family. His immigrant ancestor, Henry Wolcott, Esq., of Galdon Manor House, Tolland, Somersetshire, arrived in Boston on 30 May 1630 in the *Mary and John*, and went on to Windsor, Connecticut, to become a "chief cornerstone" of that settlement. In the first general assembly held in Connecticut, in 1637, he was elected a member of the lower house, and was annually until his death returned there or to the house of magistrates. His grandson, Roger Wolcott (1679–1767), became Chief Justice and Governor of Connecticut, as well as major general, second-in-command to Sir William Pepperrell during the Louisbourg expedition. He was, incidentally, the author of *Poetical Meditations, being some Improvement of Vacant Hours*, published at New London in 1725 (the first volume of verse to be printed in Connecticut), and reprinted by the Club of Odd Volumes in 1898 as the fifth in their series of Early American Poetry. This Roger's son, Oliver Wolcott (1726–1797), also Governor of Connecticut, who was a delegate to the Continental Congress and a signer of the Declaration of Independence, was the father of another Oliver (1760–1833), Governor, and Secretary of the Treasury under Washington and Adams, and of Frederick Wolcott, who, although resisting the family susceptibility to the governorship of Connecticut, was a member of the corporation of Yale College. Frederick Wolcott's son, Joshua Huntington Wolcott, came to Boston as a young man and entered the countinghouse of A. and A. Lawrence, in which he became a partner at twenty-six and remained until the dissolution of the firm in 1865. J. Huntington Wolcott's son Roger (1847–1900), Governor of Massachusetts, was the father of the subject of this memoir.

Our Roger Wolcott was born in Boston on 25 July 1877 and attended Hopkinson's School. When he entered Harvard College in the autumn of 1895, his father was Lieutenant Governor. When he received his A.B. *cum laude* in June 1899, his father made the last of his four appearances at Commencement as Governor. The father and son shared more than a name and a strong physical resemblance. Their early careers have a parallelism sufficiently striking to be worth noting. The father received his A.B. in 1870, standing eighth in a class of 131. After teaching French and history for a year at Harvard he entered the Law School, receiving an LL.B. in 1874 and setting up as a lawyer in Boston. He served in the Boston Common Council from 1877 to 1879, was elected to the House of Representatives in 1882, 1883, and 1884, was a Harvard Overseer from 1885 to 1895, and was elected to the Massachusetts Historical Society in 1884. The son proceeded directly to the Harvard Law School after being graduated from college, receiving an LL.B. in 1902. After four years in the law department of the Boston Elevated Railway Company, he opened an office for the private practice of law in July 1906 at 60 State Street. He too was elected to the House of Representatives in 1909, 1910, 1911, 1912, 1917, and 1918, and was an Overseer in 1921–1926 and 1927–1933.

There the patterns diverge, for the father was elected to the highest political office in Massachusetts and might well, had he not died at fifty-three, have served on the national scene, while the son never went politically beyond the House of Representatives. The difference, one suspects, is not so much in the men but in the times in which they lived. Sir Anthony Wagner once likened English society to "a lofty structure with many shallow steps by which the skilful and persistent might climb, while others slipped down and many more kept the framework solid by standing still." But, he added, "even those who stood still might find that the ground had moved under them." In Massachusetts in the first half of the twentieth century many descendants of English Puritans who climbed the steps with the traditionally confident gait of their ancestors, and with comparable skill and persistence, found themselves making as little progress as a man walking up a down escalator. This was the tragedy of Roger Wolcott. In public life and in innumerable private organizations he quietly did a great deal of dull and necessary work. He expected to do it, and, because he did, his neighbors all too often took his willingness for granted, without even troubling to thank him. In retrospect one realizes that Roger Wolcott's style, tastes, and habits of life were those of an earlier generation. In the nineteenth century his public and private services would very probably have been as appreciated and rewarded as were his father's. In the twentieth century they were not, but those of us who worked closely with him valued his skill in administration quite as much as we admired the dignity and dispatch with which he could conduct a public meeting, even when—as annually on the second floor of the Athenæum—he was silhouetted against the incongruous background of a marble copy of the Venus de Medici.

Roger Wolcott's Harvard class reports contain formidable lists of offices held and chores accomplished, enlivened by a dry humor. In noting that he he had been president of the Milton Club in 1928, of the Union Club in Boston, 1930–1932, and of the Hoosic-Whissick Club since 1935, he suggested that his "most probable epitaph will be the damning words, 'He was a prominent club man.'" He also noted: "Perhaps I am most proud of my service in three wars that have taken place since I was twenty years old, although in the last two I wore out more trousers' seats than shoe leather." His only uncle, Huntington Frothingham Wolcott, had enlisted at seventeen, served through the Civil War with distinction, and died of typhoid fever on 9 June 1865. So in the Spanish American War Roger Wolcott had quite naturally become a private, U. S. Volunteers. Thereafter he rose from private to captain and regimental adjutant of the First Regiment of Heavy Artillery, and to lieutenant colonel and inspector general, Massachusetts Volunteer Militia, retiring as a colonel on 1 September 1910. In World War I he was a major of infantry, U.S. Army, in charge of the draft in Massachusetts, giving up the seat that he had won for the sixth time in the House of Representatives because of this service. And in the last war, when past sixty, he performed thankless service as a member of the Milton draft board.

From his earliest years in legal practice, Roger Wolcott was a worker in the town and state Republican organizations. After the years 1909–1912 in the House of Representatives, he stood for the State Senate, but was defeated by the split in the vote caused by the presence of a "Bull Moose" candidate. His fifth term in the House of Representatives in 1917 was the last occasion when he held state office, but from 1924 to 1927 he was chairman of the Board of Selectmen of Milton.

On 7 June 1904 he married Claire Morton Prince, by whom he had two sons, one of whom died at four and the other at eight, and a daughter who died (before him) at forty-three. This marriage ended in divorce, and on 21 June 1928 he married Barbara Hinkley, the former wife of E. Sohier Welch. By his second wife he had a daughter Susan, now Mrs. Philip Dexter.

After his second marriage, Roger Wolcott and his wife spent the summer of 1928 in England, renting a house at Sidmouth, near Exeter, and driving themselves "over pretty near all of England west of Southampton." In the summer of 1938 they returned to Europe, visiting England and Scandinavia. They continued to live in the old house in Milton, bought by his grandfather in 1851, and spent most of their summers in hired houses at Northeast Harbor, Maine. In his fiftieth class report he noted: "The durable satisfactions of my life have come in the last twenty-one years of ideal companionship with my wife."

In 1943, on the death of Arthur Adams, Roger Wolcott became secretary of the Harvard class of 1899. This class was an unusually closely knit one, some of whose members gathered every Monday for lunch at the Union Club. Thus in the late 1940's, when he would move around the corner from the club to the Athenæum, I heard a good deal of the preparations for the class's fiftieth anniversary report and reunion, which were very close to his heart. In the decade when I saw him regularly, his appearances at 60 State Street were more likely to be concerned with Harvard than with legal business, and his life was happily centered in his home in Milton. Apart from the class luncheon, I gathered that his weekly appearances at the Athenæum and his monthly ones at the Massachusetts Historical Society, plus an occasional outing with the Society of the Cincinnati, constituted his chief tie with the world outside 1733 Canton Avenue, Milton. When he was entering his eighties Roger Wolcott suffered a stroke, which caused him to give up his offices both in this society and in the Athenæum. Although he continued to attend the class luncheons whenever he could, he never again, to my knowledge, entered either institution. I last saw him, several years later, by accident, on the steps of the Union Club. His appearance was as fine as ever, but he obviously could not bear the idea of being seen in public with any impairment of his old faculties. As his wife died on 19 March 1958, his last years were, I fear, very solitary.

CHAPTER XI

Louise du Pont Crowninshield

1877 – 1958

THE SUBJECTS of the ten previous chapters were all native New Eng-landers; Louise du Pont only became one by her marriage to Francis Boardman Crowninshield. I began to see her frequently in 1950 when she became a trustee of the Peabody Museum of Salem. Thereafter when my wife and I were driving to and from Virginia in spring or autumn we sometimes stayed with her at Eleutherian Mills in Montchanin, Delaware. Thus we came to know the re-markable museum that her brother, Henry Francis du Pont, had created at Winterthur, and the equally remarkable Longwood Gardens of her cousin, Pierre S. du Pont. As her Boston house at 164 Marlborough Street, like William Crowninshield Endicott's across the way at 163, has fallen on evil days, it gives me especial satisfaction, as a trustee of the Eleutherian Mills-Hagley Foundation, to have a share in the preservation of Eleutherian Mills. That Delaware house is today as attractive as any building can be without the occupants who gave it life and vitality.

This memoir was written for Henry Francis du Pont and privately printed by him at Winterthur in 1960. Mr. du Pont died on 11 April 1969. His last great addition to the Winterthur Museum that he created was the Louise du Pont Crowninshield Research Building, containing libraries and laboratories, which was dedicated on 12 May 1969.

LdPC

IN the fiftieth anniversary report of the Harvard class of 1891, Francis Boardman Crowninshield wrote: "I am fortunate in being married to an unusually good-tempered wife, one who spends most of her time doing kind things for other people, myself included." Forty-one years before, on 28 June 1900, he had married Louise Evelina du Pont, daughter of Colonel and Mrs. Henry A. du Pont of Winterthur, Delaware. Anyone who had the good fortune to know her would readily grant her husband's observation the status of an Absolute Truth. Louise Crowninshield was indeed unusually good-tempered and immensely kind, but that was not all. In addition, she possessed an extraordinary number of other qualities, subtly combined in a manner that was all her own. She had great administrative ability and tireless energy for getting things done. Had she been a man, she might well have run the du Pont works with conspicuous success. As it was she had a telling hand in an immense number of organizations devoted to the support of the arts, historic museums, houses and sites, and horticulture.

Her energy was boundless; she approached serious matters, and others that simply amused her, with eighteenth-century vigor and gusto. She would sit on the uncompromising cement seats of the Harvard Stadium through the worst November downpour rather than miss a Yale game, and would wear out younger friends by traveling great distances to be in more places than seemed humanly possible within the hours of a given day. The ordinary routine of a year involved her in an unusual degree of movement along the Atlantic seaboard. There were first of all two Crowninshield houses in Massachusetts, 164 Marlborough Street in Boston, a high-ceilinged red brick house on the corner of Dartmouth Street, designed by H. H. Richardson in the Seventies, and Seaside Farm at Peach's Point in Marblehead. Then came Eleutherian Mills at Montchanin, Delaware, the original du Pont house on a hillside above the Brandywine River. Finally there was a winter retreat in Boca Grande, Florida. All four houses were crowded with flowers, poodles, parrots, and great quantities of friends. When cruising and a good bit of traveling were added to the normal seasonal movements between New England, Delaware, and Florida it will be seen that Louise Crowninshield kept up a routine that would have exhausted a less vigorous person.

A stranger encountering her for the first time in a crowded room would not immediately have suspected from her appearance the remarkable and imaginative delicacy of her thoughts and the subtlety of her perceptions. In her presence you became aware that grace of person was superseded by extraordinary agility and accuracy of mind and by warmth of heart. Matters of importance she grasped with rapidity; her taste was unerring and her judgment as remarkable as was her skill in reaching with tact and consideration the goals that she instinctively sought. Perhaps because words did not come easily to her—her clear, active mind shot ahead of mere verbal felicities—her manner of speech was simplicity itself. Her natural forthrightness, however, was likely to be tempered by modesty, a diffidence almost youthful. The contrast was startling between her imaginatively generous acts of kindness and her unassuming demeanor even while she performed them.

Louise Crowninshield was a born collector who had the added gift of being able to blend possessions into an harmonious and unobtrusive whole. Her houses were packed with objects of rarity and intrinsic interest that quietly looked well together and were used, with a freedom rare among collectors, to make daily life pleasanter. Under her roof one had primarily the feeling of warmth and hospitable friendship to such an extent that one only incidentally was aware of the extraordinary beauty and quality of the individual objects that contributed to the surroundings. The talent that made these houses so agreeable to be in was often transferred to the subtle improvement of museums and historic houses with which she was concerned.

While this memoir is written to show the extent and variety of her usefulness to such institutions, some account of her early life is necessary to indicate how she developed into the unique person that she became. Louise Evelina du Pont was born at Winterthur, Christiana Hundred, New Castle County, Delaware, on 3 August 1877. Her great-great-grandfather was Pierre Samuel du Pont de Nemours (1739–1817), French economist and philosopher and friend of Thomas Jefferson, who arrived in the United States on New Year's Day 1800.

Her great-grandfather, Eleuthère Irénée du Pont (1772–1834), began the manufacture of black powder not far from Wilmington, Delaware, in 1802. Along the banks of the Brandywine River, whose water furnished power, he built a series of heavy granite powder mills, and on the west bluff above them a house, called, after the works and himself, Eleutherian Mills. From the modest beginning, the firm of E. I. du Pont de Nemours and Company expanded with the United States. Notwithstanding this growth, the company remained for a century a closely held family partnership in which descendants of the founder participated energetically in the manufacture as well as the sale of powder. Gradually the powder mills spread down the Brandywine until they stretched for three miles along its banks. Below the original Eleutherian Mills, which came to be called the Upper Yard, were the Hagley Yard and the Lower Yard. Separated from each other by safety zones, designed to reduce the danger from the explosions that were the concomitant of powder-making, a hundred granite buildings were erected with milldams in the river below, and numerous family houses on the high banks above. It was a closely knit enclave, in which members of the family settled close to the mills that furnished their livelihood, in houses owned by the firm.

Louise's grandfather, Henry du Pont (1812–1889), second son of the founder, was graduated from West Point in 1833 but served in the Army for only a year before being called home to join the company. Although at first an associate of his brothers Alfred and Victor in the management of the works, in 1850 he became the ruling partner of the powder firm, and so continued until his death thirty-nine years later.

His son, Colonel Henry Algernon du Pont (1838–1920), Louise's father, was also graduated from West Point. He, however, served for

fourteen years, through the Civil War, in which he won the Congressional
Medal of Honor, before joining the firm in 1875, a year after his marriage to

Mary Pauline Foster of New York. The newly married couple settled
several miles from the mills in Winterthur, a house built by James Antoine
Bidermann, who had come out from France in 1814 and in 1816 had married
Evelina Gabrielle, daughter of Eleuthère Irénée du Pont. In 1837 Bidermann

bought 445 acres of rolling land from the other heirs of his father-in-law. Here in 1839, upon his retirement from the firm, he built a square flat-roofed house that he named for his mother's ancestral town of Winterthur, Switzerland. On James Antoine Bidermann's death in 1865, Winterthur descended to his son, James Irénée, who two years later sold it to Henry du Pont. The latter over the years added thousands of acres on both sides of the Brandywine to the family's already large holdings. This Henry du Pont loved both land and masonry. The company steadily employed a crew of masons, whom, when they were not building new mills or repairing old ones, he set to laying magnificent stone walls around the fields of the farms that ringed the powder mills. Louise remembered hearing, as a child at her grandfather's two o'clock dinner table, a guest remark: "Mr. du Pont, those walls will be a more enduring monument to you than the Pyramids were to the Egyptians."

Louise, with her younger brother, Henry Francis du Pont, grew up at Winterthur in surroundings of extraordinary natural beauty. From the windows of this house on a hillside she saw graceful trees and rich rolling fields, marked by her grandfather's endless stone walls. She never left this scene to go to school, but was taught at home.

Ordinarily Louise only saw her grandfather at Sunday dinners when there would be so many people at table that her only contact with him would be a hasty mutual peck on the cheeks. However, from 1880 to 1889 whenever her parents went away from Winterthur she and Harry were always sent to stay with their grandparents in the old family house at Eleutherian Mills, on the bluff looking down to the powder mills and the fast-running Brandywine. During these visits Louise and her grandfather and his cat, Minette, would breakfast at seven o'clock. All three ate the same meal: pieces of bread broken in a bowl of milk, which the human breakfasters supplemented with big glasses of milk to drink.

Immediately after breakfast, the tall red-bearded Henry du Pont, followed by Minette, would walk to his office, a small stone building in front of the house, which accommodated the four clerks and one boy that he considered an adequate office force. Having no use for typewriters or stenographers, he drafted his own letters and had the clerks copy them in longhand. He sat so much at his desk that his feet wore deep grooves in the floor. Invariably in cold weather he wore a long blue broadcloth coat, coming well below his knees and buttoned straight down the front, with matching trousers and a high hat. On hot days he dressed in a similarly cut suit of pongee. While he was going through his mail, the young granddaughter would eagerly await nine o'clock, the appointed hour for a drive in a gig around the farms.

Although he seldom descended from the gig, "Mr. Henry," as everyone called him, was greatly interested in farming and would talk at length with the farmers about their problems. One day a naughty farm boy pelted Henry du Pont and his granddaughter with rotten eggs, which broke most unpleasantly over the gig and its occupants. The culprit's mother in distress of mind wiped up the mess as best she could. Henry du Pont's only comment was: "Give him a good thrashing. That is what he needs," as he drove away before it was administered.

Seventy years later Louise recalled the occasion when her grandfather was complaining that he smelled of fish. In the shad season, when boats came into the New Castle wharves, he would drive over in his gig to talk to people and buy some fish to bring home. Once he put in the back of the gig a big shad that had been given to him carefully wrapped in paper. A week later he asked his wife: "Louisa, do you smell a queer odor of fish about me? Everywhere I go I seem to smell fish." His wife attributed this to imagination, but his granddaughter disagreed. "Yes, I do, in the gig," said she. The faithful coachman was summoned and the week-old present unearthed.

One of Henry du Pont's favorite stories concerned a Wilmington silversmith, Ziba Ferris, who became so ill that his doctor finally told him there was no hope. When Ferris asked, as a last request, for a bowl of terrapin, the doctor agreed, thinking that nothing could hurt him now. Ferris ate the terrapin, felt much better; ate another bowl the next day, and in six days had entirely recovered. This, claimed the narrator, showed the miracle performed by terrapin, although in fact poor Ferris had been so weakened by medicinal gruel that what he needed was a little real nourishment. Another reminiscence concerned her grandfather's professor of French at West Point who once remarked: "Turkey is a very fine bird. He has only one great fault: he is too large for one and not big enough for two." At his own dinner table, Henry du Pont had quantities of people who came to see him on business, and his wife always had to be prepared with food for three or four extras. From these early experiences Louise profited, for later on no guest ever left her table undernourished.

Louise felt throughout her life that her grandmother, Louisa Gerhard du Pont, was one of the most marvelous people the world had ever known. The celebration on 15 July 1887 of her grandparents' golden wedding was one of the greatest events of her childhood. For two days previously she had suffered the proud but agonizing experience of having her hair for the first time rolled up in the tightest of little curls. She and Harry and their French nurse picked an enormous number of yellow daisies and wove them into a huge wreath for the celebration. On the afternoon of the 14th, Gerhard cousins arrived from Philadelphia, bringing children of Louise's age. This precipitated a crisis. Should she keep the curlers on and look very strange before cousins she had never seen, or remove them and look less beautiful at the golden wedding? Seventy years later she could not remember the decision, but only the nine-year-old's agony of choice. The music, the crowds, the unlimited ice cream were memorable.

Grandmother du Pont was tall and extremely good-looking, with great presence, charm, and graciousness of manner. Everyone admired and loved her. Louise, having been named for her and being the oldest girl in the family, considered herself her grandmother's "Pet 1." She watched eagerly for Grandmama's arrival each Sunday morning at Christ Church down the lane from Eleutherian Mills. The lady was always a little late. As Louise recalled it: "We were there beforehand and sat in the pew just behind her. The great event of the morning for me was when Grandmama came in. She always wore, except in summer when she always dressed in white embroidered mull dresses, heavy black dresses, which made a swish, swish, swish when she walked up the aisle. I waited breathless for the great moment when she reached her pew and turned around and smiled at me. After that the morning was all made. I would sit perfectly quiet and happy, particularly as I had discovered that by pressing my fingers hard into my eyes during the litany I could see hard little red balls." That greatly relieved the monotony until the happy moment just before the sermon when children could leave the church, run down into Free Park, called by them "Flea Park," and up the hill to Eleutherian Mills for a Sunday dinner of soup, roast beef, vegetables and chocolate cream in little blue cups.

As Louise's mother was a New Yorker, there were stockings and a

Christmas dinner at Winterthur. At her grandparents' house, however, presents came on New Year's, and the aunts would each take one of the parlor window-sills to display their gifts. The day was always celebrated at Eleutherian Mills with morning visits from male members of the family, bringing boxes of candy, with aunts, uncles, and cousins staying in the house, and a large family dinner with a boiled turkey with oyster stuffing at one end of the table and a roast turkey with chestnut stuffing at the other, "plum pudding and ice cream, and everything wonderful to eat."

The Sunday dinners, holiday celebrations, and other visits to Eleutherian Mills so delighted Louise that as soon as she was old enough she would ride over every afternoon on her pony, accompanied by the faithful coachman, William, to see her grandmother. As she grew older she would drive herself in a pony cart, and hardly ever missed going every afternoon. If she had a cold or was sick at home, Grandmama would always come to Winterthur, bringing Irish moss and little jars of clear soup. As her grandmother sat by the bed and held her hand, Louise would feel well straight away.

The almost daily visits to Eleutherian Mills gave Louise the opportunity to see another remarkably charming, sweet, and unselfish relation, her father's younger sister, Aunt Lina. Evelina du Pont (1840–1938) never married, and always lived with her parents during their lifetimes. As she would never allow the Civil War to be mentioned in her presence, Louise always privately thought that her aunt must have been in love with someone who had been killed during it. Aunt Lina, who particularly loved children, would do anything within her power to give them pleasure.

When Louise was twelve the pattern of life was broken by her grandfather's death. In the spring of 1889 he became very ill. She would be allowed to sit by his side and hold his hand as he lay looking so thin and long in the sleigh bed that is still in his room at Eleutherian Mills. When he observed, "You are a good girl, Louise," she would fill with pride, for he was not much given to compliments. He died on his birthday, 8 August 1889. During his funeral Louise sat upstairs, holding her grandmother's hand and following in her own little prayer book while her grandmother read the service to her. She felt very important, for she was wearing, for the first time, a black hair ribbon and a black sash, but she was also very sad. At this period ladies of the du Pont family never attended funerals.

After Henry du Pont's death his cat Minette was inconsolable. She would not eat nor stay in the house, but would go constantly to the cemetery and sit there. Grandmama would send a man to bring her home, but Minette always returned to the grave, and in the end died from lack of food.

On 7 October 1890 Louise, her brother, and their cousins the Robinsons from New York, were sitting in the big room at Winterthur making crosses on chestnuts they were about to roast. Her mother cautioned her to be very careful of a plate that she had taken, one of the best ones. "Oh," said Louise, "nothing can happen to it." At that very moment a tremendous blast sounded, the plate shot across the parquet floor in twenty pieces, every pane of glass in the five windows of the room, and most of those elsewhere, broke. Even with the greatest care, explosions are an occupational hazard of powder-making. They occurred from time to time; often enough for the mills, with their three-foot buttressed walls of granite masonry, to be built with a light wall facing the Brandywine, so that débris would be precipitated across the river rather than in more dangerous directions. This was the first in seven years. It was clearly something out of the ordinary, seven explosions within eight seconds, of a violence sufficient to break the windows of distant Winterthur. As there was no telephone in the house, no news was available. In ten minutes, William, the coachman, was at the door, and Louise's mother set off for the scene, leaving the children in the greatest anxiety for their family.

Colonel du Pont spent his mornings in Wilmington at the office of the Wilmington and Northern Railroad, of which he was president. At lunchtime he would drive out to the office at the powder mills. Having just arrived as the explosions took place, he ran down the hill toward the mills, where the roof of the big magazine was in flames. A bucket brigade was organized; Colonel du Pont went up the ladder first, followed by Tim Toomey, the boss of the Upper Yard. An echelon of men passing buckets of water from the Brandywine were able to extinguish the fire, but it was a close thing. The hundred tons of powder that had been consumed by the explosions had torn the Upper Yard to pieces, killed twelve persons, wounded twenty, and destroyed many of the workmen's houses. Five of the family houses were badly shaken. Louise's grandmother, two of her aunts, and Mrs. Bartlett, the wife of the rector of Christ Church, had just finished luncheon at Eleutherian Mills and were in the little library at the time of the accident.

When the ceiling fell they were able to protect themselves by putting sofa cushions over their heads. Mrs. Bartlett, who had lived abroad for several years and was quite *mondaine*, was on her knees praying, and actually thought it was the end of the world. By great good fortune no one in the house was hurt, but in view of the devastation of this October afternoon, the house was considered too dangerous for continued occupancy. Mrs. Henry du Pont bought Pelleport and moved there. After eighty-four years Eleutherian Mills was abandoned.

About 1897 Louise du Pont organized a group of "Willing Helpers" which met on Saturday mornings from nine to twelve in the parish house of Christ Church, to make clothes for the babies at St. Michael's Day Nursery in Wilmington. The members, girls between six and twelve years of age, were children of families that lived along the banks of the Brandywine. Louise would drive from Winterthur in her pony cart, while the Willing Helpers would arrive on foot, often carrying or dragging younger brothers or sisters for whose care they were responsible on Saturday mornings. Louise, who always opened the meeting with a prayer, taught the girls sewing and hemstitching, and encouraged them by giving prizes for their interest and the best work done. Once a year she would take them to the Nursery to see the babies and follow this outing by a "treat." Although she presided over the Willing Helpers for only three years, she had an annual reunion with the original members of the group for the rest of her life.

Louise also taught a Sunday school class at Christ Church for boys of ten. It always amused her that, whenever they were asked for any special offering, they would stoutly allege that they had only the penny for the collection, even though she could hear other coins jingling in their pockets.

Louise du Pont's girlhood, like her childhood, was centered around Winterthur. She never went away to school. There were no family migrations to Europe; at most her parents might spend a few summer weeks at a hotel in Sea Girt, New Jersey. In later life Louise moved about more than most people, but in some mysterious way carried with her wherever she went the impression of a settled existence, in which members of a large family were constantly doing kind, thoughtful, and generous things for each other. One might say that she continued the traditions of her youth in Delaware without other change than the immense extension of the family circle to include friends of all kinds in many different places. For this reason it has been necessary to give a seemingly disproportionate amount of space to her early life.

In the late Nineties Mrs. Henry du Pont had a summer house at Marble-head, Massachusetts. There by the sea Louise met Francis Boardman Crowninshield, who took her out sailing. In the autumn of 1899 he paid a visit to Winterthur; in the spring of 1900 they became engaged, and were married on 28 June of the same year. Frank Crowninshield was eight years older than his wife. He had been born in New York City on 22 April 1869; had attended St. Paul's School and entered Harvard College with the class of 1891. He did not remain for the full four years or take a degree, being, as a friend has said, like other personable and lively young men of his day, a graduate of Leavitt and Peirce's, rather than of Harvard College. He had spent some time in a Boston bank, but service in T.R.'s Rough Riders during the Spanish-American War had been more to his taste. There he had contracted typhoid fever from which he was recuperating when he met Louise.

Crowninshields had a natural affinity for the sea. They were people of strong likes and dislikes, with a mixture of the Rough Rider temperament and a flair for elegance. In the great days of Salem they had been ship-masters and merchants. Moreover, the exuberant Captain George Crownin-shield, Jr., Frank's great-great-uncle, had in 1816 commissioned the building of a magnificent seagoing yacht, *Cleopatra's Barge*, to beguile the leisure of his retirement. Unfortunately he died a year and a half later, after one transatlantic cruise, and his vessel did not long survive him. Although the bones of *Cleopatra's Barge* lay on a distant Hawaiian reef, her memory was vividly preserved in New England. The rumor of such elegance dies hard, particularly when sofas, tables, silver cups, and other sumptuous fittings, removed when the yacht was sold after George Crowninshield's death, survived as corroboration. In 1888 Frank's father, Benjamin W. Crowninshield, grandson and namesake of George's brother, who had been Madison's Secretary of the Navy, recounted for the Essex Institute the dramatic story of the building of *Cleopatra's Barge* and her voyage to Europe.

Through summers at Marblehead, Frank Crowninshield grew up with boats. He had an instinctive love of the sea that led him to embrace all opportunities for sailing and racing. From his early childhood he knew his father's forty-foot centerboard sloop, *Effie*. He and his brothers soon had their own twenty-two-foot keelboat, *Witch*, of which he subsequently wrote: "We boys did all the work on the boat ourselves—which I might say is by far the quickest and best way to learn—and after a while we couldn't help knowing something of what it was all about. We spared ourselves not at all and to the consternation of my mother we used to put the *Witch* on the beach once a week all summer and 'pot lead' her. If you are old enough to have done it I don't have to tell you what it does to you and your clothes as well as to everything in the house." Then there was *Tomahawk*, designed by Edward Burgess, not generally noteworthy for speed but remarkable for having made her maiden voyage from City Island, New York, to Marblehead without tacking. "A fresh southwester took us to Pollock Rip, where we jibed, and the port tack the rest of the way in. The tides were very considerate, changing at the most opportune times, which undoubtedly had much to do with the fast time we made, thirty-six hours, port to port." When *Tomahawk* was sold in 1893, other boats followed in rapid succession, for Frank Crowninshield was forever sailing and racing. In 1907, for example, he was skipper of *Spokane* in races at Bilbao during which the American visitors outsailed the king of Spain.

Upon their marriage, Frank and Louise Crowninshield settled at 330 Dartmouth Street in Boston. After his mother's death in 1902 they moved around the corner into her house at 164 Marlborough Street, where Louise continued to spend part of each year for the rest of her life. Frank's unmarried younger brother, Benjamin W. Crowninshield, lived with them. Part of each summer was spent at Marblehead, where Louise's Aunt Lina, who had by this time inherited Mrs. Henry du Pont's house, was a near neighbor.

In Boston Louise Crowninshield put her unflagging energy and abilities into the work of various charitable organizations. In 1915 she became a member of the Board of Lady Visitors of the Boston Lying-in Hospital; on her retirement forty years later the corporation of the hospital gave her a medal, which she always wore on a bracelet. She was a board member of the Vincent Memorial Hospital and of the Sunnyside Day Nursery, and was active in the founding and administration of Children's Island, Marblehead. One of her earliest interests lay in the Widows' Society of Boston, a charity established in 1816, for which she would often pay visits, similar to those that her grandmother had paid her when she was ill as a child. Accompanied by her Marblehead chauffeur, Henry Barry, a man highly skilled in the arrangement of Chinese export porcelain, who could also drive a car with a French poodle seated on his shoulders like a fur neckpiece, she would carry comestibles to impoverished widows in unlikely parts of Boston. One of these expeditions on behalf of the Widows' Society caused unexpected hilarity when an uninformed "well-wisher" telephoned Frank Crowninshield to suggest, leeringly, that he keep an eye on his wife, who had just been seen entering a South End lodginghouse "with a man."

In Boca Grande, Florida, she gave the town a Community House and sponsored a Health Clinic, of which she served as president. Her husband and brother-in-law first went there for tarpon fishing, staying at the local inn. About 1916 each bought a small house for further fishing visits. Gradually as the houses were enlarged the Crowninshields extended their stay until Boca Grande became their place of winter residence.

Although Louise Crowninshield's mother had died in 1902, her father continued to live at Winterthur until his death in 1926, save for a decade in Washington when he served as United States Senator from Delaware. There were consequently frequent visits to Winterthur over the first quarter-century of her married life. In her father's later years, Louise would go from Massachusetts to Delaware every fortnight to spend two days with him. One of these visits in the summer of 1923 happened to coincide with a large family party given by Mrs. Charles Copeland. As the du Pont Company had, in that year, decided to remove its works from the Brandywine, it proposed to sell to the descendants of their original owners the ancestral houses. Maps showing the land to be sold were sent to all descendants so that they might express their preferences. Louise had received one in Marblehead, but had paid no attention to it. As she was at Winterthur at the time of the family gathering that had assembled to consider the division of land, she persuaded her father to take her to it, thinking that it would be fun to see so many relatives assembled. Neither of them had any thought of buying land.

Eleutherian Mills had been abandoned by Mrs. Henry du Pont thirty-three years earlier, after the 1890 explosion. For a decade or more after 1892 it was converted into the Brandywine Club for company workmen, with a library of five hundred volumes, periodicals, and newspapers, and a gymnasium. During the Spanish-American War the militia encamped at Montchanin also used the club. Some of them cut down four beautiful tree-box in order to make a croquet court on which they never played. The superb box bushes in the gardens were dug up and given by Wilmingtonians who had charge of the Upper Yard to their friends, who let them die. The house fell into a sorry state. Its only friend was Miss Evelina du Pont, who, whenever window panes were shattered by an explosion, would have them replaced, thus preserving the interior from the weather.

With the abandoned powderworks below it, Eleutherian Mills was, in the summer of 1923, a sad sight. However, upon seeing it again, such happy childhood memories returned to Louise Crowninshield that she persuaded her father to buy her the house and the fifty-two acres of land that went with it, promising to return to live there for part of each year. This proved to be one of the happy incidents that brought extraordinary pleasure into her life. She and her husband immediately began the restoration of both house and surroundings. As the Brandywine Club had made almost no structural changes in the interior, it was not difficult to return the rooms to their former uses. Although the original furnishings had long since been distributed among the family, some pieces were returned when their owners learned of the plan to restore the house. In her purchases to complete the furnishing, Louise Crowninshield was careful to buy only pieces made in America, of a type that might have been used in this country when the first du Ponts arrived from France in 1800. She further attempted to preserve as much of the original arrangement as was possible, although her grandfather's office became a guesthouse. When I first stayed in it, I was startled to discover that, within my hostess's lifetime, the entire business of E. I. du Pont de Nemours and Company had been transacted in what made a very comfortable bedroom.

The hillside that dropped down behind the house to the Brandywine was converted into a series of gardens of unexpected variety. Steep wooded areas were planted with naturalized bulbs and wildflowers. A few of the old granite mills were preserved; others were partially or totally leveled to create a series of formal terraces, by which one descended from the house to the riverbank. Near the Brandywine, Frank Crowninshield amused himself by converting powder mills into ruined classical temples by the introduction of Corinthian columns, skillfully placed. Thus the remnants of the powder mills that had once made the house unsafe were transformed into a scene reminiscent of a Hubert Robert landscape.

The house was a remarkable tribute to the skill of its restorer. One could hardly believe that it had lain desolate for a third of a century, since it gives the impression of continuous occupancy. The quality and rarity of its contents never detracted from the comfort of its use. In good weather people were likely to be sitting on the terrace by the front door, with its tubs and pots of flowers. A parrot, brought outdoors for an airing, might be pecking through the bars of a brass cage at a box hedge until admonished by its owner. Once inside the door, the flowers that were massed along the central hall carried the feeling of the garden into the house. A variety of dogs, Pekinese and poodles of various dimensions, milled about. Their owner once observed: "Young people can't afford old rugs. In our house we have lots of dogs. They antique our rugs." The photographs of Eleutherian Mills that illustrated this memoir gave some impression of the rooms as Louise Crowninshield restored them. Without her, without people and without dogs, the scene is forever incomplete.

Normally the Crowninshields spent the spring and autumn at Eleutherian Mills. They would come from Marblehead in mid-September, but always had to leave in time to reach Cambridge or New Haven for the Harvard-Yale game. After their father's death in 1926, Winterthur was inherited by Louise's brother Harry, who had already embarked upon the collecting that was to lead to the great enlargement of the old house and to its ultimate transformation into the Henry Francis du Pont Winterthur Museum, an institution for the public good. The transformation of Eleutherian Mills and Winterthur by sister and brother led to an increased preoccupation with collecting, with the restoration and preservation of historic houses, and with horticulture.

Simultaneously Frank Crowninshield was collecting along his own lines. Like the devout fly-fishermen who spend the snowy months of the year sorting flies, recalling past exploits, and anticipating future delights, in seasons unsuitable for sailing he beguiled himself with ship pictures and seafaring memorabilia. He had a particular enthusiasm for everything surviving from his great-great-uncle's spectacular craft, and went to endless trouble to retrieve any objects relating to the vessel that wandered into the market. In 1913 he compiled from journals, letters, and logbooks *The Story of*

Louise du Pont Crowninshield

George Crowninshield's Yacht Cleopatra's Barge *on a Voyage of Pleasure to the Western Islands and the Mediterranean, 1816–1817.* This privately printed volume, which was one of the handsomest products of the Merrymount Press, would have touched even the heart of the *Barge's* fastidious and exuberant owner. To its distribution among yachtsmen and lovers of maritime history, we owe the inspiration for an exhibition held in the Peabody Museum of Salem during the summer of 1916 to commemorate the one-hundredth anniversary of the building of *Cleopatra's Barge.* From no less than thirty-five sources, largely within the Crowninshield family, pieces of furniture, tableware, silver, and other decorative elegances from the *Barge* were assembled, and a brief descriptive catalogue compiled. Some of these objects were given to the museum, but most of them, being both handsome and useful, were wanted back by their owners.

In the autumn of 1927 Frank Crowninshield characteristically recalled the memory of his ancestor's vessel by buying a yacht that he renamed *Cleopatra's Barge II.* This handsome schooner, originally *Mariette,* built by Nathaniel Herreshoff in 1917 for Frederick Jacob Brown, was not too different in size from her predecessor, for she was 80 feet on the waterline, 109 feet on deck, 24½ feet wide and 15 feet deep. For her day she was easily the equal of the first in beauty of design, but she had a far longer and happier history.

For thirteen summers, until she was taken by the Coast Guard in 1942, *Cleopatra's Barge II* was a familiar sight from Chesapeake to Penobscot bays. Her owner recorded his cruises in *The Log of Cleopatra's Barge II, 1928–1942,* privately printed by the Merrymount Press in 1948. The log indicates that nephews, nieces, cousins, and friends were as welcome and as hospitably received afloat as ashore. Its style reveals a good deal about the man who kept it, even to his political views—witness the first entry of the year "Nineteen thirty-seven—The year of Our Lord, and the 6th in the misrule of F. D. Roosevelt." Frank Crowninshield was a good sailor and a pretty fair water-colorist. He could be as generous as his wife on occasion, and would give away the coat off his back if he liked the recipient. He was also a first-rate hater when he did not like someone. The thirty-first President of the United States was his prime aversion. Someone once remarked that nothing would make him vote for F.D.R. had he not heard Frank Crowninshield denouncing him. The last entry in the log, 5 September

1940, at Marblehead, reads: "Our delightful day was actually made a nightmare by the sight of four of our destroyers en route to Canada, to be given over to the only country on earth which has ever abused us. It reminded me of the Athenian maidens sent over to be devoured by the Minotaur (if that's how you spell it), all done really to make a smoke screen for a Roosevelt third term, an act of war in itself. And what made it some hundreds of per cent more horrible was that one of the four was named *Crowninshield.*" The condition in which *Cleopatra's Barge* was returned to her owner by the Coast Guard in 1943 did nothing to improve his view of the situation. The following year he sold "the remains"—and that appeared to be the last one was likely to hear of *Cleopatra's Barge.*

Francis Boardman Crowninshield died on 19 May 1950 at Eleutherian Mills. His memory is perpetuated for all time in the galleries added by his widow to East India Marine Hall in the Peabody Museum of Salem for the exhibition of the memorabilia of *Cleopatra's Barge* the first. These were dedicated at a meeting of the Friends and Fellows of the Peabody Museum of Salem on 11 September 1953.

Working from contemporary descriptions of the yacht, the architectural firm of Perry, Shaw and Hepburn, Kehoe and Dean designed a reasoned reconstruction of the cabin of *Cleopatra's Barge*, reconciling the decorative elements mentioned with the known structural limitations of such a vessel, from which the Doane Construction Company of Beverly fashioned the exquisite woodwork that recreates so vividly the contemporary descriptions of George Crowninshield's elegant cabin. An octagonal lobby, containing Mrs. Crowninshield's remarkable collection of ship Lowestoft, serves as a kind of decorative compression chamber by which the visitor is prepared for the transition from the lofty spaciousness of East India Marine Hall to the sharply restricted area of the cabin. In the latter are the great lyre-backed sofas, the glazed cupboards for silver and glass, and the other engaging amenities by which George Crowninshield almost concealed the fact that he was at sea. A small room opening from the cabin contains his painted four-post bed, while a gallery at the rear of the wing is devoted to portraits, ship pictures, and other objects relating to the Crowninshields and their ships. In this purely functional exhibition room are shown many of Francis B. Crowninshield's best-loved possessions, the Samuel F. B. Morse portrait of Captain George, George Ropes's painting of *Cleopatra's Barge,* the Cornè oil of the Crowninshields' third ship, *America*, portraits of Mr. and Mrs. Benjamin W. Crowninshield, as well as numerous related objects given and lent to the museum by members of the family and other good friends who wished to share in this singularly appropriate memorial.

The Peabody Museum of Salem continues a collection founded in 1799 by the shipmasters of the Salem East India Marine Society. It is administered by a board of nine trustees, who, like the Harvard Corporation, elect their own successors. In 1946 Mrs. Augustus P. Loring, Jr., was elected a trustee, not from any feminist theory of the civilizing influence of women, but because she was the most qualified person available, male or female, for the post. On her death in 1950, Mrs. Crowninshield was chosen her successor for precisely the same reason. The gift of the Francis Boardman Crownin-shield Gallery and its contents was one of the most generous received by the museum over a century and a half. Nevertheless, Louise Crowninshield gave the Peabody Museum of Salem something far more precious than money and objects. She had extraordinary skill in perceiving the strengths of the institution and, in a subtle manner, encouraging her fellow trustees and her friends and neighbors to appreciate the importance of building upon these. By the breadth of her friendship she enlarged the parish boundaries, and by her imagination did away with the parochialism that often besets institutions in small cities. Moreover, she had an artist's instinct for the display of museum exhibits. She might, for example, rather diffidently suggest that some improvement might possibly be achieved by interchanging the contents of two galleries; that it might be worth trying as no particular expense or irrevocable decision would be involved, inasmuch as the objects could easily be restored to their original location if the results proved dis-pleasing. Once it was clear that no one opposed the experiment, she would appear with Henry Barry and one or two other helpers. She would seat herself in the middle of the room and immediately, with staccato rapidity, issue orders for the removal of this and the shifting of that. In a few minutes the gallery seemed reduced to débris. Then with equally startling rapidity a new order emerged from the chaos as she directed the hanging of pictures and the placing of objects in locations that had obviously been in her mind's eye long before the shift had been ever so tentatively proposed. These excursions into museum installation were remarkable to watch, and they invariably came out right.

I cite the experience of the Peabody Museum of Salem because there, as a fellow trustee, I saw her in action more repeatedly and intimately than elsewhere, even though we served on other boards together. One had to move fast to keep up with her. Although she was genuinely modest and extremely tactful in everything that she did, there was no room in her scheme of things for indecision, useless and protracted discussion, mawkish sentiment, or parochial attachment to the second-rate. Although she was a conservative and a true "preservationist," she saw no reason why things should be done as they always had been if that way were stupid. In working with a local institution, she attempted to enhance the excellence of its peculiar qualities so that the institution might be appreciated beyond the immediate vicinity. The Peabody Museum of Salem owes many of its distant friends and supporters to her energy in passing the word about its activities beyond the boundaries of New England. After her death on 11 July 1958, I became aware that a great number of organizations felt her loss as keenly as did the one in which I knew her. I soon realized that her activities, probably quite unconsciously but nonetheless effectively, fitted together into a national mosaic of an extraordinary complexity; that she had had a far wider influence in preserving the record of the American past and improving the amenities of the present and future than she herself realized. This sketch is intended to give a brief record of the extent of her activities.

In Salem, Louise Crowninshield was not only a trustee of the Peabody Museum, she had helped the Essex Institute with the decorative aspects of its houses for many years before her election to its council. In the Pingree House she furnished an entire room as a Crowninshield memorial; in other houses owned by the institute she would quietly provide curtains, refurbish rooms, produce a chair or table here, a pair of andirons or a Chinese export porcelain elephant there. In the summer of 1956, she contributed substantially to the basic restoration of the Peirce-Nichols House. Walter McIntosh Merrill, formerly director of the Essex Institute, wrote soon after her death: "Mrs. Crowninshield was always as generous with her time and skill and knowledge as with her money. It was never with her a question of the easy way, to make a financial contribution and avoid the personal effort. She was always unobtrusive about her generosity. There was never any fanfare or call for recognition. If an object were needed in one of the houses it would appear unannounced, and it sometimes required a scholar's ingenuity to discover the source. Mrs. Crowninshield had an extraordinary capacity both for details and for policy. She could remember precisely the myriad objects and their arrangement in our three houses, so that she could when she was in New York or another part of the world find exactly what was needed to complete a room or exhibit. Likewise she had the imaginative capacity for making quickly wise and far-reaching decisions on the policy level." Mr. Merrill recalled a time when the institute was considering the purchase of land needed to round out its holdings. Mrs. Crowninshield was in Florida, but she knew of the projected purchase and sent the president a telegram, which, arriving just before the crucial meeting, was most influential in helping the board to make a correct decision. In Salem she was also president of the Salem Maritime Historical Association, connected with the Derby House which is preserved by the National Park Service.

In Marblehead she was made an honorary director of the Marblehead Historical Society in recognition of her assistance in restoring the Lee Mansion. Marblehead is a deeply conservative place. When her suggestion of improving that great eighteenth-century house was first made, the society was not sure about wanting "summer people" mixing in their affairs. Crowninshields had, after all, only summered at Peach's Point for three quarters of a century. In the end she surmounted even the New England aversion to "rusticators." To the trustees of Reservations in Boston she gave Brown's Island (now Crowninshield Island), off Peach's Point, as an endowed bird sanctuary.

Within Essex County she was also a director of the First Iron Works Association, Inc., at Saugus, and a member of the Beverly Historical Society, the North Shore Garden Club, the Marblehead Garden Club, and the North Shore Horticultural Society.

President Eisenhower in 1955 appointed Mrs. Crowninshield a member of the Boston National Historic Sites Commission. She was a governor of Gore Place in Waltham, a trustee of the Society for the Preservation of New England Antiquities, with special interest in the Lyman House in Waltham and the Scotch-Boardman House, and, after it was taken over by the National Trust for Historic Preservation, president of the board of the Wayside Inn. Her other interests in Boston are indicated by her being a Friend of the Boston Symphony Orchestra and of the Fogg Museum of

Art, a member of the Museum of Fine Arts and of the Institute of Contemporary Art, of the Massachusetts Horticultural Society (which awarded her in 1937 the Albert C. Burrage Gold Vase for the most outstanding exhibit of the year), the Massachusetts Audubon Society, the Animal Rescue League, the Abigail Adams Historical Society, the Colonial Dames of America, a charter member of the Chilton Club, and a director of the Association for the Arnold Arboretum, Inc.

From the establishment of the National Trust for Historic Preservation in 1949, Mrs. Crowninshield served as a trustee; from 1953 she was a vice-chairman of the board. She served on various committees, and organized a special Committee for Historic Preservation, national in scope and divided into zones—those of the New England, Middle Atlantic, Southeast, and the Great Lakes regions—each with its subchairman and members from each state within the zones. By this device she sought to spread the word about the then little-known young organization, to secure information on preservation problems, and increase trust membership; as she put it, the committee members were to serve as proconsuls. Each year she gave a dinner at the annual meeting when reports were made; at the October 1957 annual meeting she entertained the members of the trust at a great lunch party at her house in Marblehead. Her part in this meeting did much to ease the path of the National Trust in New England, a region well studded with older organizations interested in historic preservation, where a natural distaste for bureaucracy causes anything based in Washington to be considered guilty until proved innocent. This major effort was made in the last year of her life; only a short time before, she had been in the hands of surgeons. While she was in the hospital the previous month she had arranged for the annual dinner of the Fellows of the Peabody Museum of Salem to be held at her house, as it had been for the six previous years, even though she could not attend. Consequently, her appearance at the National Trust meeting at the museum, even in a wheel chair, was the cause of great rejoicing; it was, unhappily, the last such gathering that she was to attend.

Richard H. Howland, president of the National Trust, points out the unostentatious help that Mrs. Crowninshield gave to Woodlawn Plantation, owned by the trust. "If a chair needed recovering, she would defray labor and material; if a fine piece of furniture lent to the mansion threatened to be sold, she would provide for its purchase; a check was given to the director to fill out flat silver for the historic dining table and foam-rubber carpets were purchased through her generosity to be placed under carpets." This pattern, so familiar in Massachusetts, she followed in Virginia, where she was honorary president and honorary regent for Delaware of the Kenmore Association, president of the trustees of the Wakefield National Memorial Association, and a member of the advisory committee of the National Mary Washington Memorial Association at Fredericksburg. She was a member of the refurnishings advisory committee of the Independence National Historical Park Project in Philadelphia, of the committee to redecorate the White House during the administration of President Truman, and an honorary member of the American Institute of Decorators.

After her death, Conrad L. Wirth, Director of the National Park Service, wrote: "Her active interest in historical preservation has resulted in permanent living memorials to her love of historic American furniture and the decorative arts and to her splendid perception of the value of preserving this heritage for the enjoyment of all of the American people for all time. At Salem Maritime National Historic Site, Salem, Massachusetts; at George Washington Birthplace National Monument in Virginia; at various historic places benefited by the National Trust, and wherever in the National Park Service the income from the Francis B. Crowninshield Trust Fund established by her has been used for historic preservation, the old, the beautiful and the historic legacies from the American past are owned by the Nation, either in part or largely on account of her interest and help. Because of this, her life has been of singular and lasting usefulness to the American people."

From the establishment of her brother's Henry Francis du Pont Winterthur Museum, Louise Crowninshield was a director, who followed the institution's development with close attention. She participated in the selection of graduate students for the Winterthur University of Delaware Fellowships, and maintained a keen interest in the progress of their work, and subsequent careers. She was a member of the Wilmington Garden Club and the Historical Society of Delaware, and was concerned with the preservation of the architectural amenities of New Castle, Delaware, which is perhaps the most unspoiled and engaging town along the Atlantic seaboard.

As a result of residence in Boca Grande, she belonged to the Florida Historical Society, the Historical Association of South Florida, the Florida Audubon Society, and the Florida Forestry Association.

Louise Crowninshield became a member of the Garden Club of America in 1920. At one time she was its vice-president; at others served on its policy committee, was concerned with the supervision of redwood groves, and in 1950 was awarded the Garden Club of America Medal of Achievement, an honor that she held high and one that gave her lasting pleasure. She became a life member of the American Rose Society in 1921, and took a keen interest in the New York Botanical Garden, the Horticultural Society of New York, the New York Audubon Society, and the Garden Club of Philadelphia. In New York she belonged to the Colony Club, was a member of the Metropolitan Museum of Art, and a fellow of the Pierpont Morgan Library.

To conclude this perhaps incomplete list, she was a guarantor of the Bach Choir of Bethlehem, a trustee of the Heritage Foundation, and a member of the American Association of Museums, the Society of Architectural Historians, the Marine Historical Association, the American Horticultural Council, Inc., and the American Planning and Civic Association. The blend of charity, preservation, and horticulture that has been suggested in the preceding paragraphs is perhaps best symbolized by five medals that she constantly wore on a bracelet; with the awards from the Boston Lying-in Hospital and the Garden Club of America, were the George McAneny Award of the American Historical Preservation Society of 1947, a Tribute of 1952 from the Garden Club of Wilmington, and the Preservation Society of Newport County Decorative Arts Award of 1957.

Mr. George McAneny, in presenting the award of the American Scenic and Historic Preservation Society on 4 June 1947, said in part:

> In presenting those who, at this meeting, are to receive the Society's annually bestowed medals, I am moved to say a word about the origin and significance of the medal itself. As will be observed, it bears the legend: "HISTORY, THE EXPERIENCE OF MAN, WHO PRESERVES IT IS HIS BENEFACTOR." In a sense, that writes the whole story. For it is to the selection for honor in any given year, and in our judgment, of those who have accomplished outstanding

and enduring things for the cause of historic preservation—who have, in short, added their names to the list of Man's benefactors, that we have given our attention.

The medal, with its happily expressed dedication, was established a little over a year ago, in commemoration of the Fiftieth Anniversary of the Society's existence. There were three who first received it: Dr. William Archer Rutherford Goodwin, spiritual creator and restorer of old Williamsburg, upon whom it was bestowed posthumously and received by his son; Stephen H. P. Pell, saviour and restorer of Fort Ticonderoga; and William Sumner Appleton, for his outstanding work for the Society for the Preservation of New England Antiquities.

The present year—as we shall in each recurring future year—there will be two to whom the medal is fittingly awarded: Louise du Pont Crowninshield of Delaware and Massachusetts, and Walter Evans Edge, former Governor of New Jersey, mention of whose name recalls happily our successful campaign for the acquisition and preservation of the Revolutionary Battlefield of Princeton.

Although what is said upon such a presentation is usually well summarized in the words of the set citations, I think that I should also like to speak, in this moment, at somewhat greater length, and a bit more intimately about these recipients of 1947. By them the earlier standards have been kept high. As "Benefactors," indeed, within the meaning of the legend I have read, they will long be remembered.

Particularly do I wish to speak of the fine and lasting services to our cause of the gracious lady at my right.

Mrs. Crowninshield has devoted herself actively and untiringly to the restoration and appropriate equipment and furnishing of a lengthening list of ancient houses, whose stories belong to the history of the country, notably, I should say, to the restored houses of Virginia and Delaware, and others of her affectionately adopted New England. In these undertakings she has not only been most generous in the number and the character of her gifts, but she has made them peculiarly gifts of her own, by the application both in their selection and arrangement of her own exquisite and expert personal taste. She is indeed a master of the art.

By those who have worked with her in bringing wonderful things to pass, she has seemed a Lady Bountiful, whose kindness and patriotic devotion indeed know no end. And again, as I have ventured to say, as one of those whose accomplishments in the art of restoration, she will be long and gratefully remembered.

The part taken by the women of the country in measures of historic preservation and culture has been traditionally worthy of celebration, and on this occasion may I repeat that we take keen and especial pleasure in honoring one who, individually, and in her own quiet fashion, and by the constant offer of her example, has proved one of the most forceful and one of the most helpful of this shining sisterhood.

Few other people have belonged to as great a number of organizations. When Louise Crowninshield died in Boston on 11 July 1958, the unique esteem in which they had held her was shown by the diversity of tributes paid her memory. A memorial concert was held at the Essex Institute in Salem on 30 October 1958. In the chapel of Lehigh University, on the afternoons of 8 and 15 May 1959, the Bach Choir of Bethlehem sang the choral "World Farewell" in memory of her and other guarantors who had died during the past year. The National Trust for Historic Preservation has established a fund, and the Garden Club of America has decorated a room in its New York headquarters in her memory. In Salem no less than three memorials, each of singular appropriateness, are already established. The Crowninshield-Bentley House, which was in danger of demolition on its original site, has been moved to the grounds of the Essex Institute, and is being restored through the gifts of various members of the institute, inspired by her cousin, Frederick J. Bradlee. Through the generosity of another cousin, Mrs. Arthur Wellman Butler, the Peabody Museum of Salem published in 1959 *George Crowninshield's Yacht* Cleopatra's Barge *and a Catalogue of the Francis B. Crowninshield Gallery*, while Henry B. du Pont provided funds for the addition of a Louise du Pont Crowninshield Memorial Room. The construction of this much-needed combination of a gallery and meeting room was completed in 1961.

Louise du Pont Crowninshield

Impressive though the list of organizations to which Louise Crowninshield belonged cannot fail to be, it is the nature of her participation in each that remains unforgettable. Clearheaded she always was, with a strong instinct for proportion and order. To whatever work she set her decisive hand, a desire for self-aggrandizement had no part in any activity of hers. So far was she from desiring to emphasize her own importance that she as an individual was constantly withdrawing herself. Hers was the creative spirit that darts, alights, and can decide, because it perceives more quickly and justly than ordinary mortals. The insistence of such a spirit never arises from self-conscious motives, but from a conviction of the needs of the particular situation or the special group. The influence of such a creative spirit as that possessed by Louise Crowninshield is the kind that endures.

CHAPTER XII

Jacob Wirth

1880 – 1965

THE YEAR 1968 marks the centenary of the Jacob Wirth Company, a beloved German restaurant in Boston that, for its first ninety-seven years, was operated by its founder, his widow, and then his son. In 1965 a group of friends of Jacob Wirth, the son, joined in a tribute of essays titled A Seidel for Jake Wirth, *which gave him pleasure. My contribution to that volume is reprinted here, as well as my* Remarks about Jacob Wirth 1880–1965 *for the Memorial Service at the First Church in Boston on 14 December 1965. I was touched when Mrs. Wirth asked me to participate in the memorial service for this dear and good man. Afterward two irrelevant thoughts occurred. Although my father and my Grandfather Whitehill were clergymen, this was the first time that I had mounted a pulpit; also I am certain that this was the first time in three hundred and thirty-five years that anyone had spoken so favorably of beer from the pulpit of the First Church in Boston.*

THE GERMAN RESTAURANT of the Jacob Wirth Company on Stuart Street has shown a capacity for survival and for resistance to needless change that is unique even in Boston. To have weathered the anti-German sentiment of two world wars and the fourteen-year drought of Prohibition is remarkable enough. What is even more extraordinary is that during the ninety-five years it has been in business in the same street, it has been the property of two Jacob Wirths, father and son.

I first knew the restaurant when I was a Harvard freshman in 1922. It was then customary, as it has been before and since, for students weary of university cooking to take the subway to Park Street and walk to Jake Wirth's. There in a cheerful, noisy hall with austere mustard-colored walls, with sawdust on the floor, good victuals of many kinds were to be had at honest prices, within the reach of the young. Pig's knuckles, boiled bacon, bratwurst, sauerbraten, and so forth and so on, embellished by sauerkraut and washed down by seidels of dark beer, followed by an apfelstrudel or an authoritative Limburger cheese, were a refreshing change from Memorial Hall. True, the seidels contained only near beer, for Jacob Virth was scrupulously law-abiding, but it was the best brew to be had in Boston in those arid days. So deceptively good it was that Federal agents came constantly to take samples. They were as constantly disappointed, for whenever a barrel of beer became cloudy, and hence potentially more

potent than do-goodism tolerated, it was at once knocked off and returned
to the brewery.

Jake Wirth's was not only law-abiding. It was an eminently respectable
establishment of high moral tone: *circa* 1923 I was asked to leave, because a
Radcliffe freshman dining with me lit a cigarette and was reluctant to put it
out. Loose women were not welcome, and in the mores of Jake Wirth's for
its first sixty-five years of business, a woman smoking a cigarette was very
likely a loose woman. The waiter was firm and clear on the point. We left,
but without offense being meant or taken. About the same time a journalist
whose "playmate for the evening had lit her cigarette and was called to
account for it," asked for and received the following logical explanation
from a waiter:

"There are two kinds of ladies. Those that it's all right to let them smoke
and those that it isn't all right to let them smoke. Now your friend, it
would be all right for her to smoke [we thanked him] but they are not all
like your friend. The other kind, they come in and drink beer and smoke.
They wait for what you call a pick-up. But they can't just sit and do
nothing. So they smoke. If we stop them smoking we stop them waiting
for some good customer to pay the check."

The rule is now relaxed. Thirty years ago the sign LADIES ARE REQUESTED
NOT TO SMOKE came down, to be replaced by one reading SAUERBRATEN
WEDNESDAY, without visible change in the moral tone of the establishment.

The restaurant is somewhat noisy, but solely from the honest and inevitable sounds of scurrying waiters, of dishes and seidels being planked
down on bare mahogany tables, or orders being bawled from diner to
waiter to kitchen. The quiet, orderly patrons are a remarkable cross
section of Boston, of all ages and varieties. Each enjoys himself in his own
individual way. If a man has a book to read, or a poem to write, he may
keep unquestioned title to his table as if he were in a Latin café. If he has
a train to catch, he may be sure of the promptest service. For several years
in the late Thirties, my wife and I, with two daughters under ten, invariably
supped at Jacob Wirth's on Christmas Eve. We had a family children's
party in Cambridge that rarely broke up until long after six, and we wished
to arrive at the Church of the Advent well before eight. The obvious
solution for dinner was Jake Wirth's. We would arrive breathless close to
seven. Fritz Heuser would whisk his apron over four chairs; produce

dinner with the speed of lightning; and off we would go to Mount Vernon and Brimmer streets, well fed and happy. This is a fine place to take your

girl, to take your children, to take your grandchildren. But it is probably even more appreciated by the solitary, who have no one to sup with, but who find warmth and geniality in the *Gemütlichkeit* of the restaurant. It is, moreover, a stable spot in a changing world, for the customer who returns after an absence, be it five or fifty years, would at once recognize both food and surroundings.

In 1868 Jacob Wirth, lately arrived from Germany, set up business on Eliot Street. Originally at Number 60, he moved across the street in 1878 to a red brick Greek Revival bow-fronted house, numbered 37–39, with the restaurant on the ground floor, and kitchens and living quarters for his family upstairs. If any reader is puzzled by the name *Eliot* Street, let him not rashly assume that the restaurant has ever moved from its original block. The difference in the address simply comes from the fact that the city subsequently changed the name of the street to Stuart. Next door was the granite Caledonian Hall, now, alas, replaced by a parking lot.

A plate-glass store front, extending to the sidewalk, was added on the ground floor. To the left of the entrance was a long mahogany bar, well equipped for dispensing the draught beers in which the restaurant has always excelled; above it the motto SUUM CUIQUE, a clock, and a circular medallion portrait of the founder. Simple mahogany tables, without cloths; sawdust on the floor; a few large steins and bottles for decoration; and that was all, in 1878 or now. In 1890 the ground floor of the adjoining house was added to double the size of the restaurant.

Jacob Wirth came from a family of wine-growers, with vineyards at Kreuznach, near Bingen, in Rhenish Prussia, from which he imported Rhine wine for wholesale and retail sale, as well as for use in the restaurant. He imported also German red wines, Moselles, clarets from François Cuzol et fils, Bordeaux, Rittscher champagnes from Reims, and Reginaris and Rhens mineral waters. He was also sole Boston agent for the lagers of the Anheuser-Busch Brewing Company of St. Louis, George Ehrets's celebrated New York Hell Gate Lager, Robert Smith's India Pale Ale from Philadelphia, and the products of the Narragansett Brewing Company of Providence. These, with Pilsener and Würzburger Bürger-Br¨u, were on draught; München, Guinness, and Bass's Ale were available in bottles. Incidentally, Jacob Wirth and his friend George Ehrets successfully persuaded their recently arrived compatriot, Lüchow, to go into the restaurant business in New York.

The menu in the Boston restaurant was always simple: The staples were sausages, pigs' knuckles, boiled bacon, hams, cheeses, herrings, with several special dishes for each of the six weekdays on which the restaurant was open. Daily, except Sundays, 11 to 11, was and is the timetable. This was a family enterprise. Jacob Wirth's brother, Carl, managed the Boston restaurant; his nephew, Henry R. Wirth, presided over a Hofbrauhaus in Providence, Rhode Island. His wife was responsible for many of the recipes used in both restaurants. There were bottling plants in Charlestown and in Providence, and, of course, the vineyards, vaults, shipping office, and weinstube in Kreuznach.

The comfortable and copiously moustached visage of the elder Jacob Wirth is familiar to all customers from the medallion over the bar and from a large conventional portrait that is one of the few adornments of the restaurant. A less familiar likeness appears in an advertising lithograph of the 1870's where he (in athletic undress) is portrayed sitting on a bottle borne by a prancing goat, casually balancing a keg of beer on his left shoulder, while raising a seidel in his right hand. This trophy of a victorious athlete is not unsuitable for a man who once remained on his feet while the eminent John L. Sullivan hit the deck with a resounding thud. Sullivan, who enjoyed visiting the restaurant cellar to sample the wines, was fascinated by watching barrels of beer rolling down a big skid from the brewer's dray in the street. As each barrel rolled down, Jacob Wirth would put his foot on the side of it to slow its progress, causing the barrel to spin. Sullivan had to try this trick, put his foot squarely in the middle of a barrel, and was knocked flat on his back. Parenthetically, Irish customers tend to identify the medallion of Jacob Wirth over the bar as a likeness of John L. Sullivan.

When Jacob Wirth died in 1892, his widow not only continued to live above the restaurant with her son and daughter, but carried on the business until her own death in 1899. The son, the present Jacob Wirth, born upstairs on 19 May 1880, entered Harvard College in the autumn of 1901. Having through a bout of typhoid fever lost a considerable part of his freshman year, he decided not to return to college, but to take over the management of the restaurant. Thus it has been in the hands of one proprietor-owner for more than sixty years, nearly the whole of the present century. He introduced the sale of spirits, for previously the restaurant had offered only wine and beer. He also sold the Providence Hofbrauhaus to his cousin Henry, concentrating his own efforts on the Boston store.

Otherwise the *status quo* has always been maintained, within the limits permitted by law. The restaurant is repainted every two years, but as it is always in the same color, nobody notices it. No chrome, no gewgaws have ever been permitted. At one time Mr. Wirth began reducing the amount of sawdust on the floor, thinking that sawdust on an overcoat was too much like hay on the back of a girl's dress. But when customers began to growl, "What are you trying to do? Change the place over?" he happily restored the former quota. On this, as on most other points, management and customers alike resist change, but nobody has complained about quiet introduction of air conditioning.

When the United States declared war on Germany in 1917, the Jacob Wirth Company was a Boston institution forty-nine years old. That it was clearly regarded as such is shown by an article of Reuben Greene's in the *Boston Traveler* of 14 February 1918, which began:

> Jake Wirth's is the only place I know of where you can give the waiter a nickel tip and still retain your self-respect.
>
> It is also one of the few places in America which has a German atmosphere yet is not obnoxious to the American citizen. That is because the only things connected with the place which are Teuton are the beer, frankfurts, cheese, and other articles of food. The hearts of those connected with the cafe are, and always have been, with the United States to the core. . . .
>
> Jake's is the official home of the pig's knuckle. The pea soup is masterly and the cranberry pie beyond criticism. Another absolutely characteristic Wirth dish is hasenpfeffer.
>
> Jake's is the antithesis of the modern fashionable restaurant. For example, take any one of the Back Bay eating places. You enter leisurely, languidly, the idea being to impress the door man, cloak woman, headwaiter and any others who witness your entry, that you are extremely familiar with everything in the world and impressed with nothing. Your expression should be slightly bored or mildly tolerant. When you are seated, you must ignore the waiter's presence utterly. You must take considerable time to adjust yourself to your chair and study your surroundings some minutes before picking up the menu.
>
> When you enter Jake's, particularly at noontime, the waiter

yells at you from wherever he may be when he first sees you. "What is it today, pea soup? Special? Knuckle?"

You yell back and by the time you have hung up your coat, Joe or somebody else appears, slides the soup dish across the wooden table, dumps a handful of knives, forks, napkins, spoons and rye bread beside it, and dashes off. He goes by you on the jump all the time. He never stops by your side and, presenting you with a menu, asks if you will have something more. If you want a strudel or a piece of Swiss cheese, you have to make yourself heard, or stick out your foot and trip a waiter.

Another journalist reported how a belligerent patriot, with three companions, called Fritz Früh, the headwaiter, "You damned German spy." Fritz quietly retorted: "I forbid you to call me that. I am a loyal citizen of America. I have one son in the Army and one in the Navy. I forbid you to call me that name." When invited to prove it, Fritz got his overcoat and led his hecklers around the corner to La Grange Street.—

Coming to the police station, Fritz walked up the steps. At the door he politely paused to allow his companions to enter. The courtesy was wasted. Down on the sidewalk the four were engaged in what evidently was a serious conversation. Fritz couldn't wait all night. He entered alone.

A brawny sergeant looked over the desk and saw an agitated skullcap. "Hello, Fritz, what's the matter?" "I've just been accused of being a German spy," was the indignant answer. "Where is he?" demanded the husky copper. "Outside," replied Fritz, "with three friends."

Immediately a button was pushed. The room grew rich in blue uniforms and brass buttons. This color scheme paused a moment at the desk and then flitted lightly out into the night. Soon it reappeared, darkened in spots by four splashes of plain mufti.

"These the birds?" demanded the sergeant. "They are the birds," replied Fritz, or words to that effect.

Ten minutes later he was back in the restaurant of Jacob Wirth, with an apology for each customer who had been deprived of his assistance in matters relative to the ordering of pig's knuckles and sauerkraut, or perhaps liverwurst. It is estimated that he left the police station approximately 12 hours before his overpatriotic companions.

The first World War, however, brought a major change to the restaurant by putting an end to the importation of Rhine wines from Kreuznach. With Prohibition coming on the heels of the war, Jacob Wirth sold the German vineyards. The down payment amounted to millions of marks; the cash received after exchange to $137. Throughout Prohibition the only liquid offerings were light and dark near beer, brewed by Haffenreffer in Jamaica Plain, with strict observance of the legal limit of alcoholic content. Although lacking in authority, the flavor was authentic. Many of us first acquired a taste for beer from Jake Wirth's Prohibition substitute.

A special article by C. B. Palmer in the *Boston Evening Transcript* of 12 November 1932 on the prospects of Repeal includes an account of a conversation with Fritz Früh at the "Gibraltar of Germania" in Stuart Street.

> The sum of his wise administration is this dictum: "A good glass of beer never hurt anybody." With vehemence he is willing to defend his position. "This was a family place, and we always keep it a family place. We got three rules: No politics, no war, no religion. Since 1868 this has been a place for families to come, the children and the mothers. All I got to say about beer coming back is: All right, if it comes back we sell it. If it don't, we don't. We'll go right along just the same. A good glass of beer never hurt anybody." . . .
>
> "You know this near beer costs more to make than real beer. Sure! After it's all made they have to steam it to get the alcohol out. More labor, more expense." . . .
>
> "Business? Well, I should say right after prohibition business dropped to a third what it was. A lot of places closed up. But we had our friends with our food. By 1926 we were doing I bet three times the business we were before prohibition. We've always had a good brew, made right out of Roxbury."

The brew was indeed good, for on that glorious seventh of April 1933 when liberty was restored to H. L. Mencken (and millions of other Americans), barrels and barrels of Jake Wirth's near beer were ecstatically swilled down by celebrators who mistook it for the "real thing." There had been confusion and delay in issuing liquor licenses. When the seventh arrived, Jacob Wirth Company, being still unlicensed, offered simply its usual near beer. Ignoring signs to that effect, honestly placed in the windows, thirsty drinkers swarmed to the bar. So enthusiastic were they that at 8:00 P.M. the doors were closed against future arrivals. The *Boston Evening Transcript* the following evening thus reported the doings on Stuart Street with a headline "No Trace of Drunkenness at Jake Wirth's Place—and for Good and Sufficient Reason":

The barmen were at the point of exhaustion and beer suds splattered the whole vicinity. There was not a trace of drunkenness. This absence of drunkenness was for good and sufficient reason. As a matter of simple fact not one ounce of alcoholic beverages has slid across Wirth's bar since the city went dry fourteen years ago.

Wirth's, it transpires, was a little slow in obtaining its beer license. The proprietors, being law-abiding people, consequently placed no 3.2 beer on sale yesterday or today. Being also thoroughly straightforward in their dealings, the people at Wirth's endeavored to apprise the beer-bent hordes which descended on them, that it was only near beer after all.

"This is only near beer—we haven't any license yet," Wirth's barmen and waiters repeated, but their well-meant warnings were drowned out in happy laughter and cries of "Prosit." News photographers dropped in and caught the jubilation in full ecstasy. Everyone was smiling, the customers because they were convinced they were throwing off some sort of shackles or other, the barmen because of the inherent preposterousness of the situation. The proprietors of Wirth's, meanwhile, were up against it. They put up signs that the beer was not beer, but the crowd slapped each other on the back. More news photographers arrived, and reporters chronicled the great night at Jake Wirth's. The reporters quaffed a mug and declared themselves entranced. A lot of people fell to laughing at the curious twists of a pretzel. The Wirths put up some more signs. When a new mob of bravos turned up bright and early this morning, Wirth's applied for police assistance. Still heedless of alcoholic content, the crowd packed itself solidly in front of the service bar and began drinking. In addition to the imagined beer thrill, the crowd appeared to be considerably taken by the fact that it was drinking at a bar. This is a perfectly legal way to drink near beer, but Wirth's was getting pretty sick of the whole business and two patrolmen were assigned to assist in the enlightenment of the would-be guzzlers.

One nice thing about it all, anyhow—there was not a trace of drunkenness.

FLASH—Jake Wirth's obtained its license at 10:15 A.M. today.

Once the license *was* obtained, Dawson's began brewing Jake Wirth's Special Dark, in three-hundred-barrel lots from a special formula that remarkably approximates the quality and taste of the pre-1914 imported draught beers. This, like the light beer, which differs only in the degree to which the malt has been roasted, has now given pleasure for thirty-odd years, although soon after Repeal some of the brethren who arrived on the closing of City Hall and sat, treating each other to successive rounds, until the closing of Jake Wirth's, looked back almost longingly upon the Prohibition near beer.

Ninety-five years between father, mother, and son is a remarkable record for any business. It is even more startling to see a going concern owned by a man who was born in a room upstairs more than eighty years earlier. Only a few years ago, Jacob Wirth moved from his parents' quarters above the restaurant to a house on Lime Street. Although the daily details have passed to his son-in-law, Frank Lindsey, he is daily at "the store," as he calls it, with a keen eye roving in all directions, and with determination to maintain quality unchanged. For years Carl Weitz, a butcher a few doors up Stuart Street, made sausages, as well as buying top-quality beef directly from packers and aging it for the restaurant. Although Carl Weitz, in his white coat and straw hat, has died, his firm still supplies Jake Wirth's. Sauerkraut is made every three weeks in great wine hogsheads, numbered from 1 to 10, and used in strict numerical order. It gives pause to think that thirty tons of sauerkraut are made, and consumed, each year. The pastry comes from a small bakery in Jamaica Plain—with Roxbury and Roslindale the chief residence of Boston Germans —while the bread is baked especially for the restaurant by Green and Freedman.

The employees of the Jacob Wirth Company have had records almost equaling, and in one instance surpassing, that of the present owner. On 7 February 1875 Frederick Früh, known invariably as Fritz, frequently quoted on previous pages, then a green lad fresh from Germany, was hired as waiter by the elder Jacob Wirth. Save for the bartender, he was, at this early period, the only employee serving in the dining room. Later he became cashier. When Fritz Früh died, at the age of eighty-six, as manager of the restaurant, he had been sixty-seven years in the employ of the Wirths, father and son. In 1890 Jacob Wirth gave Fritz a gold watch bearing the inscription, "For Fifteen Years of Faithful Service," with the remark that if still there in another fifteen years he "would fill it with diamonds." Although he was not, his son in 1905 gave Fritz a bouquet of violets for his wife, with a silk purse of gold pieces hidden beneath it. On his fiftieth anniversary in 1925 Fritz received a loving cup, flowers, and a diamond ring. This devoted little man, unique among headwaiters in wearing a black skullcap, shook hands genially with thousands of customers, yet could, in later years, grumble to his employer: "You know, Jacob, it's got so if I want to send a fool on an errand, I've got to go myself." By 1910 Fritz was so much of a Boston fixture that a postcard, mailed with no other address than a water-color sketch of him, complete with skullcap, was promptly delivered at the restaurant. On his fiftieth anniversary in 1925, he told a reporter:

"Yesterday it was the fathers who were my friends. Today it is the sons. Yesterday a man came in and brought his boy. Today that boy's son comes in and calls me Fritz just as his grandfather and father did before him. Are they different? I don't know. Sometimes I think they don't take as much time to eat as their grandfathers did. But then, the world moves faster today. They like to sit at the same table, each noon and night, but so did those who have gone. Sometimes I look at a young man and see the father, and then my memory goes back to many things when I should be thinking of frankfurters or pumpernickel bread."

It was, I am sure, Fritz Früh who asked me to leave Jake Wirth's forty years ago, but I have a less clear recollection of him than of another Fritz, the diminutive Frederick T. Heuser, five feet two inches, one hundred fifteen pounds, who first came to work in 1893, and retired in 1948, after a mere fifty-five years' service. It was Fritz Heuser who made our hasty Christmas Eve suppers so agreeable in the late Thirties. It was he who estimated that, during his first years, he had served at least six million seidels of beer, and from this extensive experience ruled: "You have to drink it through the foam to get the flavor. Nine out of ten blow the head off and so they blow the best part away." He further observed: "They can't put no bum beer in front of me, I like it thick enough to chew."

After fifteen years of service, Fritz Heuser received a gold watch; after fifty a thousand-dollar war bond and a silver tray. On 1 October 1948, after fifty-five years and six months as a waiter, Fritz Heuser retired. When he died on 1 July 1949, Lawrence Dame of the *Boston Herald* wrote the following verses:

> *Tiny man with ready smiles,*
> *Who walked more than million miles*
> *Giving cheer to young and old,*
> *Bringing food and seidels cold.*
>
> *There are grooves along the floor*
> *Where he did his daily chore*
> *Oh, at Wirth's the beer still flows,*
> *But Fritz no more on errands goes.*
>
> *You miss him coming up the aisle*
> *With his hands all full and his face all smile,*
> *Yet surely somewhere, no need to give odds,*
> *Our dear little Fritz is serving the Gods!*

And the incomparable W. A. Dwiggins drew in his best style a sketch of "Fritz Heuser in Asgard," which shows the diminutive waiter quenching the thirst of the Norse gods with the seidels that were so welcome to Dwiggins, Dame, and thousands of other mortals.

Both Fritzes have gone to Asgard, but others are fast running up records that match theirs. In 1961 Jacob Wirth gave silver salvers to six waiters with thirty or more years' service: Joseph Fettig, Carl Neugebauer, and

Jacob Wirth

Karl Bischoff, who came to work in 1919, Hugo Kopke (1923), Herman Fehrmann (1924), and William Lyons (1931), as well as a gold wrist watch to Maria Schlaich, a cook since 1924.

For thirty-odd years I ate at Jake Wirth's without stopping to consider who Jake was, or how the restaurant had become, and had remained, what it was. Then one day I encountered Mrs. Jacob Wirth reading in the Boston Athenæum, and thus came to know the man whose establishment I had so long enjoyed. It was, as Ray Billington of the Huntington Library remarks in a piece that follows, "legend brought to life." So the various friends who have joined to commemorate the ninety-fifth anniversary of this Boston institution, join with Dean J. P. Elder in saying to its owner: "Tibi et tuae dominae omnia omnes bona fausta prospera precamur."

DAY BEFORE YESTERDAY, 12 December [1965], in the early light of a gloomy snowy Sunday morning, our friend Jacob Wirth died quietly in his home at 32 Lime Street, a little more than halfway through his eighty-sixth year. Countless thousands of Americans throughout the country know affectionately the name that he shared with his father, but only a relatively small number of New Englanders were honored by his personal friendship, for he was a modest and retiring man. A little over a year ago, seven friends joined with me in producing a little *Festschrift* titled *A Seidel for Jake Wirth* in recognition of the many seidels of his Special Dark beer that we had enjoyed over years and decades. David McCord wrote a ballade, concluding with the line: "A seidel of dark on the side of life." The classicist John Petersen Elder, Dean of the Harvard Graduate School of Arts and Sciences, offered birthday greetings in resonant Latin, with translation appended for those ignorant of ancient tongues. Lucien Price of *The Boston Globe*, who died before his contribution appeared in print, started with a description of the Stuart Street restaurant, and, from that reasonable launching pad, rocketed off into the Empyrean, borne aloft for twenty pages by a rhapsody on Wagner, Schubert, and Goethe. Other friends contributed briefer but no less feeling reminiscences

· 139 ·

of the pleasures of dining at Jake Wirth's, while I provided not only an affectionate tribute to my own forty-one years in Stuart Street, but an historical sketch of this remarkable institution.

This greatly beloved Boston institution has survived in a changing world because it was, in the highest spirit of European craftsmanship, the lifework of our friend Jacob Wirth. In the family quarters upstairs over the restaurant, our friend Jacob Wirth was born on 19 May 1880, and here he lived for nearly three quarters of his long life. The place has changed as little as anything in Boston. It was simple, sensible, and excellent when Jacob Wirth inherited it, and so it has remained. So it will remain, I feel sure, under the management of his son-in-law, Frank Lindsey.

When the United States declared war on Germany in 1917, the Jacob Wirth Company was a Boston institution forty-nine years old, and was clearly recognized as such. However German the cooking, the proprietor was a native-born American of unquestioned loyalty. The late President Kennedy, in his book *A Nation of Immigrants* remarked:

> . . . Every American who ever lived, with the exception of one group, was either an immigrant himself or a descendant of immigrants. The exception? Will Rogers, part Cherokee Indian, said that his ancestors were at the dock to meet the *Mayflower*. And some archaeologists believe that the Indians themselves were immigrants from another continent who displaced the original Americans—the aborigines.

So it comes about naturally that I, the grandson of a Scot born in Paisley on the Clyde, should be paying tribute to the son of a German from Kreuznach in Rhenish Prussia, in the pulpit of the First Church, founded by those earliest immigrants, the Puritan Englishmen of the Massachusetts Bay Company who came to Boston more than two centuries earlier. And so it is equally natural that this German restaurant has become part and parcel of Boston, equally loved by residents, old and young, and by visitors.

Yet Jacob Wirth was so modest a man that few of the people who knew his name and his establishment also knew *him*, or even, in later years, realized that there actually *was* a Jake Wirth. I began to frequent the restaurant as an undergraduate in the early 1920's, but thirty years passed before I came to know its proprietor. The historian Ray Allen Billington, now of the Huntington Library in California, also came to love the restaurant when he arrived at Harvard as a graduate student in 1927. But he knew nothing of the man behind the name until a few years ago, when he returned briefly to Boston and met the Wirths. The moving essay that he contributed to *A Seidel for Jake Wirth* concludes:—

> The theatre is gone now . . . and the old friends scattered. But Jake Wirth's is still there, with the menu just the same, and the beer as supreme as ever. To be taken there, as I was recently, with Mr. and Mrs. Jake Wirth in person, was an experience that might well climax a lifetime. For here was legend brought to life; I am sure that no ancient Greek could have been more thrilled if he had been invited to dine with Zeus. Long may Jake Wirth's give substance to the dreams of Harvard graduate students: Boston should venerate that cradle of thought as it does the Old South Church or Faneuil Hall.

Jacob Wirth devoted his life to the great simplicities. In youth he came into a man's responsibilities, and built an outstandingly successful business by patient, constant, sensible attention to all details. For long years he was single, and of necessity absorbed by the demands of work. When he married, his imagination found new scope in loving care of his family.

Although city-born, he loved both the country and the sea. He summered in Farmington, Maine, where he owned the local newspaper, the *Franklin Journal*. He loved dogs, and was a good sailor. It was characteristic that in World War II he not only turned his yacht *Frou Frou* over to the Government, but had, at sixty-three, gone to sea (with other good sailors too old for Navy commissions) as a petty officer in the United States Coast Guard Reserve.

Modest, unobtrusive, almost austere in his personal wants, it was happiness for him to give generously and thoughtfully to his family, his friends, and his employees. When we think of Jacob Wirth, we recall him as one who over a long life brought his qualities to a rare perfection; we remember him as a simple, a good, and especially a *gentle* man. When Henry Thoreau lay dying one hundred and three years ago, his aunt Louisa pretentiously asked him if he had made his peace with God. He answered: "I did not know we had ever quarrelled, Aunt." Had anyone put such a question to Jacob Wirth, he might have given a similar answer.

Dr. William Sturgis Bigleow, in an Ingersoll Lecture, "Buddhism and Immortality," wrote more than fifty years ago:

> There is a Japanese proverb that says, "There are many roads up the mountain, but it is always the same moon that is seen from the top." The Japanese themselves, with a liberality worthy of imitation, apply this saying to different forms of religious belief. The mountain may well typify matter, and the summit the highest accessible point on which a climber can stand and maintain his separate individual existence in terms of consciousness drawn from the material world. This peak may be accessible by any religion, or without any religion; but Buddhism and its generally associated systems look beyond.

What lies beyond the grave remains a mystery not susceptible of proof. Whether death is the end or the beginning, none of us can ever know until we ourselves set upon that road which our friend took on Sunday morning. Man's mind has envisioned everything from the shades beyond Styx to ineffable light. Whether individual consciousness survives, or whether, as Dr. Bigelow's Buddhists would have it, the peace of limitless consciousness is unified with limitless will in Nirvana, no good man is ever dead when he is remembered in the minds of those who knew him with the affection with which we treasure the memory of Jacob Wirth. Of this degree of immortality there can be no doubt.

Let us pray.

Almighty God, we entrust all who are dear to us to thy never-failing care and love, for this life and the life to come, knowing that thou art doing for them better things than we can desire or pray for; through Jesus Christ our Lord. Amen.

O God, whose mercies cannot be numbered, accept our prayers on behalf of the soul of thy servant Jacob departed, and grant him an entrance into the land of light and joy, in the fellowship of thy saints; through Jesus Christ our Lord. Amen.

May he rest in peace.

CHAPTER XIII

Ernest J. King

1878 – 1956

FROM NOVEMBER 1942 until June 1946 I was on active duty in the Office of Naval Records and Library, Navy Department. I had been commissioned in the Naval Reserve at the request of its Officer in Charge, Captain (later Commodore) Dudley W. Knox (1877–1960), for archival-historical duties in connection with operational records of the current war, which were my chief concern during these three and a half years. But an unanticipated occurrence in the autumn of 1943 led to additional duty in the headquarters of Commander in Chief, United States Fleet, which, in its turn, led to an equally unanticipated friendship with Admiral King. During my first six years at the Boston Athenæum I collaborated with him in the writing of Fleet Admiral King: A Naval Record *published in this country in 1952 by W. W. Norton & Company, Inc., and in abridged form in England by Eyre & Spottiswoode the following year. In "A Note on the Making of this Book" (pp. 647–697 of the American edition) I gave an account of our collaboration. After Admiral King's death I published the piece that follows,[1] under the title "A Postscript to* Fleet Admiral King: A Naval Record," *in Massachusetts Historical Society* Proceedings, *LXX (1950–1953) 203–226.*

The circumstances accompanying the achievement of the March 1945 photograph that is here reproduced are described in Footnote 12 at the end of this chapter. My reflections on the passage of time in the last paragraph of the chapter become even more pertinent when one recalls that since these sentences were written naval vessels bearing the names of Fleet Admiral King, his classmate Rear Admiral Julius A. Furer, and Commodore Dudley W. Knox have been built, commissioned, and joined the fleet.

E J K

THE Daily Personnel Report of the United States Naval Hospital, Portsmouth, New Hampshire, for 25 June 1956 contained among its statistics of patients the laconic entry:

KING, Ernest Joseph   FADM   USN   Discharged by death

which recorded the end of nearly sixty years of single-minded devotion to the United States Navy. Admiral King's death at 2:45 P.M. on that early summer Monday afternoon, from an acute heart failure brought on by high blood pressure, ended nearly nine years of determined struggle against physical obstacles that would have years before completely defeated a less determined man.[2]

Upon his relief as Chief of Naval Operations by Admiral Nimitz on 15 December 1945, Admiral King was ordered to duty in the office of the Secretary of the Navy. Free of crushing responsibility for the first time in five years,[3] he returned to the spacious but Spartanly barren office on the third floor of the Navy Department building on Constitution Avenue that he had occupied during the war.[4]

Five-star officers have the right to remain on active duty if they choose, and after more than forty-eight years of service no other life attracted King. He did not know how to loaf gracefully, and had no desire to learn. Nor had he any inclination to sell his name as an ornament to industry or the popular press or to seek public office. He wisely chose to remain in character, doubtless realizing that the qualities of direct and logical action that permitted him to achieve the impossible in wartime would have proved a serious handicap in civilian or political life in peacetime. He had never cultivated the art of diplomatic address, and he had no aptitude for political bargaining. The most withering term of contempt in his vocabulary was "fixer," which he occasionally applied in conversation when referring to officers who particularly enjoyed duty in the Bureau of Naval Personnel and remained too long there.

While King was the greatest man that I have ever known on terms of friendly intimacy, or am likely to encounter in the future, I should be the last to deny that he was an unevenly developed man, for while his intellect and will power were towering, his human emotions were rudimentary in comparison to the Olympian magnitude of other sides of his character. Admiral W. V. Pratt summed matters up rather well in 1933 when he wrote to the Secretary of the Navy:

> Captain King has certain characteristics which make him an outstanding officer—
>
> (a) He is highly intelligent.
> (b) He is extremely active and energetic.
> (c) He is very forceful.
> (d) He is a flyer and pilot.
> (e) He is a man of great decision of character.
> (f) He is a good strategist and tactician.
> (g) He is not as tactful as some men but he is very direct.
> (h) He is trustworthy.
> (i) He is due for promotion to the position of Rear Admiral.[5]

These were the qualities which were to carry him through World War II when he had to attempt to make something out of nothing by doing the best he could with what he had. Under such conditions the simplicity of his emotions became one of his greatest strengths, for he was able to concentrate the portentous power of an iron will upon enforcing a carefully reasoned decision, without being distracted by considerations that would have affected a man of more complex character.

One of his successors as Chief of Naval Operations, the late Admiral Forrest Sherman, recalled in an address at the Naval Academy on 5 December 1947:

> In December 1941 it happened that I was with Admiral Stark in his office when Admiral King, then Commander in Chief of the Atlantic Fleet, arrived in the Navy Department and first learned the full extent of the damage at Pearl Harbor. I shall never forget the emotions evidenced by the face of Admiral King—an initial expression of sorrow—with some moisture visible in his eyes— followed immediately by an expression of cold determination, a determination which continued unrelaxed while for four years he overcame all obstacles, did his best with initially inadequate forces, gathered men and material, created and directed the greatest Navy ever conceived, and drove through to victory. Never overlook the part played by that great man in the distant victories which brought fame to others.[6]

Sometimes, when resources were lacking, matters had to be put in motion by sheer force of personality. Samuel Eliot Morison described a clipper ship coming into port, "crew leaping into the rigging to furl the sails as if shot upward by the blast of profanity from the mate's bull-like throat."[7] Something similar is indicated in Admiral R. S. Edwards's recollection of how the Bora Bora convoy was speeded toward its goal by Admiral King:

> This convoy was hastily got together in January 1942 to carry base material, SeaBees and a small Army garrison to Bora Bora. Some of the transports and cargo vessels that had to be used were in very poor condition. In consequence there were appeals to delay sailing to give time for repairs. Admiral King, sensing that here was an opportunity to inculcate the spirit of regarding difficulties

Ernest J. King

as a challenge, blew the roof off in a series of heated exhortations to all concerned, principally the Director of Naval Transportation Service and the Commandant of the Navy Yard at Charleston, S. C., the final port of departure. The resulting speed-up of preparations was little short of miraculous, considering the conditions that existed at the time. The incident is of some interest because it established the fact that the newly installed Cominch was Bull of the Woods and intended to exact the utmost in performance.[8]

To me the most perceptive observation ever made about Admiral King are the words italicized in the statement[9] issued on the day of his death by the present Chief of Naval Operations, Admiral Arleigh A. Burke.

> Coupled with the penetrating mind of extraordinary brilliance Adm. King was blessed with complete intellectual integrity and the undeviating courage of his convictions. His conclusions were logical and his beliefs unshakeable. Many times he adhered doggedly to his reasoned beliefs in the face of tremendous opposition and *no pressure except the pressure of logic could make him back down.*[10]

A similar thought was amplified in the tribute from King's classmate and close friend, Rear Admiral Julius A. Furer, that was published in the August 1956 issue of *Shipmate*.

> In dealing, during World War II, with his superiors and high ranking opposite numbers in other services his forthrightness saved much of the wear and tear that goes with the polite circumlocutions characteristic of upper level conferences. It also prevented the misunderstandings that so often are fatal to effective collaboration between allies. No one was ever left in doubt as to where King stood on any question. He had no pride of authorship if he could be shown that the position he had taken was in error. From the time he entered the Naval Academy he had no liking for bowing the head or bending the knee and his boiling point was always low. Even Franklin Roosevelt changed the subject when he saw the color rising in Ernie's face. He had tenacity of purpose,

an inflexible courage, and an unbending will which never flinched before any antagonist or difficulty. His determination not to allow the war in the Pacific to be relegated too far to the rear in the overall war effort and his courage in taking the calculated risks that were necessary early in the war undoubtedly brought the war with Japan to a much speedier victory than had at first been considered possible. Thereby, thousands of American lives were saved.

His overall contribution to the greatest naval war in history was second to none. Ernest King was a towering figure in those crucial years of national peril; a towering figure in bringing victory to the whole Allied world.

In theory King was after the war an adviser of the Secretary of the Navy, but it seemed, at least to an outside observer, that little use was made of his incomparable abilities and experience. King and James Forrestal, although they respected each other, thought differently on many points and were temperamentally incapable of a mutual liking. A letter that King wrote on 18 May 1944 to Frank Knox's close friend, Rawleigh Warner, suggests the climate of relations between King and Forrestal from the moment that the latter succeeded to the Secretaryship.

> Despite your expectations I was *not* consulted as to the filling of the big vacancy.
>
> I am sure that it will be of interest to you to know that, after due reflection, I went yesterday afternoon to the new incumbent and laid the situation on the line, as I saw it, about my feeling as to the agencies and activities of the Navy in general and the Navy Department in particular. It was an unpalatable job for me but I am bound to say that it was, all things considered, received amiably enough. Anyway, I have done what I thought I had to do. Among other things that I took up was the matter of what I have called the "cleavage" organisation in the Navy Department, on which it was said that my judgment in the matter was accepted, so I hope there will be no more of that.

Although they worked together to good purpose during the next nineteen months, the end of the war brought problems that accentuated rather than minimized the difference in King's and Forrestal's approaches. Thus during the first two years after the war, few official demands were made upon King's time or thoughts. During 1946 and the first half of 1947 he remained chiefly in the Navy Department, quietly reviewing the crowded events of the preceding years and planning a narrative of the international conferences in which he had participated.

From the autumn of 1943 I had been doing chores for Admiral King's successive Flag Secretaries, Captains Orem and Dietrich.[11] At the desk that I occupied in their crowded office—Room 3047—across the corridor, I had come to know the thoughts and personality of Admiral King through his papers—including those formidable yellow chits with a very few penciled words followed by the initial "K," which were capable of setting mighty events in motion—but I was entirely without personal knowledge of him. Just as a pair of footprints or a vacant chair served to represent the Buddha in the earliest Buddhist art, so the sound of a buzzer summoning the Flag Secretary to Room 3048 was the only symbol of Admiral King in Room 3047, yet his unseen presence dominated the room. Had there been time, one could have written a play, with a chorus of WAVES yeomen, about this office that would have given considerable insight into the character of the man for whose service it existed.

I had in 1945, from the comfort of a hideaway normally used for visiting flag officers, which was one of the few quiet and peaceful places in a fantastically confused and overcrowded building, drafted the Admiral's second and third reports to the Secretary of the Navy on the progress of the war. In thoughtful acknowledgment I had been sent a copy of Maurice Constant's fine photograph[12] of the Admiral, inscribed "with appreciation and with best wishes" and an official letter of commendation for my "efficient performance of duty" which stated that I had "displayed soundness of judgment and unusual aptitude to vary [my][13] writing style to conform to that used by Fleet Admiral King." I had heard him speak at a massing of the colors ceremony outside Washington Cathedral on 21 May 1944.[14] I had passed him in corridors, as on that spring morning in 1945 when news of the sinking of the Japanese battleship *Yamato* was being broadcast over the public address system in the Navy Department. Admiral King and Admiral Edwards emerged from one third-floor doorway and disappeared shortly into another, so deep in conversation about the future, that neither of them ever observed hundreds of officers, enlisted men, WAVES, and civil servants piling into corridors in an excitement that foreshadowed the V-E day that was so soon to follow.

In the summer of 1944 I had been ordered to assemble the documentation for a history of the establishment of and succeeding changes to the organization of COMINCH headquarters.[15] As the files were scanty, particularly for the early months of 1942 when everything was happening at once, there were many points of organization that could be determined only by talking with Admiral King.[16]

Thus it came about that on Lincoln's Birthday in 1946 I was ushered into the vastly empty 3048 Navy Department for my first meeting with him. He received me with an air of leisurely cordiality, gave me a cigarette and waved me to a leather armchair. The physique of the man I saw revealed both lifelong habits of self-discipline and British ancestry. His lean body did not sag or bulge. Photographs represented his face exceptionally faithfully, for there was little variation of hue in his healthy skin; it was not the color but the keenness of his brown eyes that struck you; the pointed nose, the firm mouth and chin were what you remembered. A voice that was neither resonant nor richly modulated carried conviction from his decisive manner of utterance. In routine social interchange he spoke quickly and quietly without emphasis. When he was absorbed in his subject, words would explode impatiently from him in phrases as laconic as a set of signals. Upon occasion, though, when he was conveying contempt, there might be a slackening of pace and a suspicion of nasal twang to his speech. When out of uniform he wore tweed jackets and flannel trousers with ease, but a gray felt hat never sat on his bald head with quite the felicity of a naval cap.

It was a curious experience to compare the man with the portrait that I had formed of him from his papers, and find that the two exactly agreed. During the next four months, I often returned to 3048 Navy Department for long and fascinating conversations in which he not only answered my numerous questions with succinctness, simplicity, and candor but voluntarily reminisced about the earlier years of his naval service. The unerring accuracy of King's memory, combined with his structural gift for stripping away all but the truly significant details, made these afternoons memorable.

From notes scribbled in rapid longhand, I would type a memorandum of the conversation and submit it for verification and correction. It seemed to me, as winter passed into spring, that the Admiral enjoyed these conversations quite as much as I did, for they gave him an opportunity to speak quite freely and informally about matters that interested him. From the time a man commands a ship he of necessity has to become used to his own company, and in high naval command loneliness increases with responsibility.[17] The tradition of isolation, combined with the necessity of rationing time during the war, caused most of the Admiral's visitors to pay rather brief and formal calls. I, on the other hand, was seeking information for legitimate and official reasons. Because I was in uniform, with some knowledge of what had gone on in his headquarters, he could assume that I would understand the significance of what he said, yet as I was only temporarily in that uniform I had no preconceptions or personal interests to hamper the freedom of conversation. Aside from the facts that my grandfather had been born in Paisley, Scotland, and the Admiral's grandparents had lived a few miles down the Clyde at Bridge-of-Weir; that we both valued the friendship of Commodore Dudley W. Knox, and both enjoyed Douglas Freeman's books and the fictional exploits of Horatio Hornblower and Colin Glencannon, we had nothing of a personal nature in common. Our lives and experiences could not have been more different, yet very early in our acquaintance I found that I was regarding King not only with respect and admiration but with a strong admixture of personal liking, which increased proportionately with the passage of time.

During the spring of 1946 I became convinced that, upon leaving the Navy Department, I should try to write Admiral King's life. While he had no particular enthusiasm for the idea, he acquiesced gracefully enough, for, much as he disliked publicity, he knew that something of the kind was inevitable. He had seen enough of me to know that I shared his distaste for ballyhoo and sensationalism, and so, considering that my proposal was the least undesirable form of a necessary evil, agreed to it. Once again he decided quite simply in his own way what he wished to do, without reference to the commercial blandishments of publishers or magazines.

The piece of work that had originally brought us together was completed in June 1946 and forwarded by Admiral King to the Director of Naval History on the 19th with a characteristic letter.

Ernest J. King

1. A History of Headquarters, Commander in Chief, United States Fleet, from 30 December 1941 to 10 October 1945, prepared by Commander W. M. Whitehill, USNR, and approved by me, is forwarded herewith for the use of the Office of Naval History.

2. A classification of RESTRICTED is considered adequate for the present.

E. J. KING

At this time minor commands were sending in bulky narratives, sometimes in many volumes, classified SECRET or higher. For the top command, by contrast, there came 178 pages of text, plus 158 pages of supporting documents, personally approved by COMINCH, and classified in the lowest rank of the security scale.

On 21 June 1946 Admiral King flew to England to receive on the twenty-sixth the degree of Doctor of Civil Law from Oxford University—one of the honors that he valued most highly.[18] On the 24th I was ordered to inactive duty and headed immediately for Boston and the Athenæum. I next returned to Washington early in 1947 when Rear Admiral John B. Heffernan asked representatives of various universities and institutions to inspect the activities of the Office of Naval History. Having gone back to the Navy Department in civilian clothes for the somewhat Gilbert-and-Sullivan reason of examining what I had been involved in doing while in uniform, I called on Admiral King, who was to speak to the assembled visitors at dinner that night. Waving some papers at me, he remarked that Dudley Knox had written his speech for him. Later in the morning, when Commodore Knox said that it would be interesting to hear what King had to say at dinner, I suggested that it could hardly prove a great surprise to him. To this the Commodore replied that, although he had given the Admiral a few notes, King would use them in his own way. In the end both were right. After dinner Admiral King delivered himself of some well-reasoned observations on naval history that clearly bore the Knox touch; then, shoving his hands in his jacket pockets, he gave firsthand recollections of Stalin at Teheran that were equally clearly pure King.

Admiral King accepted in 1946 the presidency of the Naval Historical Foundation, which had been the personal creation of Commodore Knox, but otherwise he showed no willingness to hold office of any kind. His public appearances were few. On 28 April 1946 he addressed the Veterans of Foreign Wars in Columbus, Ohio; on 7 May he made a statement before the Senate Naval Affairs Committee in opposition to Senate Bill 2044 proposing a single department of national defense; on 27 February 1947 he spoke at the Winter Forum of Elgin Academy, Elgin, Illinois, on "The Navy and National Security." He gave a major summary of the grand strategy of the war at the Town Hall Meeting in Pottstown, Pennsylvania, on 21 March 1946, and on 29 April 1947 addressed the National War College on "Some Aspects of the High Command in World War II." While perfectly prepared to state his views if requested to do so in a civil manner, he showed no readiness to push himself before the public. Most of his days were passed in an inconspicuous self-imposed routine in his office in the Navy Department.[19] Thus matters stood until August 1947, when, as a delayed consequence of the strains and exertions of the war, he suffered a brain hemorrhage that for a time deprived him of the power of speech and caused him to take up residence on the seventeenth floor of the Naval Medical Center at Bethesda. There, at his bedside, President Truman presented the gold medal voted to him by the Seventy-ninth Congress "on behalf of a grateful nation."

King's illness was of a severity that would have made a helpless invalid out of a less determined or less physically strong man. Wartime commanders who had borne lighter loads than he were dying with distressing frequency. Gradually by sheer determination he recovered his speech,[20] and before the end of the year was making regular trips from Bethesda to the Navy Department in a modification of his old routine. Once again he had demonstrated the power of will over seemingly insuperable obstacles.

During King's illness I temporarily suspended work on his biography, for while I could have drafted a brief life with the material then in hand, it seemed undesirable to do so if there were a possibility of getting further data from him. I therefore waited, and in mid-December 1947 was told by his aide that his convalescence had reached the stage where he was anxious to proceed. Therefore I began to go to Washington whenever I could spare the time, and spent many hours talking with him and reviewing documents that he lent me. While words sometimes eluded him, the quality and clarity of his thought remained unaltered, and the accuracy of his memory survived, as I was able to check from documents that I turned up independently. We would often drive out into Virginia, for he liked to be in motion, and enjoyed the rich farming landscape. He would have the car stopped at a rustic four corners and explain to me the details of a minor Civil War cavalry action, for he had remembered everything from his early exploration of the Virginia battlefields. Every feature of the landscape suggested some military use. Once when he pointed to a hillside as a likely place for artillery, I suggested that if he put guns there he would obviously be a Confederate, defending the Shenandoah Valley. "Not necessarily," he replied, "just repelling Russians or anybody you please." He drove me past General Marshall's house in Leesburg, and then showed me many sites that he would have preferred, had he been buying a house in the vicinity. Between visits he would write out in laborious longhand recollections of his early life, in strictly inexorable chronology, which would, after typing, be sent on to me to supplement material that I had gathered on my own.

On 8 July 1948 the late Douglas S. Freeman wrote me:

> As I may have told you, I have been so impressed by the difficulties of handling in scientific spirit any documents written by living men concerning the Second World War that I have declined all overtures to write or to edit the work of others. Knowing you to be a scholar I do not see how you can do anything except in one or the other of two lines of action—to write the memoir and fight out the revision with Admiral King, or to have him write it and you revise it. Any compromise between these alternatives is almost certain to confuse future readers.

To this I replied on 13 July 1948:

> My relations with Admiral King in this venture are eminently satisfactory, as I am writing this memoir and giving it to him for revision. He submits in a most amiable fashion to my requests for information and is himself sending me copious memoranda concerning his recollections of his early life.
>
> The difficulties of handling contemporary documents are indeed great, but I feel that I am in a fortunate position in this particular case because of the straightforwardness and clarity of the Ad-

miral's character. I have never known a man who was less of a politician and who said more clearly what he meant, come hell or high water. The problem becomes, therefore, one of simple exposition, for which I am relieved.

Thus it remained to the end, without change. Two incidents in the course of the work seem to be of sufficient historiographical interest to warrant mention.

I had known King from his papers for a considerable time before I came to know him in person, yet when I met him I found that he corresponded to my mental picture of him. This experience with a living man suggests, as Charles P. Curtis pointed out to me in 1951, the possibility that the portrait of someone long dead, reconstructed by an historian from the subject's writing and correspondence, may be a respectably accurate likeness. Although by no means certain, it is at least a possibility, particularly with a monolithic and single-minded subject.

The second point is less reassuring, for it introduces an element of doubt in the interpretation of supposedly unimpeachable documents. When the Army monograph on the Guadalcanal campaign was nearing completion, a copy of the manuscript was sent to Admiral King for comment. He returned it with the criticism that too much space was wasted on low-level planning papers that were of no importance. When it was pointed out to him that the documents he depreciated were all the work of Joint Chiefs of Staff planners, King countered by the irrefutable observation that no use had been made of them in planning the operation, which he and Marshall had had to do in such haste that they had had no time even to look at them; hence they were of no importance in establishing the evolution of the plan. This introduces the disquieting possibility that, without the personal testimony of participants as a guide, the historian may place undue importance upon a seemingly reliable document that is, in fact, nothing more than a red herring.

King had been taken sick in extremely hot weather, and, very probably because of this, the summer heat of Washington became exceptionally distasteful to him. During a visit that I made in the spring of 1949 we conceived the idea of his coming to the United States Naval Hospital at Portsmouth, New Hampshire, for the summer. There he would find a more tolerable climate, and also be more readily in touch with me. Thus it came about that during 1949 and succeeding summers he came frequently to our house in North Andover for week-end visits. While it might have seemed to those unfamiliar with his ways that putting up Admiral King would be a little like domesticating the Washington Monument, he was one of the easiest and most considerate of guests, for his wants were simple and he always said what he meant and meant what he said without affectation or pseudo consideration. If asked when he would like breakfast, he would say, "At eight o'clock, please." You could then be certain that at eight o'clock precisely—not at 7:59 or 8:02—he would present himself at the breakfast table.

Sir Arthur Bryant, in *The Turn of the Tide*, quotes Sir Ian Jacob's impressions of King at the Casablanca conference of January 1943.

> He seems to wear a protective covering of horn which it is hard
> to penetrate . . . His manners are good as a rule, but he is angular
> and stiff and finds it difficult, if not impossible, really to unbend.
> I am convinced, however, that there is much more to him than
> appears on the surface, and that if one could get beneath the horn
> shell that one would be surprised at what one would find beneath.[21]

The horn shell appeared so opaque to many who were King's colleagues in great matters, that it seems worth recording what I, for one, found beneath it.

One attribute of a great man is the ability to make complicated matters seem simple. From all my relations with King, I chiefly carried away a sense of wonder at the inexorable simplicity and directness of his thoughts and expression. Admiral Richard S. Edwards once observed to me that it was Admiral King's "custom to encourage free and uninhibited debate until he had absorbed all points of view. He would then come forth with a clear-cut scheme, usually so obviously applicable as to cause all concerned to wonder why they had not thought of it themselves." My greatest problem in reducing his views to paper was to do so in a way that would make it clear that these deceptively simple-sounding ideas, and these alone, were the principles that had guided to speedy victory in a war of unprecedented magnitude the greatest fleet the world had ever known.[22]

My problem was further complicated by the monolithic simplicity of King's character, for here was a man who was all of a piece, without any of the endearing chiaroscuro that lightens the biographer's task. When Sir Winston Churchill disposes of a cold grouse and a bottle of white wine as a prebreakfast snack before sunrise, even his political enemies cannot repress a momentary admiration for so heroic a figure. A single-minded Scot does not afford his biographer such easy assistance. King, although born in Ohio, was entirely British in origin. Northern Ireland, Devonshire, and Cornwall were in his background, but the influence of his Scottish father—an able, uncompromising Clydeside sailor turned mechanic—predominated.[23] So far as his home life was concerned, Ernest King might just as well have grown up in Renfrewshire as in Ohio. He went to the Naval Academy in identically the spirit that has sent many an ambitious young Scot to Edinburgh with little beyond a sack of oatmeal and an unswerving determination to excel in his profession. Throughout his life there was scant time for anything save his profession. His friends were mostly fellow officers; his chief diversion the study of military history. While Lord Alanbroke was seeking relaxation from the burden of World War II with a set of Gould's birds, King was reading and rereading *Lee's Lieutenants*. King's ideal was the Earl of St. Vincent, "who"—in his words—"forged the weapon that Nelson wielded—who approved Nelson's initiative at the Battle of St. Vincent—who chose Nelson, a junior, for the operation that culminated in the Battle of the Nile—whose discipline was strict, even harsh, but just and necessary."[24]

Lord Cunningham and Lord Alanbroke—King's British colleagues in the Combined Chiefs of Staff—have, while admitting his abilities, spoken of King with an asperity that he never reciprocated. Lord Cunningham wrote of him: "A man of immense capacity and ability, quite ruthless in his methods, he was not an easy person to get on with. He was tough and liked to be considered tough, and at times became rude and overbearing . . . On the whole I think Ernest King was the right man in the right place, though one could hardly call him a good coöperator. Not content with fighting the enemy, he was usually fighting someone on his own side as well."[25] Sir Arthur Bryant reflects Lord Alanbroke's view when he refers to "the tough and stubborn King—the old crustacean as one of his countrymen called him—the ablest strategist on the American Chiefs of Staff."[26]

A persistent, but entirely unfounded, legend attributes anti-British sentiments to King. From my repeated conversations with him, nothing seems to me further from the truth. Witness, for example, the concluding sentences of the special Introduction to the English edition of *Fleet Admiral King: A Naval Record*:

> In the years since 1945 I have often pondered, as I have indicated in the last sentence of this book, upon the need, for the peace of the world, of assuming the permanence of the Anglo-American alliance of 1941–1945. I ask my British readers to keep this thought constantly in mind while examining this record of how the United States and the British Commonwealth accomplished *together* what neither of them could have singly.[27]

and the final page of the Epilogue.[28] When King's admiration for Lord Cunningham's fighting qualities caused him to describe that officer as "a spiritual successor of the Earl of St. Vincent,"[29] he had no higher form of praise.

In *The Turn of the Tide*, Lord Alanbroke seems to find it difficult to believe that King was actually—as I entirely believe him to have been— consistently faithful to the strategic decision requiring the defeat of Germany first, while Lord Cunningham repeatedly makes heavy weather of King's reluctance to employ a British Pacific Fleet in the closing phase of the war against Japan. What is overlooked in both cases is that King, having no political preoccupations, thought purely in military terms of what could be accomplished with the tools available. Although sincerely committed to the defeat of Germany first, he was keenly aware that the Japanese were unlikely to wait passively to be defeated at a time and place of the Allies' choosing. Consequently, while pressing for an acceleration in European operations, he was reluctant to commit forces and ships urgently needed in the Pacific if there were a possibility of their lying unemployed for an extended period in Europe. His views regarding the British Pacific Fleet sprang, not from any jealousy or anti-British sentiment, but from the simple military belief that, as there would be enough American ships to do the job without them, there was no point in straining supply arrangements by the addition of a fleet unaccustomed to operating at great distances from land bases.

Coöperation between allies is never simple. In World War II relations between naval allies were, to a great degree unconsciously, complicated by the reversal of traditional strengths between the Royal Navy and the United States Navy. This was, again quite unconsciously, made no simpler by the fact that the Commander in Chief, United States Fleet, was, without realizing it, a complete Scot. Family disagreements are singularly acrimonious, for charitable allowances made for obvious "heathen" are rarely extended to one's cousins. Some of King's actions must have proved more unpalatable than otherwise to his British colleagues because he was often, all unaware that he was doing so, operating as they might have, had they been in his place.

The popular notion of King's toughness sprang not only from the austerity of his appearance, but from President Roosevelt's delight in Arthur Walsh's gift to King of a scale model of a blowtorch for use as a razor.[30] In consequence of this jest, King was presented with a four-foot brass crowbar inscribed A TOOTHPICK FOR BLOWTORCH and the President circulated the rumor that King cut his toenails with a torpedo-net cutter. It was also widely reported that, upon his appointment as COMINCH in December 1941, Admiral King had observed: "Yes, damn it, when they get in trouble they always send for the sons of bitches." This tale had such currency that Captain (now Vice Admiral, retired) John L. McCrea, meeting the Admiral in a Navy Department corridor in January 1942, ventured to inquire into its authenticity. King replied: "No, John, I didn't say it, but I wish I had."

King's standards were exacting, but his belief in the initiative of the subordinate, and his practice of saying *what* was to be done, and *when*, but never *how*, made him a good man to work for. As I observed in the final chapter of his life:

> He would tolerate almost anything in an officer except incompetence, laziness or verbosity. His major concern was with getting work done promptly and correctly, and as he was singularly indifferent to everything else—including personal publicity, repute or popularity—his Headquarters were happily free from preconceived ideas, affectation or empire building.[31]

Most of the members of his wartime staff were in COMINCH Headquarters solely because they were available at the time, and were, on the basis of their record of past performance, considered competent by the Bureau of

Naval Personnel to be ordered there. If any old acquaintance happened to be among the number, he knew fully that he would be judged impartially by his performance, that friendship would permit no allowance for laziness or stupidity.

During our postwar collaboration King and I would talk whenever we were together, almost entirely on professional subjects. Between visits he would send me notes and documents which I would use in drafting chapters. When I went to 1078 Navy Department, I might pass him thirty or forty pages of such a draft. He would take it, without comment, put on his spectacles, swing around in his chair and read at lightning speed. On conclusion he would hand me back the draft with either "That will serve," or a suggestion or two. There was never a word of thanks, but once he had approved a chapter, that was that. I could then go on to the next with complete assurance that there would be no afterthoughts or changes of mind. Knowing his standards, the absence of unfavorable comment with the corresponding feeling that you had done your job correctly, meant more than conventionally polite remarks from other men. Vice Admiral McCrea told me of an incident when he was in command of the destroyer *Trever*, operating with the carrier *Lexington* in the early Thirties. During night maneuvers one of *Lexington*'s planes crashed in the water. McCrea rescued the pilot and so reported to Captain King in *Lexington*. The night was extremely dark. A strong wind was blowing and there were many whitecaps. Weather did not bother *Lexington* but it was very troublesome to *Trever*. A second plane crashed; this time McCrea rescued not only the pilot and an additional officer observer but succeeded in salvaging the plane. Feeling rather proud of himself, he was somewhat downcast when he received in return for his second report only a signal from King reading: "Night flying excercises canceled. Return to port." Then, on reflection, McCrea concluded that, being in command of a guard destroyer, he had simply done his duty, and that, in King's view, one did not offer any thanks or congratulations for that. But when they met in the Coronado bank the very next day, King called McCrea "John" for the first time, and thenceforth treated him with a subtly different air as the result of that night's work. In their many subsequent conversations during the next quarter of a century, the incident was never referred to by either of them.

Even though King was not accustomed to thank anyone for doing his duty, he was a thoughtful and considerate person in social relations. Whenever he came to stay with us he would unfailingly produce a book, a bottle of whiskey, or jars of country preserves, jams or honey bought from roadside stands during his drives in Maine or Virginia. When he came to the Boston Athenæum, even when sadly ill, he would remember where members of the staff had their desks, and go to greet them. There is ample evidence of personal consideration in an interchange of messages at Newport in 1941 when King, with four stars, as Commander in Chief, Atlantic Fleet coming into port in the cruiser *Augusta* received a signal from Rear Admiral E. C. Kalbfus, President of the Naval War College, reading: "At what time may Rear Admiral Kalbfus call upon Admiral King?" Three years before, King, as Commander Aircraft, Battle Force, with the rank of vice admiral, had served under Kalbfus, who as Commander Battle Force temporarily wore the four stars of an admiral. The reversal of former rôles was minimized in the reply: "Admiral King will call upon the President of the Naval War College at whatever time it is convenient for the President to receive him."

King loved a joke, and enjoyed teasing with a straight face, but his sense of humor was somewhat forthright and rudimentary. A photograph taken over a cup of coffee in New Orleans in 1944, showing King guffawing heartily, came as a surprise to those who had seen only serious likenesses of him.[32] The story that produced this boisterous reaction concerned the strength of Louisiana coffee. Someone had remarked that you tested it by putting a pewter spoon in the pot. When the spoon melted, the coffee was ready. The countersuggestion that when a large iron bolt floats, the coffee is ready, had just been made when a photographer snapped his shutter.

Hearing a commotion in his outer office one day during the war, King asked his flag lieutenant what was going on.

> FLAG LIEUTENANT: "Admiral Ingram is there, sir."
> ADMIRAL KING: "What's he doing?"
> FLAG LIEUTENANT: "Talking to New York, sir."
> ADMIRAL KING: "Tell him to use the telephone."[33]

Arriving in the Navy Department from Boston one March 17th, I found King sporting a green tie and green pullover, worn, so he alleged, to make me feel at home.

It used to give King pleasure to maintain, with a perfectly straight face, the fiction that I was a slave driver who made him work. In our guest book for 28–29 July 1951 he wrote: "Whitehill seems to be a driver." This I was expected to regard as a compliment, for "driver" was a favorite word of King's, frequently used in personal characterizations with an inflection diametrically opposed to that of "fixer."

The rumor that Admiral King occasionally dined on raw ensigns undoubtedly sprang from a misunderstanding of his teasing. He enjoyed making disconcerting remarks, partly for the fun involved and partly as a test of the person he was dealing with. In the spring of 1949 I was in 1078 Navy Department—in uniform, having been on two weeks' training duty—to say good-bye to Admiral King. We were discussing his summer visit to Portsmouth, and he politely inquired what part of the summer would be most convenient for us to have him come to North Andover. I suggested July, as I had planned to go cruising with Gus Loring in August. King frowned and snapped: "What, loafing on the job again?" I answered, without change of expression, that I had always understood that in the Navy it was well thought of to take any opportunity of going to sea. An aide looked worried by this frivolous retort, but it was the right answer. A hearty laugh and, "You win," followed.

Vice Admiral Howard E. Orem once told me of a similar conversation that took place early in 1941 between Admiral King and Rear Admiral Robert C. ("Ike") Giffen, who was commanding a cruiser division of the Atlantic Fleet. Giffen came into Newport early one morning in the cruiser *Wichita* at a time when King was putting pressure on all Atlantic Fleet ships to get out to sea and stay there. At 0900 as Giffen was punctiliously making his way up the gangway of King's flagship, *Augusta*, to call on CINCLANT, he was greeted, before he had said a word, with a blast from King: "What the hell are you doing in port?" Giffen, instead of answering, turned to the officer of the deck and said, "Will you call my barge alongside."

KING: "Why the hell do you want your barge alongside? Didn't you come to see me?"

GIFFEN: "I'm going to sea."
KING: "Come on, Ike, cool down. Come in."

And off they went to an interview that was all the more friendly for Giffen's correct response to the opening gambit. Such a form of pleasantry might easily prove confusing to the uninitiated—particularly young men calling upon daughters at home—and give rise to an undeserved reputation for ferocity.

Only once in ten years did I ever hear King's voice raised in genuine irritation. He had been staying with us over a blistering week-end. We had sat in our barn, with all doors open and electric fans at work. We had driven along country roads hoping to kick up a synthetic breeze. We had eaten ice cream and drunk beer without avail. Finally about 10:30 at night King asked me if it would be too much trouble to drive him back to the Naval Hospital at Portsmouth, where there *might* be a breeze from the sea. I assured him that it would not, but before getting the car, asked if I should telephone ahead to announce his arrival. "Thank you for thinking of it, but it is not necessary." After Newburyport the heat broke, and for some miles we ran through a heavy thunder shower. It was close to midnight and the storm was dying away when we reached the gate of the Naval Base, where the way was barred by a very young Marine sentry who seemed entirely ignorant of the identity of my passenger. Twice the Admiral gave his name; twice the Marine stared blankly. Then for a few seconds King ceased to be a tired and hot invalid. For a moment the Olympian Zeus returned; lightning flashed and thunder roared; the gate opened and the sentry saluted. The most accomplished actor could not have simulated the speech; only a Commander in Chief could have made it.

In 1953 and 1954 I saw King less frequently than in preceding years. His life had been published in November 1952, and with that accomplished his infirmities appeared to take stronger hold of him. During the preceding five years he had driven himself to complete the record that he wished to leave of his thoughts and decisions. He had persuaded me to undertake a life of Admiral Henry T. Mayo, the Commander in Chief in World War I, on whose staff he had served from December 1915 to April 1919, and whom he greatly admired. I had sought out Admiral Mayo's son, Captain Chester

G. Mayo, a retired officer of the Supply Corps, living in Huntington, Vermont, who had generously lent me his father's papers. I had hoped that my work on Admiral Mayo's life might prove of continuing interest to Admiral King, but as months passed his hearing and speech deteriorated to a point that made communication extremely difficult. I last saw him in 1078 Navy Department during the winter of 1955–1956. He came to Portsmouth as usual in June 1956. William G. Wendell had invited the Colonial Society to lunch in Portsmouth on Friday, June 29th. I had planned to see Admiral King at the Naval Hospital that morning, but instead I attended his funeral in Washington.

On Tuesday noon, the 26th, King's body was flown in a Navy plane from Portsmouth to Washington, where it was placed in the crypt chapel of St. Joseph of Arimathea in Washington Cathedral. I flew to Washington Thursday afternoon, the 28th, and drove out to the cathedral in the long light of the June evening. As I passed the Japanese Embassy, which had looked so sad and deserted during the war, the courtyard was well raked and a manservant stood in the open door awaiting guests. Nearly eleven years had passed since King had disposed of the Japanese fleet. It was a cool sunny early evening. The Bishop's Garden was full of fragrant herbs, roses, delphinium, and madonna lilies, and the cathedral grounds were quiet and peaceful. In the massive Norman crypt, King's coffin, covered with a flag, was flanked by an impassive honor guard of six Air Force men.

Washington Cathedral began to fill soon after noon on Friday, June 29th. The coffin was now in the crossing, with an honor guard, and Marines in blue jackets and white trousers. Flag officers in whites, with mourning bands, and generals of the other services, filled the south transept, although the ushers, being young, did not always recognize retired admirals in civilian clothes. At one o'clock the funeral began, the Bishop of Washington using the Book of Common Prayer simply and correctly, without rhetorical flourishes. "Eternal Father, strong to save, whose arm hath bound the restless wave" was the only hymn, and by 1:20 the procession was moving out of the cathedral. It went by car to Fifteenth Street and Constitution Avenue, where the main funeral procession formed to march to the Capitol.

My ever-helpful friend, John Heffernan, realizing that I would see more out than in, drove me straight to the Capitol, where he made arrangements to join the "motorcade" to Annapolis. I walked out on the terrace behind the Capitol and looked down the Mall to the Washington Monument. The day was cool but sunny, one of those rare moments in early summer when Washington is still at its springtime best. In the distance one heard drums and the sound of marching; bands playing funeral marches, "Onward Christian Soldiers" and (with wonderful flourishes of trumpets) "God of our fathers, whose almighty hand." The music came nearer as the procession marched along Constitution Avenue; as it turned into Pennsylvania, and came down toward the Peace Monument, I could see a V-shaped wedge of motorcycle policemen with red headlights, riding very slowly; then the Navy Band, followed by the Battalion of Midshipmen from the Naval Academy in whites with rifles, their officers holding drawn swords with black crape streamers; a company of infantry; the Marine Band, a company of Marines, a squadron of airmen, a company of Waves, Wacs, and the like, another band, the national colors, King's five-star flag; then the body on a horse-drawn caisson, followed by cars. As the procession started up Capitol Hill, I went back to John Heffernan's car in the square before the Capitol, and watched it arrive. When the caisson reached the steps of the Capitol, the Navy Band played "Lead, kindly light," as the body was transferred to a motor hearse. The troops dispersed, and some fifty cars formed for the drive to Annapolis.

All along North Capitol Street, New York Avenue, the Baltimore Parkway and Route 50 to Annapolis traffic was cleared in every direction. As the procession approached Annapolis, carrier planes appeared overhead. When it reached Gate Eight of the Naval Academy at half-past four, the planes flew to and fro in formation during 'the movement to the Naval Academy Cemetery by College Creek. As the hearse entered the cemetery, the first of a seventeen-gun salute was fired. Midshipmen, Marines, and band were in position by the grave on a lovely tree-shaded hillside where King and his classmates had walked on Sunday afternoons close to sixty years before—the Secretary of the Navy, the Chief of Naval Operations, and honorary pallbearers standing near. As the bearers brought the body from the hearse, the Escort Commander ordered "Present Arms"; the band played four ruffles and flourishes and the hymn "Eternal Father, strong to save" as the body was carried to the grave. The music ceased; the troops came to Parade Rest as the chaplain read the committal, ending with Cardinal Newman's "Lord, support us all the day long" and "May the souls of the faithful departed, through the mercy of God, rest in peace." Then, as the troops again presented arms, the firing squad fired three volleys, and as the bugler sounded "Taps," the last of the seventeen-gun salute boomed out from across the river. The bodybearers folded the flag, gave it to King's son, and, after a few minutes of quiet conversation, the mourners scattered. Nothing could have been at once simpler and more magnificent, or more appropriate to the man.

But to most of the midshipmen at the grave, King—and indeed Nimitz, Halsey, and Hewitt, who were among his pallbearers—must have seemed as distant figures as Dewey, Farragut, or even the sailors of the earliest wars of the Republic. The class of 1959 is two full generations removed from the class of 1901, and to a very young man this degree of remoteness borders on that of eternity. So rapidly do great men cease to be people and become instead names, portraits, or statues, curiously familiar, yet personally unknown. The speed of this process has led me to offer this perhaps discursive tribute of affection and respect to a figure of naval history that I had the good fortune, in his last years, to know as a man, rather than as a name.

NOTES

[1] At the 12 April 1951 meeting of the society I had reported on the progress of Admiral King's biography, on which I had been working since 1946. As *Fleet Admiral King: A Naval Record* was published in New York by W. W. Norton & Company, Incorporated, in November 1952, and in London (with considerable abridgment as to Books One and Two) by Eyre & Spottiswoode in 1953, it would be pointless to print the paper that I read at that time, for its contents were summarized in the final chapter, titled "A Note on the Making of this Book." Instead, I took the opportunity to complete the record by a brief account of Admiral King's last years, accompanied by a few things that I felt deeply, but could not appropriately say while he was my co-author.

[2] I am grateful to Mr. Joseph W. P. Frost, of Kittery Point, Maine, for sending me this and other similar ephemeral Portsmouth reports of Admiral King's death that I would not, save through his thoughtfulness, have seen.

[3] He took command in the Atlantic on 17 December 1940, just two days short of five years before his relief by Admiral Nimitz.

[4] Illustrated in *Fleet Admiral King: A Naval Record*, opposite 368. King's headquarters as

Commander in Chief, United States Fleet were hastily improvised in December 1941 on the third floor of the Navy Department. When, upon Admiral Stark's departure for London in March 1942, King became Commander in Chief, United States Fleet and Chief of Naval Operations, he remained on the third floor in Room 3048 and installed Vice Admiral F. J. Horne, Vice Chief of Naval Operations, in the traditional second-floor office of the Chief of Naval Operations. King felt so strongly that the Chief of Naval Operations should be the top man in the Navy (see *Fleet Admiral King,* 355, 631–632) that one of his main concerns after the victory over Japan was the abolition of the function of COMINCH and the strengthening of the Chief of Naval Operations. When this was accomplished on 10 October 1945 King very characteristically at once moved himself and the principal members of his staff to the second floor, although this physical transfer (useful chiefly as a symbol to civil servants) involved him in considerable personal inconvenience. For a few days no one knew where anyone was. I recall meeting one of his Guamanian stewards, bearing a pot of coffee, hopelessly adrift in a second-floor corridor, saying to me with a despondent look on his face, "Can't find Admiral Edwards."

5 King, from the beginning of his naval service, always had a legitimate desire to reach the top of his profession. On 13 April 1933, after seven years' experience in naval aviation, he wrote the Secretary of the Navy requesting that he be considered for appointment as Chief of the Bureau of Aeronautics. Admiral Pratt, the Chief of Naval Operations, who had suggested that he make this formal application, gave this analysis in his forwarding endorsement. King got the job in less than a month.

6 I owe a copy of the draft of this address to Admiral D. B. Duncan, who, during his years of able and inconspicuous service as Vice Chief of Naval Operations, had (like Admiral R. S. Edwards before him) kept alive the spirit of Lord Barham. Admiral Sherman in this address had quoted Sir Julian Corbett's description of Barham in *The Campaign of Trafalgar*: "Unseen and almost unnoticed he was gathering in his fingers the threads of the tradition which the recurring wars had spun, and handling them with a deft mastery to which the distant fleets gave sensitive response."

7 *The Maritime History of Massachusetts* (Boston, 1921), 373.

8 Personal letter from Admiral R. S. Edwards of 24 August 1951.

9 Published, among hundreds of places throughout the naval service, in *The Portsmouth Periscope* 29 June 1956 with the report of Admiral King's death.

10 The incident at the TRIDENT conference, described in *Fleet Admiral King: A Naval Record,* 441, is typical. "It was pointed out to him that everyone else was in agreement against him, *but he did not consider that relevant when a matter of principle was involved.*"

11 Now Vice Admiral Howard E. Orem, USN (retired), and Rear Admiral Neil K. Dietrich, USN.

12 In this study, contrary to the wishes of the photographer (who did a fine series of photographs of Flag Officers) the subject wore his cap. King had so little time for or patience with posed portrait studies that most of his wartime likenesses were caught by civilian or naval news photographers in passing. Notable exceptions were Lieutenant

Ernest J. King

Constant's black-and-white portrait, Edward Steichen's color photograph of October 1943 (reproduced in *Fleet Admiral King: A Naval Record*, opposite 496), and the March 1945 color photograph taken in the conference room at COMINCH Headquarters (reproduced opposite 592). The latter was achieved under typical circumstances. For some weeks following King's promotion to Fleet Admiral in December 1944, public-relations officers had been clamoring for a photograph showing him wearing the extra stripe of the new five-star rank. Finally in March 1945 King grudgingly agreed to give a very few minutes to this uncongenial operation. Knowing that he was as good as his word, everything had been set up in advance so that the subject could practically walk in front of the camera and out the door. King arrived, stepped into position, and, just as the shutter was about to click, some unfortunate character nervously tripped over a cord and blew the lights. Precious seconds slipped away, but just as the time was up and King was about to leave, the damage was repaired and the lens caught COMINCH-CNO with an expression that—in ancient Chinese military tactics—would have proved invaluable for frightening the enemy. During the years 1952–1956 when I was Allston Burr Senior Tutor of Lowell House, Harvard University, I paired this photograph of Admiral King with D. C. Sturges's etching of Dean Briggs on my office walls to keep my mind in balance while dealing with undergraduate breaches of industry or decorum.

[13] In the original of 23 March 1945, "his."

[14] When, as was his usual practice, he read from a prepared text. See *Fleet Admiral King: A Naval Record*, 543. When letters or speeches were prepared for him, as was necessarily often the case, Admiral King would have no truck with them if their contents or expression were out of character. In November 1942 a fulsome journalist in Public Relations drafted a flowery message of congratulation to the Chief of Staff of the U.S.S.R. Navy, which King summarily returned with a yellow chit reading, "Tone this down—I don't talk like this! !"

[15] Admiral Edwards, in a memorandum of 15 July 1944 to Admiral King, concluded: "At present your headquarters is the only naval activity in Washington that is not being embalmed in historical amber, and it might be well to change this status. Shall I have Orem implement his plan?" A penciled "Yes K" sent me to work on this project and opened all doors in a headquarters that otherwise was exclusively concerned with the present and the future.

[16] See *Fleet Admiral King: A Naval Record*, 353, for Admiral Edwards's inspired description of his first day in Washington.

[17] Admiral Forrest Sherman in his previously cited address said: "The life of Barham illustrates rather forcefully what has been called the loneliness of responsibility. It is unfortunately true—it even seems to be an inescapable law—that the greater our responsibilities the less prospect there is of sharing them."

[18] During the war he had received an LL.D. from the College of William and Mary (8 June 1942) and degrees of Doctor of Science from Bowdoin College (2 June 1945) and Harvard University (28 June 1945). His other postwar degrees were D.Sc., Northwestern University (26 October 1945), LL.D., Princeton University (22 February

1946), LL.D., Miami University (2 June 1946), and LL.D., Columbia University (21 February 1947).

[19] With the shifts and changes of the postwar years, when the Secretary of the Navy and the Chief of Naval Operations moved to the Pentagon and the Army took over parts of the Navy Department building on Constitution Avenue, King gave up his spacious office in Room 3048 and compressed himself into Room 3046, which during the war had been occupied by some of his aides. In 1949 he moved downstairs to Room 1078, next to offices provided for Fleet Admirals Leahy and Halsey.

[20] I have been told that he showed little interest in the hospital's suggested therapy. One day, however, when a hospital corpsman dropped a tray of dishes, the Admiral expressed his opinion of such clumsiness in a clear, succinct and typical way. At this point it was concluded that he would make progress in his own particular way, if let alone; he did!

[21] (London, 1957), 544*n*.

[22] In a Founder's Day address titled "The Break in the Circle," delivered at the Henry E. Huntington Library and Art Gallery on 2 March 1953, published in *The Huntington Library Quarterly*, xvi (1953), 223–235, I mentioned Admiral King, Sir Richard Livingstone, and President Conant as examples of men able to express the most varied thoughts without recourse to the jargon that afflicts certain academic disciplines today.

[23] See *Fleet Admiral King: A Naval Record*, 10–11.

[24] *Ibid.*, 639.

[25] *A Sailor's Odyssey* (New York, 1951), 466.

[26] *The Turn of the Tide*, 614.

[27] (London, 1953), xvi, dated 24 January 1953.

[28] 646 in American edition; 438 in English edition.

[29] *Fleet Admiral King: A Naval Record*, 409.

[30] *Ibid.*, 306, 413.

[31] *Ibid.*, 649–650.

[32] *Ibid.*, opposite 592.

[33] King's love of teasing is well shown in the incident of the name of Ingram's flagship— *Big Pebble*. See *Ibid.*, 527–528.

CHAPTER XIV

Fred Anthoensen

THE FOLLOWING ACCOUNT of my thirty-year friendship with this great printer was given on 23 February 1966 as one of a series of lectures on the graphic arts arranged by Dr. Robert R. Leslie at the Composing Room, 130 West 46th Street, New York City. Later in the year it was handsomely printed by the Anthoensen Press in an edition of three hundred eighty-five copies under the title Fred Anthoensen A Lecture.

IN NOVEMBER 1936 I met Fred Anthoensen for the first time when he came to my office at the Peabody Museum of Salem to discuss the printing of a museum publication. I knew nothing of him or his work, for I had returned to New England the previous spring after spending the better part of nine years in Spain, and was out of touch with recent developments in fine printing. He was then in his early fifties—a short, stocky, trim, gray-haired man, dressed in dark sobriety that suggested an established doctor or lawyer rather than artist. He was—and still is—a quiet, shy man, totally without the false *bonhomie* and mendacious blandishments of The Salesman. What he said was brief and to the point. And it was clear from the beginning of this first meeting that he instinctively understood what the Peabody Museum wanted, and intended to use the full extent of his crafts-manship to give us *that*, rather than something quite different, however good that something different might be.

It was fortunate for me that I met Fred Anthoensen when I did, for I was in the awkward situation of knowing the difference between good and bad printing when I saw it, without having the slightest technical knowledge of how this difference was achieved. In this first meeting we briefly looked through the typescript of a mid-nineteenth-century journal of travel in South America that the museum wished to publish, chatted a bit about books and the world in general, and that was that. Fred returned to Portland, and shortly submitted some sample pages, which delighted me. When proofs came, they were clean and handsome, free of printer's errors. In due course there appeared what became one of the Fifty Books of the Year 1937, achieved at a fair and mutually satisfactory price, without hassles of any kind. So began a friendship, based on trust and sympathetic under-standing between craftsman and customer, that has enriched my life and made my work easier over the past thirty years.

As a Harvard freshman in the academic year 1922–1923, I wandered into the Widener Room in the library and encountered George Parker Winship, who had a singular genius for infecting undergraduates with a love of books and fine printing. I often returned, and as a junior enrolled in Winship's Fine Arts 5e, History of the Printed Book. Through George Winship I came to know the work of Daniel Berkeley Updike and Bruce Rogers, and eventually made the acquaintance of the printers themselves. To me Updike's work was particularly sympathetic, and the Merrymount Press the ideal of twentieth-century American achievement in bookmaking.

Thus, when I found myself at the Peabody Museum of Salem in need of having a book printed, I would instinctively have turned to the Merrymount Press, and was not wholly enchanted when my boss, Lawrence W. Jenkins, seemed inclined to turn to a printer in Portland, Maine, of whom I knew next to nothing. As matters turned out, nothing could have been more

fortunate than this somewhat accidental encounter, for Fred Anthoensen's tastes in bookmaking and mine were very similar. He and I were both striving for perfection in our different ways. The museum had things that needed publishing, which he instinctively knew how to clothe in appropriate dress. And as the work that we gave the press was unaccompanied by hampering restrictions, it gave him a useful opportunity to exercise his talents in design to the fullest extent.

Few men are still active in the same printing office that they entered some sixty-eight years ago. Fred Anthoensen is a native of Denmark, born on 14 April 1882 at Tonder in Slesvig, but at the age of two was brought by his parents to Portland, Maine, where he has been ever since. In 1898, after completing his grammar-school education, he was apprenticed in the composing room of the Southworth Printing Company. This firm began in 1875 when the Reverend Francis Southworth bought a small press and a few fonts of type to produce a religious newspaper and tracts for distribution among the seamen who then abounded in Portland. Originally his four sons manned this press, but after a time outside work was taken in and a printing business established.

"This was," as Fred Anthoensen recalls, "the era in printing history when the use of twisted rules in imitation of lithographic effects was much in vogue, and taste in printing called for a different type for each display line." Moreover, the outside work of the company was not stimulating, for it consisted largely of Sunday-school lessons and law books, but it proved the means of learning the craft. In 1901 Fred Anthoensen became a full-fledged compositor; in 1917 he was made managing director of the Southworth Press. In 1921 he gained his first out-of-state client, and in 1923 his first book to design and print, a narrative of shipwreck in the Fijis, edited for the Marine Research Society of Salem by Lawrence W. Jenkins. By the time I came to know him, Fred Anthoensen was not only managing director but part owner of the establishment, which hyphenated its name as the Southworth-Anthoensen Press. Eventually he bought out the family interest and became the sole owner of the Anthoensen Press.

This is a very American nineteenth-century performance which, if edifying tracts were still in vogue, would have furnished the Reverend Francis Southworth with a good subject—the son of Danish immigrant parents who, without established friends, rose by consistent hard work and self-education, to the top of a craft that he entered as an apprentice, and became an extremely cultivated gentleman into the bargain. The key to all this is that, although Fred Anthoensen's formal schooling stopped at sixteen, his education has never ended.

In a recent letter to me, he remarked: "In learning to be a printer I discovered there was both good and bad printing, and I soon decided which I wanted to do. I also knew it would take study to perfect myself." In notes on the press that he wrote in 1943, he observed that when he became a compositor, "Mr. D. B. Updike and Bruce Rogers were working in Boston and Cambridge, well on the road to distinguished careers. It was through the specimens of their work shown in *The Printing Art*, that handsome and scholarly printing journal without a peer, before or since, under the editorship of Henry Lewis Johnson, that I became interested in fine printing. I have always felt that this journal never received due credit for its share in the revival of American fine printing. At that time it was the best source of study for the apprentice who had but few dollars to spare for books. It was to this journal, too, that I owe so much in determining and shaping my own career."

He owed even more to his habit of reading widely in good literature of every kind. As a young man he bought volume after volume of Everyman's Library, and gradually read his way through the series. Thus to meet Edward Gibbon, Herodotus, Plato, Richard Hakluyt, and Jane Austen—to name only a tiny fraction of the riches there available—provided a broader education than many institutions achieve in conveying. The English eighteenth century especially attracted him, both in prose and typography, and gradually he began to assemble favorite authors in contemporary editions. His studies of literature and book design went hand in hand, and thus gave him the basis for the uncannily intuitive sense of appropriateness in design that marked his mature work. When I received proofs of the October 1942 meeting notice of the Club of Odd Volumes, at which Professor F. N. Robinson was to speak on the "Poetry of Dafydd ap Gwilym, a Welsh contemporary of Chaucer," I found with them a note that I had better ask the speaker whether the decoration—a pair of medieval lovers kissing in a tight clinch—was appropriate to the subject. I telephoned Fritz Robinson to say that Fred Anthoensen wanted to know whether a medieval necking party was a suitable symbol, and received the answer: "Absolutely. That is all Dafydd ap Gwilym ever wrote about." Over and over again I have had cause to be delighted by the subtlety with which Fred Anthoensen has caught the spirit of what he is putting into type, no matter how abstruse the subject may be.

His process of self-education was a solitary one, for he worked long hours and he knew few people who shared his interests, as he seldom left Portland. A few years before World War I, he revisited Denmark and had pleasure from the fanciful rococo palace façades of Copenhagen, as well as from the admirable Danish food and drink. In 1924 he made a second trip abroad, visiting Kelmscott House, the Caslon Letter Foundry, the British Museum, and other sources of typographical inspiration. Although in the 1920's and '30's, when he was developing the kind of business that he had always wished the press to do, he made occasional trips to Boston and New York in search of orders, such excursions eventually became unnecessary. Instead, customers came to 105 Middle Street, Portland, and climbed the steepest and most vertiginous stairway in New England to the third floor of an unexciting loft building in order to see him. Only occasionally could he be persuaded to vary a routine which was happily filled by his printing office, his library at home, and his garden with its yew and lilac hedges. Although he has long been a member of the Club of Odd Volumes in Boston and done most of its printing for the past quarter of a century, his appearances in the convivial surroundings of 77 Mount Vernon Street have been all too infrequent.

Early in this century Fred Anthoesen decided what kind of printing he wanted to do. He then spent twenty-five years of unremitting work to reach the point where he could do it. From 1923, when he began to design and print books that were to his taste, he was continually seeking types and ornaments that would enable him to carry out his ideal. Following his visit to the Caslon Letter Foundry in 1923 he acquired a supply of the Caslon fonts, complete with accents, ligatures and swash characters. In 1931 he printed for the Mergenthaler Linotype Company a *Specimen* of George W. Jones's new cutting of the Baskerville face. Through friendship with Paul A. Bennett and C. H. Griffith of that company, he followed with especial interest the recutting for the Linotype of such essential book faces as Caslon Old Face, Janson, Baskerville, and Scotch to conform to the original fonts, and the creation for the Linotype of new faces by W. A. Dwiggins and Rudolph Ruzicka. Although he made extensive use of the constantly improving resources of the Linotype, he nevertheless consistently sought castings from original matrices for hand composition whenever possible. In 1931 the press acquired the Binny and Ronaldson "Roman No. 1"; in

1932 some of John Bell's types from Stephenson, Blake and Company of Sheffield, England; in 1933 Joseph Fry's double small-pica italic of 1766, and a stock of Anton Janson's types, cast from the original matrices by the Stempel foundry at Frankfurt-am-Main. From Stephenson, Blake and Company were also obtained a remarkable range of eighteenth-century type flowers and ornaments, which gave Fred Anthoensen the material for the evolution of the engaging decorations that have enlivened so many of his books.

The evolution of this stock of original types and ornaments, and of the use that Fred Anthoensen made of them, is simply and delightfully set forth in a 170-page volume titled *Types and Bookmaking* that the press issued in 1943, on the twentieth anniversary of the first book completed that represented the type of work that he wished to do. For this he wrote a 68-page essay, commenting on the search for types; the late Ruth A. Chaplin—long a faithful assistant—prepared a bibliographical catalogue of the two hundred and sixty-five books printed in these two decades, and specimens were given of the types and ornaments. Here is the autobiography of twenty years of the work of the press, similar in concept to the volume that Mr. Updike and Julian P. Smith prepared in 1933 on the fortieth anniversary of the Merrymount Press. I have always hoped for a sequel. I know that Ruth Chaplin had it in mind until her death, and I strongly suspect that bibliographical entries from Number 266 and beyond were somewhere in her desk. I hope that Fred Anthoensen may have jotted down some further notes, or, if he has not, that he will do so now that he is leaving more and more of the daily routine of the press to his able ally, Warren F. Skillings. Twenty-three years have passed since *Types and Bookmaking* appeared, and there should be a new edition.

Several things have combined to make the Anthoensen Press a uniquely useful institution. There has been first of all Fred Anthoensen's meticulous striving for perfection, which has gone beyond design and presswork to the training of singularly able compositors and proofreaders, who relieve the customer of anxiety and drudgery. The second is the remarkable intuition of this printer-designer that leads him to propose the appropriate treatment of any kind of material that may be submitted to the press. Copy sent with only the most general instructions, or with no instructions at all beyond the number required, is translated into type that seems inevitable in its appropriateness. The third is the ability of the press, through the presence in the same building of John W. Marchi's bindery, not only to produce a complete book under one roof but to distribute it, if required. The fourth, and by no means the least, is its willingness to attempt to achieve a sound piece of work at a price that the customer can afford to pay. Thus an important part of its work has come to be done for learned institutions and for individuals who wish to have something printed for noncommercial distribution.

There has scarcely been a week in the last thirty years when I have not had at least one job of some kind in process at the Anthoensen Press, yet in this time I have visited Portland very seldom, had extraordinarily little correspondence with Fred Anthoensen, never had a disappointment in the result, or a disagreement about price. The notion that one has to be near one's printer is erroneous if the printer is good enough. When I have had books to do, Fred would give me an estimate for budgetary purposes and a sample page, or general indication of his plan. When the bill came, it was almost always less than the estimate, unless I had made unanticipated additions to text or illustrations. It has never been necessary to dot i's and cross *t*'s in giving instructions, or even to spell out financial considerations with the detail that is customary in general business. Such a relationship has greatly simplified my work over thirty years, as it has that of many other bibliographers, librarians, and learned institutions.

Miss Margaret Bingham Stilwell, in the preface to *Incunabula in American Libraries, a Second Census of Fifteenth-Century Books Owned in the United States, Mexico, and Canada*, printed by the press in 1940, observed of this listing of more than thirty-five thousand incunabula: "The fact that copy for the main text of the *Census* was set up and read within seven months from the time it went to press has been due, in no small part, to the efficiency of the Southworth-Anthoensen Press and of its compositor, Mr. Warren F. Skillings, who with a minimum of error set the main text single-handed." In the same year, Fred Anthoensen worked out for me the format of *The American Neptune, A Quarterly Journal of Maritime History*, set for the most part in 12-point Linotype Baskerville, with certain sections in smaller sizes in double columns. After twenty-five years this format has accommodated the most diverse types of material, always readily and handsomely. Statistical tables, architectural drawings, fit into its pages as readily as articles for general reading. By such performance the press became an indispensable ally of the Bibliographical Society of America, the Peabody Museum of Salem, the John Carter Brown Library, and many other institutions. After the closing of the Merrymount Press in 1949, many of its long-standing customers, like the Massachusetts Historical Society, the Colonial Society of Massachusetts, and the Boston Athenæum, moved their work without question or hesitation to Portland.

The variety and skill of Fred Anthoensen's design is most readily seen in small compass in the work he has done for the Club of Odd Volumes over the past quarter-century. The notices of monthly meetings, usually printed on short notice, are as varied as they are numerous. As I have had to come to New York by way of Washington, I could not readily bring any books with me, but have instead placed in the cases a selection of these Odd Volumes notices as a microcosm of the work of the Anthoensen Press.

In 1947 Bowdoin College, by the conferring of an honorary degree, made Fred Anthoensen technically what he has already been for many years in fact—a Master of Arts. Colby College conferred the same degree upon him in 1951. It is singularly appropriate when a man is honored by his neighbors rather than by distant admirers. We were all delighted when Yale University made Harold Hugo of Meriden an honorary alumnus. It is equally fitting that two Maine colleges, both of whom have benefited by the typography of the press, should have enrolled Fred Anthoensen on their lists of graduates.

But honorary degrees pale beside a little volume titled *In Tribute to Fred Anthoensen Master Printer*, containing bibliographical essays by Paul Standard, Carl J. Weber, Charles R. Capon, Rudolph Ruzicka, E. Harold Hugo, Edward F. Stevens, Lawrence C. Wroth, Paul A. Bennett, Edward Page Mitchell, and myself. It bears the uninformative imprint: "1952 Portland, Maine," but the remarkable thing is that it was printed under Fred's very nose, in his own shop—where his eyes were then accustomed to inspecting the inking of every form put on a press—through the amiable conspiracy of his own employees. The organizer and generalissimo of this benevolent plot was Ruth Chaplin, who proved herself as able in a cloak-and-dagger act as in the customary routine of a printing office. In the Preface, where her fellow conspirators were named, I wrote: "One of the soundest principles of administration is what is called in the United States Navy the 'initiative of the subordinate,' which involves the premise that all members of an organization are competent in their several duties unless and until they themselves prove otherwise. Those who know The Anthoensen Press cannot fail to admire the manner in which everyone knows his or her job and deals with it—a situation far too uncommon in 1951." Parenthetically, even more uncommon in 1966. Continuing, I said: "It is not surprising that friends of Fred Anthoensen should wish to honor him by the publication of this series of essays. Neither is it surprising that his staff should have devised the means of printing the present volume without his knowledge or guiding hand."

This little volume inspired a chain reaction of benevolent conspiracies. Two years later Julian P. Boyd, Lyman H. Butterfield, and I produced a little tribute to Harold Hugo that, although printed at the Princeton University Press, was illustrated by collotypes produced under Harold's nose at Meriden. Then in 1958 Lyman Butterfield joined forces with Fred Anthoensen and Harold Hugo to print a handsome account of my varied writings and confused activities, the material for which was extracted from my office and house, again without arousing suspicion. In 1959 Wendell and Jane Garrett and I, with the assistance of the Harvard University Press, paid Lyman Butterfield back by printing his letters home during a research trip to Holland in the manner and style of *The Diary of John Adams*. Only four nights ago, when Wendell Garrett was leaving the Associate Editorship of The Adams Papers to come to New York to assume a similar post with *Antiques* magazine, Lyman Butterfield presented him with another surreptitious volume, strongly resembling The Adams Papers, containing various extracts from the writings of several generations of Adamses concerning New York City. Thus the tribute to Fred Anthoensen established a pattern by which printers and historians have been honoring and mystifying their friends ever since.

The naval principle of the "initiative of the subordinate," which I came to know during wartime service with the late Fleet Admiral Ernest J. King, has more applications to printing than the one which I indicated above. It amounts in essence to believing that a naval commander should tell his subordinates *what* to do, and *when* to do it, but never, under any circumstances, *how*. It is the business of a competent subordinate to know *how* to carry out his duties; if he doesn't, he isn't worth having, and the sooner one gets rid of him the better.

Fred Anthoensen

It is equally the business of a master printer to know *how* to do his work, without being told, or without the intervention of an outside designer. If he doesn't, he is not a master printer. The client should confine himself to *what* and *when*, and have confidence that a real craftsman knows the *how*. I suppose, in retrospect, that an unconscious recognition of this principle—long before either of us had ever heard of it in naval language—explains the singularly happy relation of mutual confidence that Fred Anthoensen and I have enjoyed for thirty years.

In closing, I permit myself a final naval analogy in regard to the work of Fred Anthoensen. In the last chapter of my biography of Admiral King, I quoted a striking passage from John Buchan in which he analyzed the qualities invariably found in "great captains." There are three powers, Buchan wrote, "which raise their possessor to the small inner hierarchy of leadership." The first, in brief, is "visualizing power or synoptic power" or better still "the power of seeing a battle-front as a whole." The second is "the power of reading the heart of the enemy." These require some explanation in reference to bookmaking, but I translate the first as the ability to see a manuscript in all its implications of historic style, present-day use, and practical cost before devising a plan for its printing. The second is more quickly translated as "the power of reading the heart of the client"; of knowing instinctively what he wants and offering him that rather than something else. Buchan's third quality needs no translation. It applies as well to a master printer as to a great captain in arms. It is "the power to simplify, the capacity to make a simple syllogism, which, once it is made, seems easy and inescapable, but which, before it is made, is in the power only of genius. No great step in history, whether in war or in statesmanship"—and I might add in printing—"seems to us otherwise than the inevitable in the retrospect. The ordinary man flatters himself that he could have done it too, it seems so easy."

Fred Anthoensen died on 13 August 1969 as this book was going to press.

W. M. W.

CHAPTER XV

Rudolph Ruzicka

WHEN I WAS an undergraduate, George Parker Winship first showed me the enchanting wood engravings of Boston that Rudolph Ruzicka annually made for the New Year's greetings of the Merrymount Press, but it was only after returning from Spain that I first met the artist. I was as enchanted with the man as I had been by his work, and for thirty years have sought opportunities to enjoy his company and to benefit by his consummate skill in design, engraving, and calligraphy. The greater part of the piece that follows was written for the catalogue of a 1948 Grolier Club event, The Engraved and Typographic Work of Rudolph Ruzicka, An Exhibition. *Soon after this exhibition, the Ruzicka family moved from New York to Concord, Massachusetts, and then to Boston, where they lived for some years on Pinckney and Marlborough streets. Since the death of his wife, Rudolph Ruzicka has lived in Hanover, New Hampshire. Consequently although born in Bohemia and resident in Chicago and New York for more than fifty years, he is an adopted New Englander of two decades' standing, and an adopted Vermonter as an honorary Master of Arts of Marlboro College. The photograph of him at work was taken in 1953 while he was living in Concord.*

Early in 1951 the Boston Public Library held an exhibition of Ruzicka's work. Although smaller than the Grolier Club show of 1948, it had the advantage of including recent work of the previous two and a half years, including two new type faces. For this I wrote a piece titled "The Ruzicka Exhibition at the Library," which was published in the Boston Public Library Quarterly, *III, 1 (January 1951) 6–14. Although a few paragraphs of this have been woven into the 1948 text written for the Grolier Club to make the picture less incomplete, this chapter, alas, contains no reference to Rudolph Ruzicka's very considerable artistic production of the past seventeen years. To have attempted that would have led me into extensive rewriting, which is beyond the scope of this series of reprints. But I cannot forbear mention of the appearance in 1952 of* Boston Athenæum Six Views Drawn by Rudolph Ruzicka, *printed in an album by Fred Anthoensen, or of the numerous calligraphic bookplates by Ruzicka that now adorn many books in the Athenæum. It is a delight to me that he designed my* Fleet Admiral King: A Naval Record *(1952) and my* Boston Public Library: A Centennial History *(1956). At the age of eighty-five he is as busy as ever, and his work still has the freshness of a spring morning.*

Et vigilia sua ornabit in perfectionem

THE EXHIBITION that is described in the Grolier Club catalogue represented the results of four decades of work by that singularly versatile artist, Rudolph Ruzicka. The club was fortunate in being able to present examples of his art in all its varied phases. It was also particularly fitting that it should show his works in 1948, at the flood tide of his achievement, because thirty-three years earlier his first major undertaking—*New York, a Series of Wood Engravings in Colour*—was published by the club.

Born in Bohemia in 1883, Ruzicka came to Chicago with his parents in the early Nineties. Of his school days he once wrote in a private letter: "The thing that most stands out in my mind, when I think of my early years in this country, is my struggle with the English language and the resulting sense of loneliness. But I got on famously in the Public Schools after the rather humiliating experience of having to start in the first grade at 11 years of age. I went to school just three years, passing through seven grades; rapidity of progress I ascribe to my ability to draw. I decorated the black-boards of nearly all the school rooms and I gained thereby much favor with the teachers. Saturday afternoons I attended drawing classes at the Hull House. Then at fourteen years I had to seek a job and found one at com-mercial wood engraving, in a large engraving house. I took my work extremely seriously and remember that when the firm which employed me was denounced for employing a minor—(I was found doing a journeyman's job)—I argued very heatedly in Court, claiming that I was not doing factory work, but art work, much to the amusement of everyone in the court room. This happened after about six months in this shop—all that time I received no salary; they then 'raised' me $1.00 a week. . . . In another six months I gave up wood engraving and took up designing. In the meantime I at-tended night classes at the Art Institute."

In 1903 Ruzicka moved to New York and worked for a time in an ad-vertising agency, while continuing his studies. It was in New York around 1906 that he started again to engrave on wood, this time designing his own pictures and pulling hand-rubbed proofs on thin Chinese paper. This was not done without some sacrifice, as, for the first few years, all time given to engraving had to be outside normal working hours. His earliest subjects were found near the East River, and the Queensboro Bridge was his Fujiyama. A series of views of New York engraved in chiaroscuro, illus-trating an article in *System* in 1908, was his first published work, and in the same year he contributed a title page and two woodcuts to *A Portfolio of Prints*, issued by the Graphic Arts Club.

In 1907 Ruzicka first met Daniel Berkeley Updike in New York, having been recommended to him for the engraving of a title-page decoration in-tended for a volume of *The Humanists' Library*. Two or three years later he made his first visit to Boston, chiefly to see W. A. Dwiggins, then working in a Cornhill studio. Having advised with Dwiggins as to the wisdom of doing so, Ruzicka called at the Merrymount Press on Summer Street to show Updike a dozen or so of his engravings. At this meeting he found

Updike simple, appreciative, and pertinently critical. From it began a friendship of thirty years' duration and a collaboration which produced singularly felicitous results, for many of the most attractive books of the Merrymount Press were enhanced by Ruzicka's illustrations and decorations, and the Annual Keepsakes which he engraved for the press furnished Ruzicka with the occasion for preparing a series of topographic views of

Boston and vicinity which are unrivaled in interpretative insight as studies in the character of a city. The first of these, representing the Old State House, was issued for the year 1912; the last of them, with the waves breaking against Minot's Light off Cohasset, was received by at least some friends on the very day in December 1941 on which they had attended Updike's funeral at the Church of the Advent in Boston.

In an appreciation of Ruzicka's work, written for the September 1917 issue of *The Printing Art*, Updike wrote, with particular reference to the early views of New York: "One of the qualities in Ruzicka's work is its actuality. He seizes the picturesque side of a 'Gospel tent' at night, with its violent contrast of light and shade, or a gasometer, or a Ferris wheel, as some others have done; but actuality is not all, for he makes them pictorially his own, presents them always *more suo*. To be able to see picturesque qualities where other people see nothing is the power of the seer; to convey them to others is the power of the interpreter."

Having set up his own press in a back parlor near Sutton Place, in the days when the East River was full of coal pockets and that kind of romantic thing, he made full use of the picturesque elements of the waterfront, and odd corners of the city. In referring to his press he recalls that "it went with me wherever I moved and became an integral part of my technical equipment—indeed I am not sure if I did not often spend as much time over press, paper and ink as I did over the wood block." In his earliest wood engravings he sought to achieve the utmost effect out of a very few colors—often reds and browns—and relied for his results upon the combination of intricately engraved blocks painstakingly printed by himself. This is readily seen in the small night-pieces of the "Gospel tent" and of a concert in Bryant Park, behind the New York Public Library, that were engraved for Dr. and Mrs. William S. Dennett's Christmas cards. Yet from the same period dates the magnificent engraving of St. John's Chapel in Varick Street—the largest of his black-and-white blocks—which is, in its British classical dignity, an unsurpassed rendering of an architectural subject.

The quality of Ruzicka's work was soon recognized by others than Updike, for in 1912 he was invited by Auguste Lepère, whose engravings had in a large measure led him to return to the medium, to send examples of his wood engravings to the first exhibition of the Société de la Gravure sur Bois Originale, held at the Pavillon de Marsan in the Louvre at Paris, and in 1913 the Grolier Club commissioned him to begin work upon *New York, a Series of Wood Engravings in Colour*. This book, consisting of ten full-page and twenty smaller wood engravings, accompanied by "A Note on the Development of Colour Printing from Wood Engravings" by Ruzicka and prose impressions of the city by Walter Prichard Eaton, appeared in 1915. The text was printed by the De Vinne Press, and the full-page engravings by Emile Fequet. Ruzicka had originally intended to print the blocks himself, but having set out for Rome in November 1913 before doing so, he left the blocks in Paris with Fequet—at one time Lepère's own printer—who did an excellent job, following Ruzicka's sketches, flat proofs, and instructions. This magnificent portrayal of New York City inspired the members of the Carteret Book Club to seek a similar interpretation of their own "huge, uncouth and unthinking industrial Frankenstein." In the introduction to *Newark, a Series of Engravings on Wood*, published in 1917, John Cotton Dana justly observed that "it is necessary to speak only of the one thing already noted as significant of the city's long delayed reflections on its own possibilities of excellence—the publication of this volume." In this instance, Ruzicka printed the five full-page engravings himself; the text, with twelve black-and-white wood engravings, was printed by Updike at the Merrymount Press. The combination of text and illustrations is of the happiest kind, as was true in Thomas Robinson Hazard's *The Jonny-Cake Papers of "Shepherd Tom"* and *The Fiftieth Anniversary of the Opening of Vassar College*, which Updike had printed in 1915 and 1916, respectively. In the Vassar volume the illustrations consisted of four full-page linecuts after pen drawings by Ruzicka, with a single color, engraved on and printed from wood. These four illustrations were chosen from a group of twelve views published in a portfolio of *Sketches of Vassar College*, in 1915. His drawing of Main Hall must have surprised many Vassar alumnae by its beauty quite as much as the illustrations of *Newark* must have astonished those residents who had never before appreciated the artistic potentialities of gasometers and a grimy industrial riverfront.

Alas, the unsurpassed joining of Updike and Ruzicka was not achieved in the publication of Mrs. Charles Mac Veagh's *Fountains of Papal Rome* (New York: Charles Scribner's Sons, 1915), for which Ruzicka had been commissioned in 1913 to prepare a series of wood engravings. Although Updike had made preliminary typographical designs, the book was printed elsewhere, with indifferent press work which marred the sparkling brilliancy of the illustrations. This is the more to be regretted, for, as W. M. Ivins, Jr., justly observed: "In these prints, without the aid of color [Ruzicka] has, by a very beautiful and brilliant handling of his masses of black and white, and a quite extraordinary virtuosity in the use of slender line, captured the robust exuberant fantasy of the Imperial City." In this exhibition, however, one sees the artist's own proofs and can appreciate the magnificence—and almost feel the cold water—of the Tartarughe, the Tritone, and the other fountains of the Eternal City. One cannot help feeling that Bernini would have rejoiced to see his work so subtly although so simply engraved.

In these engravings of Rome, New York, Newark, and Boston one sees the breadth and catholicity of Ruzicka's appreciation of the essential qualities of cities. The baroque exuberance of the Roman fountains and the breathtaking caverns and skyscrapers of lower Manhattan are conveyed with equal appropriateness. Of the Merrymount Press Keepsakes Mr. Ivins remarked that "such woodcuts as the Louisburg Square, Faneuil Hall, and Old State House are correct in every Bostonian sense of the word, a little dry, a little precise, quite restrained, and just a little backward looking to the older times of the shallow, straight-backed chair which forbade lounging, in a word, charming records of a prime provincial elegance which seems about to depart." That is equally true of the prospect of the State House, seen across the *rus in urbe* of the Walnut Street garden that was then Ellery Sedgwick's, or the view of the idyllic summer house, designed by Samuel McIntire, that the late William Crowninshield Endicott moved to the gardens of Glen Magna Farm in Danvers. On the other hand, the engravings of St. Stephen's and Christ Church, looking east and west from "The Prado," show the North End as it is today, while there is no nostalgic trace of a "prime provincial elegance" in the very contemporary picture of children wading and bathing in the Frog Pond. In the Weeks Memorial Bridge across the Charles a recent and primarily utilitarian monument proved to be an equally appropriate subject, while the last of the series shows the boisterous waves breaking against Minot's Light. Altogether here is not Boston from a single angle, but from many. The carefully engraved Latin inscriptions, supplied by D. B. Updike, added a touch of subtle wit which in some cases has become abstruse with the passage of years. *Venite ad aquas, et qui non habetis argentum* [Isaiah lv.1] applies to the

Rudolph Ruzicka

Frog Pond quite as well today as it did in 1935, but the incomplete quotation of Song of Solomon i. 4 on the engraving of the Charles Street Church—*sed formosa, filiae Ierusalem*—is less clear now that the building has passed from an African Methodist Episcopal to a Universalist congregation. Similarly one would have to recall the agressive tactics of the Watch and Ward Society in the late Twenties to enjoy to the full the *Vigilate ergo: nescitis enim, quando dominus domus veniat* on the view of Lowell House. To the Bostonian these views seem perfection, in proof of which I must descend to personal testimony. In 1946, while still in naval service, I accepted the direction of the Boston Athenæum, and one of the thoughts which first crossed my mind was the delightful prospect of inducing Ruzicka to do a series of drawings of the interior of that library.

Mr. Ivins further observed that the Boston engravings took a place in Ruzicka's work "quite by themselves, as in them he has given supple expression to a local psychology quite different from that with which he is more familiar." That, when written in 1917, was unquestionably true, but in the fifty years that have passed, Ruzicka has mastered so many techniques, and by means of them given supple expression to so many local psychologies that it is no longer possible to suggest that he is more familiar with one than with another. It is because of this that, while his work is so universally admired by practitioners of the graphic arts and discriminating collectors, his engravings have had relatively little circulation among casual buyers of prints. He has changed his technique so much that he has never become the ideal "duck artist," who promptly carves a niche for himself in popular esteem by his constant repetition of something that everyone can recognize.

In book illustration one quickly sees the versatility of Ruzicka's technique and inspiration. For the edition of Washington Irving's *Notes and Journal of Travel in Europe*, issued by the Grolier Club in 1921, he turned to aquatints, with details heightened in watercolor. Soon after this a book on Czechoslovakia, illustrated by wood engravings, was projected by Chatto and Windus, but unfortunately it was never published. Ruzicka made numerous sketches and watercolors of his native country for this volume. The wood engraving in five colors of the Charles Bridge at Prague was to have been the frontispiece, and some other blocks were cut. After this project was abandoned, a few of the subjects—of which the Powder

Tower at Prague is one—were engraved separately in a larger size. *The Fables of Jean de la Fontaine*, produced for the Limited Editions Club in 1930, are illustrated by copper engravings. In the bookplates, Christmas cards, and smaller works included in the Grolier Club exhibition, the thoughtful visitor readily detected an unerring choice of the medium that was best adapted to the business in hand. With Ruzicka technical ability is applied to a specific piece of work; it is not vaunted for its own sake. Consider, for example, the wood engraving of a watercolor of Tantalus by Hans Holbein the Younger, which Philip Hofer wished to reproduce in a little booklet. Here no less than seven colors were used in an engraving barely two inches in diameter. The result is a miraculous facsimile of Holbein's watercolor, of such apparent simplicity that one must see the proofs of the progressive states to appreciate the intricate processes of wood engraving by which it was produced.

It is not alone through such prodigies of technique that Ruzicka is known. Particularly in recent years he has devoted himself to problems of design of wider application. In his earliest wood engravings he strove to get the utmost effect out of a very few colors. As he greatly enjoyed pulling proofs —deriving pleasure from the combined smells of printing ink, benzine, and old rags—he was able to experiment with intricately engraved blocks in which each color was forced to play a hero's part. But these early chiaroscuros had to be printed by Ruzicka himself; they could not be safely entrusted to another printer. Consequently in the Twenties, when his engravings were demanded for larger editions and more colors were introduced, the lines were kept relatively more open, so that other people could print them without resorting to dampened paper, and could occasionally even smash in the blocks without achieving too much damage. Similarly, from having produced illustrations for books printed in very restricted editions, he broadened his activities to the designing of books that were made fine chiefly by his participation in their production. *A Series of Monographs on Color*, published in three volumes by the International Printing Ink Corporation in 1935, is a case in point. There the problem was to translate data from the sciences of chemistry and physics of color into acceptable form. By imaginative yet straightforward handling of the very uncompromising material, he produced a book of both beauty and utility, where one might normally have expected little beyond a work of scientific reference. In an experimental project for *The Reader's Digest* in 1944 and in cartographic designs for the *Encyclopaedia Britannica* the same principles were applied to unpromising material which had to be printed in great quantity.

Similarly his first venture in type design—the legible and distinguished Fairfield face—was produced, not for a Kelmscott, Doves or Ashendene type of hand press, but for the Mergenthaler Linotype Company. In Ruzicka's "Note on the Fairfield Face" in the announcement of its availability for the Linotype in 1940, he observed: "Theories have been expressed about type and will continue to be expressed. Type has been viewed as an ingenious mechanical imitation of calligraphy; as abstract pattern, one of the elements of the 'book beautiful'; as a vehicle for self-expression, etc., etc. Its design has been exhaustively analyzed; it has been anatomized and even, very recently, collectivized! Whatever the theories, all of them necessarily reflections of those who gave them voice and of the shifts of time, not one disputes that type is made to read . . . Here, however, we come upon two interrelated problems, one physical and the other esthetic: problem of fatigue and problem of monotony of appearance. For extensive reading there must be furnished some degree of stimulation and pleasure to the eye, to overcome fatigue and give the eye its due satisfaction. In the excellent phrase found in a recent publication, type should be designed 'to submerge type consciousness and invite reading.' To submerge consciousness of type, all obvious cleverness must be ruled out. There should be a kind of impersonal ease about type—type is after all only a medium between writing and reading. But to invite continuous reading, type must have a subtle degree of interest and variety of design."

Ten years after the appearance of Fairfield come Ruzicka's second and third Linotype faces—Fairfield Medium and Primer—specimens of which were publicly shown for the first time in the 1951 Boston exhibition. Both are clearly conceived as means of expression—as bridges between writing and reading—rather than as ends in themselves. Fairfield Medium, as its name implies, is a slightly heavier form of the earlier design. Primer is a "modern" design, more strictly utilitarian in character and without historic suggestions, which it may be hoped will take the place of textbook afflictions of the "Century" family. It is remarkable for the sturdy quality of its roman and the tightness of its italic.

In sharp contrast to the practicality of the new Linotype faces are

Ruzicka's marginal illustrations for Mrs. Chester N. Greenough's *The Bible for My Grandchildren*—another product of 1950. This sumptuous two-volume edition of passages from the King James version of the Bible, selected by and printed for Mrs. Greenough, was designed by John Bianchi of the Merrymount Press and is illustrated by full-page reproductions of William Blake engravings and watercolors and by marginal designs by Rudolph Ruzicka. In these marginalia—printed in one color from line-cuts—one sees both Ruzicka's ability to translate literary perception into artistic forms and his knack in expression even under the most restricted conditions. Although each design is scarcely larger than one by one and one-half inches, they convey far more of the essence of Holy Scripture than the full-page colored inanities that have, since the days of Tissot, travestied the sacred scenes that they purport to represent. Here, in the smallest of compass, is a return to a great tradition of imaginative biblical illustrations.

The ideals of ruling out cleverness and maintaining a subtle degree of interest and variety of design represent not only what Ruzicka was aiming at in designing the Fairfield face, but what he has achieved throughout his work. Cleverness is the lazy man's escape from drudgery, from getting to the bottom of a situation. Throughout Ruzicka's life he has shown abundant evidence of the subtlety that is attained only by unremitting hard work, both over form and content. In the matter of content, I wish to place on record something of the background of the wood engraving in three colors which was made to illustrate Charles Edey Fay's *Mary Celeste, the Odyssey of an Abandoned Ship*, published by the Peabody Museum of Salem in 1942. No picture of this vessel existed, and it seemed desirable to reconstruct one. I therefore furnished Ruzicka with photographs of several brigs of similar dimensions and age, together with data from documents concerning the condition in which *Mary Celeste* was found abandoned on 4 December 1872. From this evidence he made a drawing, which was subjected to rigorous examination not only by Mr. Fay but by the late Lincoln Colcord of Searsport, Maine, whose knowledge of the minutiae of nineteenth-century sailing vessels was unsurpassed. When all possible nautical corrections had been made the drawing was engraved. The result is not only a most attractive wood engraving but a document which genuinely illustrates the text of the book. This kind of meticulous reconstruction could never have been achieved by an artist of the "take-that-and-be-damned-to-you" school of thought.

Rudolph Ruzicka

Philip Hofer, in an address at the opening of the Ruzicka exhibition of the American Institute of Graphic Arts in 1935, said with justice that "Ruzicka, the artist and craftsman, is only a fraction of Ruzicka, the Scholar, the Humanist and the Man." The Grolier Club exhibition showed his insight into the character of works of literature as different as John Donne's *Devotion* upon the tolling bell and Thoreau's *Walden*. No exhibition can even suggest his knowledge of where the best flowering dogwood is to be seen in the spring; the literary skill of his "Fragments of Memory," written for the Club of Odd Volumes' *Recollections of Daniel Berkeley Updike;* the acuteness of his study of the typographical qualities of the first edition of *Tristram Shandy;* or the companionable qualities with which his fellow members of the Grolier, Odd Volumes, and Century clubs are happily familiar.

Rudolph Ruzicka has been elected an Honorary Member of the Grolier Club and the Club of Odd Volumes and has been awarded the Gold Medal of the American Institute of Graphic Arts. The Boston Public Library show in 1951 was the ninth major exhibition of his work. He has not sought these honors; they have come to him. The reason that they have done so can best be expressed in the words of three critics whose judgments command respect.

In 1917 W. M. Ivins, Jr., wrote: "The first thing that impresses one in Ruzicka's prints is their workmanlike competency, a quality which, considered with his notable common sense, creates the comfortable feeling that the artist who made them knows not only his business but his own mind. Having found himself, and in so doing having acquired simplicity of thought, he is content to make his designs directly and calmly, without resort to forcing or over-emphasis, confiding fully in the telling power of terse veracity. His work is thus cast in the quiet form that comes of perfect self-possession, and nowhere is vociferous or theatrical."

In W. A. Dwiggins's opinion, Ruzicka's "outstanding quality is sanity. Complete esthetic equipment, all managed by good sound judgment about ways and means, aims and purposes, utilities and 'functions'—and all this level-head, balance-mechanism added to the lively mental state that makes an artist. Fortunate equipment, in a disordered world. . . ."

Finally, I quote once again from Daniel Berkeley Updike: "Through every piece of Ruzicka's engraving and design runs a secure and sufficient quality—the sane, self-respecting individuality of a man who has something to say and says it simply, directly, calmly, and felicitously. In an hour of intellectual mob-thought and artistic mob-fashion, of open advertisement of self or tacitly permitted exploitation by others, he has the poise to let his work speak and be himself silent. He reserves his strength for his task and dilutes not his talents in criticism of others' performance, or explanation of his own. . . . We can all learn from him not merely the technique of engraving, but (incidentally) the technique of good manners, and admire a man whose work shows that he possesses that rarest of all possessions—himself!''

CHAPTER XVI

L. H. Butterfield

LYMAN HENRY BUTTERFIELD, born in Lyndonville, New York, on 8 August 1909, was graduated from Harvard College summa cum laude *in 1930. The circumstances that brought him to the Massachusetts Historical Society in 1954 as editor in chief of* The Adams Papers *are described in the sketch that follows. He taught English at Harvard from 1930 to 1937 and at Franklin and Marshall College from 1937 to 1946. In 1945 he edited for that college* A Letter by Dr. Benjamin Rush Describing the Consecration of the German College at Lancaster in June, 1787, *and from this beginning proceeded to collect and edit all available letters of that Philadelphia physician. The two volumes of his* Letters of Benjamin Rush *were published by the American Philosophical Society in 1951. Lyman Butterfield left teaching in 1946 to join Julian P. Boyd at Princeton as associate editor of* The Papers of Thomas Jefferson, *and, save for the years 1951 to 1954 when he was director of the Institute of Early American History and Culture at Williamsburg, Virginia, has been engaged in historical editing ever since. The fifteen volumes of* The Adams Papers *that have thus far been published by the Belknap Press of Harvard University Press are definitive proof of his consummate mastery of that exacting aspect of historical learning.*

The pages that follow were written as a Postscript to Butterfield in Holland, A Record of L. H. Butterfield's Pursuit of the Adamses Abroad in 1959 *privately printed at Cambridge in 1961 in the format of* The Adams Papers, *but without the knowledge of the editor in chief. This volume was one of the instances of benevolent conspiracy honoring a man behind his back which have already been mentioned in Chapter XIV. Inspired by the success of the clandestine tributes to Fred Anthoensen and Harold Hugo, Lyman Butterfield in the spring of 1958 embarked on an even more ambitious masterpiece of white magic, for behind my back he and fellow conspirators produced an exhaustive bibliography of my writings, illustrated by personal photographs (purloined from my own house).* Walter Muir Whitehill A Record Compiled by His Friends, *printed by Fred Anthoensen, illustrated by Rudolph Ruzicka and Chiang Yee, was presented to me at a great surprise party at the Butterfields' house at The Glades, Minot, Massachusetts, on 13 September 1958. Julian Boyd wrote the Foreword; David McCord contributed a poem, "The Man with the Vellum Valise," and Lyman furnished a Postscript on the making of the book. No man was ever more generously, affectionately, and elegantly honored than I was on this occasion.* Butterfield in Holland *was an attempt that Wendell and Jane Garrett, Harold Hugo, and I made to surprise Lyman Butterfield in his own coin.*

The footnote reference to "congresses" gives me an excuse to include as an extended note at the end of this chapter my Foreword to Frank H. Wardlaw's "I Have That Honor": Tributes to J. Frank Dobie, *printed in 1965 at the Congressional Press, Paisano, Texas, and Biddeford Pool, Maine. Alas, I only saw Frank Dobie on this one occasion, but I loved him.*

L. H. Butterfield

LHB

ONE DAY in the late Forties Lyman Butterfield turned up in the Boston Athenæum seeking a clue to the whereabouts of certain Jefferson letters that he had reason to believe were privately owned in Massachusetts. With succinct accuracy he told me what he knew about their previous history. I added my scraps; he thanked me courteously and departed, all within a very few minutes. I remember the visit as a model of a scholar seeking information in a library, for he clearly knew what he was about, and accomplished his business without wasting his time or mine. I had never seen him before, for his Harvard class was 1930 while mine was 1926, and I had been in Europe during most of his years as a graduate student.

It was at Williamsburg in May 1951 that I next saw him, when, as director-elect of the Institute of Early American History and Culture, he spoke to the council of the need for further editorial projects similar to the Jefferson Papers. Such was his conviction and breadth of vision that I thought with sorrow of the Adams manuscripts, whose great bulk had long defied any reasonable plan for arrangement and publication. The impression made by his casual remarks on this occasion was so strong that it was clear that Lyman Butterfield would be an essential member of the committee being assembled to advise upon the future of those papers. When Thomas Boylston Adams, who had succeeded his uncle Henry Adams 2d (1875–1951) as the principal trustee of the Adams Manuscript Trust, called a meeting at the Stone Library at Quincy on 9 August 1952, Lyman again took an active part in the discussions. Plans were laid for microfilming the papers. When the interest aroused by the microfilming had led Thomas J. Wilson to propose that the Massachusetts Historical Society edit an edition of the Adams Papers for publication by the Belknap Press of Harvard University Press there was no doubt in anyone's mind that Lyman Butterfield was not only the ideal but the only possible editor. In the spring of 1954 I had the pleasant task of conveying this conviction as we sat on a bench by the pond in the garden of the Governor's Palace at Williamsburg, and in the autumn he joined the staff of the Massachusetts Historical Society. Nothing that I have done has given me greater satisfaction than having had a hand in persuading Lyman Butterfield to settle in Massachusetts.

In a paper at an American Historical Association session in December 1954, he described thus his initial impression of the material committed to his charge:

Keats in his sonnet on Chapman's Homer pictures "stout Cortez" and his companions on a peak in Darien looking at one another "with a wild surmise." The phrase is splendidly applicable to one just beginning the exploration of the Adams manuscripts as they stand in serried rows of leather bindings differently colored for the several generations, or spill from boxes, bundles, cases, drawers, portfolios, and every other sort of receptacle, including packets of papers that are tied up in other manuscripts. (Parchment laws and commissions, being oversize and durable, make handy wrappings; and being plentiful among this family's papers, they were sometimes used for this purpose.) It will be impossible to tell for some months to come with any reasonable accuracy just what is going to be found in this immense accumulation of the records of a peculiarly record-keeping family over a period of more than two centuries. A brown-paper parcel may contain several hundred retained copies of Abigail Adams' letters written throughout her lifetime and evidently not examined during the last half-century. Next to it may stand a ledger of kitchen accounts kept by John Quincy Adams' cook in St. Petersburg. A box stuffed with loose papers with Henry Adams' name affixed to it yields long sequences of letters from Mrs. Henry Adams to her father in the 1870's and 80's—the very sequences, a quick check shows, that were supposed lost when a volume of Mrs. Adams' letters was published in 1936. These discoveries are interestingly amplified by further contributions from living members of the family, who are now ransacking their desks and cupboards, and from friends and even perfect strangers,

who have been sending in stray Adams letters and papers by ordinary mail. (One Christmas card brought two Adams letters of different generations attached to it.)

But even at this stage Lyman Butterfield offered his listeners a coherent outline of the working plan for the edition. By March 1955 he had completed the first inventory ever attempted of the collection, and in the following November established a transcription assembly-line. Gradually the chaos described in the paragraph above gave way to a controlled and disciplined order that assured definitive editing, but only those who have had the luck to look over the editor's shoulder during the past six and a half years can have any conception of the task that he has accomplished with a limited budget and with a small and changing staff. His quarters in the overcrowded building consist of a small circular office that doubles as a passageway between the stair landing where his staff precariously roost and the stack where the manuscripts are housed. Despite inconveniences that might have discouraged a less single-minded man, Lyman from the first has shown that he knew what he was about and was accomplishing his aims without wasting his time or that of anyone else.

For the intelligent handling of the Adams Papers, vastly unwieldy and diverse as they were, one of the first requirements was a variety of filing and control systems. These could only have been devised and adapted by a man whose memory resembled a filing cabinet ever being replenished from his reading. Not only had he to call to mind the multifarious facts of his historical knowledge, but to supplement that knowledge for himself and for his staff by gathering a library of reference books. Yet even so the whole enterprise might well have turned into a pedestrian affair, a mere ramble through the brambles. Besides knowledge, the editor must possess patience to a degree matched only by the inexhaustibility of human error. But even that is not enough. Above all the editorial vision must be the steadfast twenty-twenty sort that snaps up trifles and still can sharply see contours and colors all the way to the horizon. And let no reader, so fortunate as not to be himself an editor, suppose this is a fancy and idealized portrait. Indeed it is no theoretical description, but a factual one, based upon a sober observation of the editor of the Adams Papers at work.

Lyman Butterfield literally lives with his work. He refuses to leave the Massachusetts Historical Society at the accepted closing hour and is all too likely to return there on days when it is normally shut. Moreover he summers among live Adamses at The Glades, a rocky peninsula at Minot, Massachusetts, where many members of the family have congregated for the past eighty years. He has somehow found time to inspire the reorganization of the library of the Massachusetts Historical Society, to serve as a director of the Council on Library Resources, Inc., and to have a hand in many projects that show genuine promise of advancing the cause of learning.

L. H. Butterfield

For some years he and his wife have conducted a spring book sale in Cambridge that has proved phenomenally profitable to the Bryn Mawr College Scholarship Fund. Friends and neighbors are encouraged throughout the year to dump unwanted books on the porch of 5 Berkeley Place, which are stored until April in the cellar, where Lyman spends long evening hours sorting and arranging them.

Unlike the businessman who forgets his occupation on the golf course, Lyman Butterfield's most complete form of relaxation is to attend one of the congresses in which he holds office (*see* the extended footnote that follows), where his fellow officers are scholars and printers. On two occasions he has instigated the compilation of the bibliography of the writings of one of his fellow congressmen, and conspired with others so as to surprise the subject with a handsome book containing the record of much that he had forgotten writing. Julian Boyd in 1950, on his tenth anniversary as librarian of Princeton University, was the recipient of one such tribute, and I in 1958 of another. These clandestine enterprises, which require a singular blend of human warmth, meticulous research, and impeccable typography, are so characteristic of their instigator that the milestone represented by his completion of the diary of John Adams could not be passed without some attempt, however inadequate, at imitation.

Mr. and Mrs. Wendell Garrett conceived the idea of converting extracts from Lyman Butterfield's letters to his family and friends, written during a research trip to Holland in 1959, into the form of a diary. This they have edited in the form established by its author for the *Diary and Autobiography of John Adams*. To complete the illusion, Harvard University Press agreed to have the volume printed in the format of *The Adams Papers*, while E. Harold Hugo undertook to supply the illustrations.

By the time publication date is reached any author is heartily sick of his own book. He has completed his work, read the proofs, checked the index weeks, or, as in this case, months before it is printed and bound. Consequently the staff of the Adams Papers wished to congratulate their editor in chief at a gathering of close friends in North Andover on Sunday, 11 June 1961, before he had forgotten all about the diary of John Adams and become completely immersed in the family correspondence that is his next project. *Butterfield in Holland* was prepared for presentation to its author on that occasion. The compilers and contributors hoped that they had covered their tracks as successfully in the preparation of this mock-heroic token of affection and esteem as he had succeeded in covering his on occasions in the past when he surprised some of them.

On 12 August 1959 Lyman Butterfield wrote Julian Boyd, "I do promise to give you a narrative of my European adventures one day." Now he has, without realizing that he has fulfilled this promise!

AN EXTENDED FOOTNOTE

THE IMPRINT of this work, like that of the *Atalzaide* of Crebillon fils—"Imprimé où l'on a pû"—calls for a word of explanation, for neither the Biddeford Pool nor the Paisano Congress will be found in any of the works of reference usually consulted by librarians, bibliographers, or Ph.D. candidates. In fact the only description that I can recall appears in a footnote in a privately printed work, *Butterfield in Holland, A Record of L. H. Butterfield's Pursuit of the Adamses Abroad in 1959* (Cambridge, 1961) pp. 20–21, which I quote:

> In this instance the 6th signification [of the word Congress] of the *Oxford English Dictionary* is applicable: "A formal meeting or assembly of delegates or representatives for the discussion or settlement of some question." The Bear Lake Historical, Typographical, Gastronomical, Marching, Singing, and Grouse Poaching Congress, Inc., of which LHB has been Treasurer since its organization in 1955, convenes annually at the call of its Chairman, Julian P. Boyd. LHB is also Editor and Scrivener of The Camel's Hump (or Rump) Congress, held at Starksboro, Addison County, Vermont, for the Promotion of Typography and Calligraphy (established 1957); Founder and President of the Glades Congress (established 1958), with headquarters at the Butterfield Villa, The Glades, Minot, Massachusetts; and on occasion a participant in the older Biddeford Pool Congress, which convenes annually in September at Biddeford Pool, Maine. All congresses conduct their business with appropriate formality and issue publications, which, as in the case of the *Bear Lake Songster* [*Contributions to Historical, Typographical, Gastronomical, Marching, Singing, and Grouse Poaching Knowledge*, Fascicle No. 1 (1957)], sometimes confuse library cataloguers. The typographical standards of all three congresses are high. Their publications will eventually be listed in a supplement to Arthur Dinaux, *Les sociétés badines, bachiques, littéraires et chantantes, leur histoire et leurs travaux*, Paris, 1867, 2 vols., that the Bear Lake Congress, Inc., has in preparation. The congresses of the New England-Pennsylvania axis maintain cordial relations with the Paisano Congress of Austin, Texas, of which J. Frank Dobie is Founder and President.

L. H. Butterfield

The essential ingredients of a congress are (1) a few congenial scholars and printers, (2) a secluded country house in a pleasant landscape, and (3) an adequate supply of food and drink. Thus the Biddeford Pool Congress came to convene in Herbert Farrier's seaside cottage at Biddeford Pool, Maine, well after Labor Day so that the participants might have a superb stretch of sandy beach to themselves and sing, if moved, without disturbing neighbors. Inspired by this prototype, others developed at Julian Boyd's mountain hideaway in the Poconos, at mine in the Green Mountains, and at Lyman Butterfield's house at The Glades. When Harold Hugo of the Meriden Gravure Company found his way to Frank Dobie's ranch at Paisano some years ago, he immediately recognized that the assembly there of such cronies as Walter Prescott Webb, Roy Bedichek, Frank H. Wardlaw, and Glen Evans exactly paralleled the proceedings of the New England–Pennsylvania congresses, of which he was a member. From that discovery sprang an interchange of visits. Frank Wardlaw, during a New England trip, was unanimously elected to the Biddeford Pool Congress. When I paid my first visit to Austin, Texas, in late February 1960 a session of the Paisano Congress was organized.

Frank Wardlaw drove me out to Paisano on the afternoon of Saturday, the 27th. It was a cold day for the region, with light rain turning into fog. I almost thought myself in the Dordogne, for the cliffs above Barton Creek startingly resembled those around Les Eyzies. It was in a sense a rump session, for Roy Bedichek had recently died, and Walter Webb was unavoidably absent, but Glen Evans drove four hundred fifty miles from Midland for the session. For a couple of hours we drank Jack Daniels and told stories. About five o'clock we got into the car and drove around the ranch. In dry country one can forgo roads in a comfortable way. We would drive for a few minutes, get out and listen to the creek, collect lichens from a dead tree, admire the shape of a stunted live oak as it could be seen through the fog, and look for deer. We didn't see any, although once we saw the white striped tail of a hog-nosed skunk, trotting through the tall grass with the motion of a dog. Evans, who was spending the night before returning to Midland, was seeking out good spots for fishing. We looked at the cliffs from the riverbank; we drove to the tops of cliffs and looked down across the river to the house, and generally had a happy time until dark. When we returned indoors, Tomás began to produce dinner—a superb steak, a kettle of frijoles, salad, and baked sweet potatoes, washed down with bock beer—for dessert, local honey on fresh hot rolls. Then more talk until after eleven, when Frank Wardlaw and I started back through a pea-soup fog to Austin.

Although I never again saw Frank Dobie, he has been often in my mind ever since that visit. We exchanged letters now and then. I would find in his books passages that vividly conveyed the sound of his voice and the quality of his mind. Some of these I freely appropriated as ammunition against pedants and those who exaggerate the significance of local history. When Frank Wardlaw sent me new publications of the University of Texas Press, I read them eagerly, always measuring them against my recollections of Frank Dobie at Paisano. These memories were vividly enhanced by Frank Wardlaw's article in the 24 July 1964 issue of *The Texas Observer*. Of all the sections of that perceptive tribute, none was more moving to me than the account of the gathering at

Paisano soon after Roy Bedichek's death. The sense of this same unbreakable kinship between the living and the dead permeated the remarks made by Frank Wardlaw at Frank Dobie's funeral on 20 September 1964 in the Hogg Memorial Auditorium of the University of Texas.

CHAPTER XVII

John Otis Brew

I FIRST MET John Otis Brew close to thirty years ago when we engaged in the congenial occupation of uncorking bottles at a party given by Hugh and Thalassa Hencken. Through his instigation I became in 1951 a member of the faculty of the Peabody Museum of Archaeology and Ethnology, Harvard University. On his retirement from the directorship of the Peabody Museum in the autumn of 1967 I was asked to prepare a memoir of his services for the minutes of the faculty. This was printed for distribution at a dinner given Jo Brew at the Club of Odd Volumes on 15 February 1968 by the visiting committee and staff of the museum and the Department of Anthropology, and is reprinted here without change. As this memoir was written as a matter of formal academic record, it is somewhat less personal than most of the chapters in this book. It is therefore worth noting here that at the 15 February 1968 dinner Jo was presented with a set of silver cups and a cocktail shaker inscribed with this couplet by David McCord:

J.O.B.

THESE THREE FOR NAME AND FAME BELIE THE BOOK OF

BUT BLESS FOR YOU JO'S BREW TO BE PARTOOK OF

This is appropriate for one who is a congressman par excellence *(in the terms of the Note to Chapter XVI), and whose company in the Club of Odd Volumes, the Senior Common Room of Lowell House, the Massachusetts Historical Society, and other places has added greatly to my pleasure over many years. The time in the year when I see him with the fullest opportunity for conversation is when we journey from Chicago to Santa Fé by train in late January to attend the annual meeting of the Museum of Navajo Ceremonial Art, founded by our late friend Mary Cabot Wheelwright, of which he is president and I am a trustee.*

The photograph that is here reproduced was taken at the Club of Odd Volumes on 15 February 1968 for the Harvard Alumni Bulletin. *Jo Brew is unwrapping the gifts that are being presented to him by the present Augustus Peabody Loring, a member of the Visiting Committee and the eldest son of the subjects of Chapters IV and V. I am on Jo's right; on my right is Ernest Stanley Dodge, Director of the Peabody Museum of Salem, of which Gus and I are trustees.*

JOB

JOHN OTIS BREW, Director of the Peabody Museum of Archaeology and Ethnology, Harvard University, from 1948 to 1967, was born in Malden, Massachusetts, on 28 March 1906. Although at Dartmouth College, where he received an A.B. in Fine Arts in 1928, his particular interest was in classical archaeology, he has been a part of the Peabody Museum for the forty years since his graduation. He came to Harvard as a student in anthropology in the Graduate School of Arts and Sciences in 1928. After 1931, when he completed his residence requirements, he was actively in the field with the museum's expeditions in the Southwestern United States. In 1931 he was scientific director of the Claflin-

John Otis Brew

Emerson expedition, and in 1931–1933 director of the Peabody Museum Southwestern Utah expedition. Following this he briefly changed scene by excavating in Ireland in 1934 as assistant to Dr. Hugh O'Neill Hencken, director of the Harvard Irish expedition, but was the next year back in the Southwest for five years of field research as director of the Peabody Museum Awatovi expedition. Toward the end of work at Awatovi, on 11 June 1939, he married Evelyn Ruth Nimmo, a member of the expedition staff. Of their two sons one has become a lawyer, the other an anthropologist. Having received the Ph.D. degree in 1941, from 1941 to 1945 J. O. Brew served as assistant curator of Southwest American Archaeology in the Peabody Museum, and as curator of North American Archaeology from 1945 to 1948. In the latter year, upon the retirement of Professor Donald Scott, he succeeded to the directorship of the Peabody Museum. In 1949 he was appointed Peabody Professor of American Archaeology and Ethnology— a chair that he still holds.

In seeking detailed information about J. O. Brew's highly varied activities, I have consulted scholars in various parts of the country, and have in consequence gleaned much from private letters that are quoted throughout this memoir. Thus Dr. Richard B. Woodbury, Curator, Office of Archaeology, Smithsonian Institution, gave me the following appraisal of J. O. Brew's archaeological expeditions in the Southwestern United States:

> His work can be described as outstanding for two reasons: the first his skill in selecting relatively neglected or misunderstood areas for research, and second, the thoroughness with which the research was organized and directed. The areas on which he has focused his interest are southeastern Utah (particularly the great Alkali Ridge site, which was recently designated a National Historic Landmark), the Hopi country of northeastern Arizona (Awatovi and the many prehistoric sites near it), and west-central New Mexico (centering on Quemado), and in each of them he was responsible for major advances in knowledge of permanent significance.
>
> At each of these areas he was responsible for a major advance in knowledge, not only of the area directly concerned, but of the Southwest as a whole. Each of these archaeological programs was

a multi-season field investigation with a large, carefully selected staff and crew which had a wide range of scientific specialties and was able to attack a broad range of problems, extending far beyond the usual tradition of archaeological limitations of excavating rooms and burials, and examining the associated architectural and artifactual details.

The results of the Utah work were published entirely by Brew himself in 1946 [*Archaeology of Alkali Ridge, Southeastern Utah*, Volume XXI, *Papers of the Peabody Museum*] in a volume that has become a keystone in the understanding of the Four Corners area, including Mesa Verde, just to the east, to which Brew's work contributed more basic clarification than had the previous half-century of digging the Mesa Verde itself.

The Awatovi Expedition's results were too complex and extensive for any one person to write up individually. Brew himself contributed a major portion of the 1949 volume on the Franciscan mission [*Franciscan Awatovi*, Volume XXXVI, *Papers of the Peabody Museum*], which is outstanding for its significant blending of archaeological, ecclesiastical, historical and architectural data to form a meaningful whole. Also of major importance was the remarkable series of well-preserved paintings of ritual subjects found in the kivas of Awatovi, published by Watson Smith in 1952, another landmark in Southwestern archaeological studies. The participation of the late Kirk Bryan and of his then student (John T. Hack, '51) resulted in important publications on the physiography and aboriginal farming of the area. Two other volumes have reported on a particularly rewarding pit-house site of early date that was dug in establishing the full occupational sequence of the Awatovi area, and on the stone implements of all of the sites excavated, a frequently neglected aspect of the prehistoric cultures of the Southwest. In addition, the published reports on the animal bones make basic contributions to the identification and interpretation of this kind of archaeological material. In sum, the Awatovi Expedition, conceived and directed by Brew, was one of the most comprehensive, ably executed, and productive programs of archaeological research ever carried out in the United States.

Brew deserves the major credit for both its intellectual and practical aspects.

Dr. Edward B. Danson, director of the Museum of Northern Arizona, has commented upon the manner in which the Awatovi expedition gave to Southwestern archaeologists for the first time sound archaeological knowledge about early colonial culture.

> The expedition gave archaeologists an historical picture of the Hopi contacts with the Spanish. The archaeological record found there is brilliantly used to clarify the documentary accounts of the Spanish mission period on the Hopi mesas. Besides presenting the archaeology of the religious establishments, Brew's observation of disputes over land rights and his comparison of Hopi behavior as recorded in 1780 with modern Hopi conduct is particularly illuminating.

The directorship of the Peabody Museum did not bring an end to J. O. Brew's field work in the Southwest, as Dr. Danson points out.

> Brew's third major expedition was the Peabody Museum's Upper Gila Expedition, which began immediately after the war and lasted until 1954. It included large-scale archaeological surveys, excavations of the famous Bat Cave, studies ranging from early ceramic sites through large pueblos in the Quemado area of New Mexico—an area where little was known but which was important in the prehistoric Zuni and Acoma cultures. The archaeology of the Red Hill site near Quemado helped illuminate the development of the pit house in the Southwest prior to cultural amalgamations that came after the A.D. 900's—and led to more formalized house types.
>
> Dr. Brew has, in all of the expeditions under his direction, arranged to work in areas of importance and areas where studies were needed to help answer blanks in Southwestern prehistoric knowledge. His Alkali Ridge excavations gave, for the first time, a clear picture of the Anasazi area archaeology for Pueblo I. His work on Antelope Mesa and Awatovi not only gave students a picture of the development of culture in the Hopi country from the

John Otis Brew

Early Basket Maker sites up through Spanish contact, but, what is even more important, his work tied the historic period into the prehistoric and thus pushed the history of the Hopi back in time.

The excavations resulting from the Upper Gila Expedition produced knowledge of an area of great importance where practically no studies had been made before.

Another of Dr. Brew's important contributions to archaeology was the number of students whom he helped train. His breadth of vision and knowledge was a constant source of stimulation to his students, and his enthusiasm and love of the Southwest added to the pleasure of studying under him. No student of Dr. Brew's was allowed to be pedantic or petty. He wanted his students to be careful but not meticulous, imaginative but not fanciful, enthusiastic but not extremists. He wanted his students to be well-rounded anthropologists, and a reflection of his archaeological standards are the numerous publications produced under his aegis that are of significant importance.

When a scholar becomes the head of an institution, he inevitably devotes the greater part of his time to encouraging and supporting the work of others. This is especially true of an institution with such universal ramifications as the Peabody Museum. Although the chair that J. O. Brew still holds—Peabody Professor of American Archaeology and Ethnology—is appropriate for a scholar active in Southwestern archaeology, the institution has never limited itself geographically. It has excavated in Ohio, the Mississippi Valley, the Southwest, Mexico, Guatemala, and Peru. Members of its staff are quite at home among the pygmies of the Kalahari Desert of southwest Africa and in the jungles of New Guinea and the Solomon Islands. They dig at Les Eyzies in the Dordogne, measure skulls in the Caucasus, and collect masks in Liberia. All of this activity throughout the world requires support; moreover, it swells the exhibition cases and storerooms, and eventually the publications, of the Peabody Museum. And as its activities are as intertwined with the Department of Anthropology as the Fogg Art Museum is with the teaching of the fine arts, the Peabody Museum is a seat of instruction as well as of collection and research. In this connection it is worth recalling the remark of the late Professor Roland B. Dixon:

In most branches of learning that are pursued in Harvard University, laboratories, museums, and libraries are the outgrowth of teaching and research. In anthropology, the order is reversed; and for the obvious reason that anthropology is so young a science that the overwhelming need was to discover and classify data, rather than to present conclusions which were purely tentative. Most of the significant history of anthropology has occurred since the Peabody Museum was founded in 1866.

In commenting on J. O. Brew's support of research and publications in all aspects of anthropology during his nineteen years as director of the Peabody Museum, Dr. Richard B. Woodbury observed of the museum's accelerated publication program:

Although its quality is its important aspect, it is also impressive quantitatively. There are few scholarly series that have issued more important series of monographs than those appearing since Brew's directorship began.

H. M. Worthington, curator of archaeology, Denver Museum of Natural History, after commenting on the importance of Dr. Brew's own work at Alkali Ridge and Awatovi, continued:

Equally important is the aid and encouragement he has given to other scholars working in many areas and concerned with many periods. In the Early Man field, with which I am most familiar, Dr. Brew's outstanding contributions include his support and his aid in obtaining funds for the years of excavation at the Hell Gap site, Wyoming, and the work done on ancient sites in the vicinity of Puebla, Mexico. The former, a deep stratified site, has provided invaluable data concerning the sequence in the Plains over some three millenia beginning about 9000 B.C. The latter have, in my opinion, provided the earliest evidence of man yet found in the New World.

The awards that Dr. Brew has received and the offices he has held are a matter of record, but many of his activities have been known, in general, only to those who have benefited from them, and he has not always received the credit which he deserves.

John Otis Brew

With severely limited space that is each year overtaxed by the collections that grow from the field activities of its curators, the Peabody Museum poses nearly insoluble problems of housekeeping. Although continued research, publication, and teaching are the first obligations of its staff, great improvements were made during J. O. Brew's administration. In 1950 the Hall of North American Ethnology was reinstalled by Frederic H. Douglas of the Denver Art Museum, who devised a manner of exhibiting, within limited space, a large number of specimens, logically arranged by culture areas, entirely visible to the visitor, and adequately labeled for the student. The purpose in this hall, as in the many other galleries that were subsequently reinstalled by various curators, was to present material in a manner that would be instructive to any intelligent person who took the trouble to examine the objects and read the labels. The object is not to dazzle the eye—as in the department store window—but to excite the mind, and to do so with restricted space and funds. Such a theory makes it possible to keep many objects on exhibition, where they can be seen without handling, for fragile artifacts cannot be pulled out casually from storage, as books can be conjured up from the shelves of a stack. Thus the Peabody Museum galleries are conceived of somewhat in the terms of the book stacks of a research library, where qualified users can find their way about unaided, with ample resources to stimulate the mind. An opportunity for more public display of the examples of primitive art that abound in the Peabody Museum was developed in 1958 by a coöperative agreement with the Museum of Fine Arts in Boston. In that year under Dr. Brew's guidance, with the help of Mr. Eliot Eliosofon, a brilliant exhibition of "Masterpieces of Primitive Art"—the first of its kind to be held in Boston—was mounted at the Museum of Fine Arts. Since that time, changing displays of primitive art, borrowed from the Peabody Museum, have continued to be shown at the Boston Museum.

An instance of J. O. Brew's activities in an area of anthropology somewhat remote from his chief interest as a field archaeologist is furnished by his colleague, Professor Evon Z. Vogt, who writes:

> From 1949 through 1955 Professor Brew served as a member of the Advisory Committee of the "Comparative Study of Values in Five Cultures Project" that was funded by the Rockefeller Foundation and jointly sponsored by the Peabody Museum and the Lab-

oratory of Social Relations at Harvard. Along with the other two members—the late Professor Clyde Kluckhohn and Professor Talcott Parsons—of this Advisory Committee, Professor Brew helped establish the basic intellectual directions and administrative policy of this Values Study Project which carried out field studies of five cultures in New Mexico. These five cultures—Navajo, Zuni, Spanish-American, Mormon, and Texas Homesteader—were studied by some 40 fieldworkers, representing the disciplines of Anthropology, Sociology, Psychology, Government, Human Geography, and History. The published results appeared not only in several notable monographs in the Peabody Museum Papers series, but also in numerous books and articles in technical journals. Throughout the project Professor Brew not only provided much appreciated administrative and technical advice, but also took an active rôle in directing graduate students along more productive lines as they coped with the intricacies of carrying out field operations in various communities which he had come to know so intimately during his long experience with the cultures of the Southwest.

His breadth of interest has gone far beyond his immediate colleagues at Harvard. Mrs. Marjorie P. Lambert, Curator, Division of Research, Museum of New Mexico, in a piece titled "Dr. John Otis Brew, Anthropologist and Humanitarian," wrote:

It is difficult to give a completely accurate appraisal of Dr. Brew because of the fact that his interests and contributions to our civilization are so wide and varied. He is indeed an unusual and gifted human being.

One only has to consult *Who's Who in America* and *American Men of Science: The Social and Behavioral Sciences* in order to visualize the scope of his contributions in the past few decades to world art, anthropology and history. But as impressive as this record is, it in no way describes the quality and warmth of this scientist's personality.

Probably no other American has a wider knowledge of museums and departments of anthropology in this country and abroad. No matter where, or how busy he is, he has never been known to spurn the young person who has needed his advice. The same holds true in the case of the hundreds of professionals who constantly call on him for help and advice. His loyalty, integrity, and warm personality are legend. The students and professional anthropologists, and museum employees whom he has assisted or who have felt his influence are *countless*. In this respect alone, he is one of Harvard University's greatest assets.

His broad attitude toward the field of anthropology is significant, an important fact in this day of specialization. Every discovery, wherever it is made, and whether it pertains to something of man's simplest beginning, or to that which is spectacular and sophisticated, is to him equally exciting and important.

Dr. Brew is a conservationist in the true sense of the word.

Perhaps no other person has been as influential and active as he in launching and helping to maintain a world-wide program of salvaging archaeological and historical remains, as well as the art treasures throughout numerous countries, all of which might otherwise be lost forever were such an endeavor not made.

Those of us who have worked with him, and who have his friendship look on him as one of the great men of our generation.

On the theme of salvage archaeology, Professor Richard D. Daugherty of Washington State University observes:

Many years ago Jo Brew, Fred Johnson, and a few others were perceptive enough to see the critical problems facing this nation with regard to the loss of prehistoric resources through the various mechanisms of an expanding industrial society. They also had the foresight to begin doing something about it. Through their efforts the Committee for the Recovery of Archaeological Remains was formed (Jo is the present chairman) which was very successful in stimulating Congressional action to provide funds and the necessary legislation to salvage those sites and materials in danger of being lost. One can trace the evolution of the attitudes and efforts regarding salvage archaeology from this early beginning, through the establishment of a number of boards, councils, and commissions that now exist throughout the structure of the Federal Government. In back of this expansion in funds legislation and public awareness has been the ever-moving, persuading, arguing, and stimulating figure of Jo Brew. Without doubt, Jo has had more influence in the development of salvage archaeology, nationally and internationally, than any other man. He has the sincere respect and admiration of the entire profession.

In a similar vein, Dr. Emil W. Haury of the University of Arizona writes:

Jo, more than any other person, has made salvage archaeology his main crusade. He has been most effective in promoting guidelines and policies through UNESCO and as chairman for many years of our domestic Committee for the Recovery of Archaeological Remains. He, more than any other member on that committee, must be given credit for the level of annual Federal support we now have in the United States for this activity, about $1.1 million.

Jo knows his way around in Washington, on the Hill and wherever else it counts. His dealings with tough-minded Senators, Representatives, and people in the Bureau of the Budget, have been done with a finesse that has paid off.

All one needs to do is to sit through one of our annual CRAR meetings in Washington, when fifteen or twenty representatives of as many Federal agencies are present, to catch the enthusiasm Jo has instilled in them for an activity that is far from their main line of interest. I seriously doubt whether as many representatives of government agencies have ever been brought together in one room who are thinking constructively along the same line.

The long and the short of all of this is that we have in the United States the best organized and the most ambitious salvage program in the world and its state of good health is due to Jo's tireless activity. No other American archaeologist has bothered or committed himself so deeply to this cause. A special medal should be struck for him and him alone.

By emphasizing the foregoing aspect of Jo's career, his capabilities as an archaeologist and a scholar are not being minimized. He has made valuable and significant contributions in his own right to American archaeology, both through his own writing and in providing opportunities for others to go into the field to conduct research and to publish. That latter aspect is eventually the fate of the administrator and most of the time these efforts go unsung.

Dr. Richard B. Woodbury comments on the good use to which J. O. Brew's earlier experience in planning complex archaeological field programs has been put in his rôle as adviser on and creator of national and international programs of archaeological salvage and preservation.

He is one of a handful who appreciated that large-scale research need not slight the myriad minute details that prove significant in the long run, and he has, through his persuasiveness and personal experience, convinced many doubting scholars that research could maintain the highest standards even while meeting incredibly tight schedules. This has been a profound and little-noticed revolution in archaeological thinking, and without it the major programs to "save the past from the present" would have been ineffectual. I am sure that Brew deserves more credit than will ever be generally realized for this application of research skill to major archaeological salvage work.

J. O. Brew ably served his fellow scholars as president of the Society of American Archaeology in 1949 and 1953, and as president of the American Anthropological Association in 1954. In 1952 the Secretary of the Interior invited him to serve on the Advisory Board on National Parks, Historic Sites, Buildings and Monuments, established by Act of Congress some years before. The effect that he had upon his colleagues during his six-year term, which ended in 1958, is best shown by the comment from one of them, F. E. Masland, Jr., a businessman of Carlisle, Pennsylvania. Mr. Masland, whose first year on the advisory board, was Brew's last, writes:

I had become somewhat interested in conservation as a result of my travels in country that Jo had "dug up" in his early days as a field archaeologist and as a result of the battle to save Dinosaur from the devastating hands of the Bureau of Reclamation.

It was, however, that first year on the Advisory Board, during which I was able to sit at Jo's feet and listen and learn that both opened my eyes to the battle that needed to be fought to save the remainder of our natural heritage and how to fight it.

That was in 1956. From then to date I have devoted a major portion of my time to conservation activities. Jo's inspiration and

his words of advice led me to a new way of life, led me into conservation activities throughout our own land, South of the Border,
in Africa and the Middle East. I cherish Jo's friendship and I owe
him a debt of gratitude beyond the possibility of evaluation.

Since 1958 J. O. Brew has served on the consulting committee to the
Director of the National Park Service for the selection of Registered National Historic Landmarks. Ronald F. Lee of the National Park Service
writes:

> The quiet labors of this Committee of which Dr. Brew is Vice-
> Chairman have materially assisted the Secretary of the Interior in
> the official designation of over 800 national historic landmarks,
> now protected by law from many adverse influences.

> National recognition of the value of Dr. Brew's public service
> has been accompanied by requests to serve international organiza-
> tions in a similar way. In 1952, Dr. Brew was invited to become a
> member of the International Committee for Monuments, Historic
> Sites, and Archaeological Excavations then newly established by
> UNESCO. This is a permanent Committee and since 1956 Dr.
> Brew has served as its Chairman. Among the Committee's world-
> wide interests, it has played a central rôle in the program to con-
> serve archaeological sites and monuments in the Nile Valley. Dr.
> Brew headed a special UNESCO technical mission which laid the
> groundwork for the rescue of archaeological and historical sites in
> Egypt and the Sudan which has contributed to preserving the
> record of over 500,000 years of human occupation in the valley of
> the Nile. Because of the special problems of Abu Simbel, this pro-
> gram has received world-wide attention and has made international
> conservation history.

Dr. Edmundo Lassalle, vice-chairman of the International Fund for
Monuments, adds further details on this activity:

> A key moment in the history of international cultural coöperation
> was marked in 1960 when the governments of the United Arab
> Republic and the Sudan made an international appeal, through
> UNESCO, to the world to save their threatened archaeological
> monuments in Nubia. J. O. Brew, notwithstanding his full load of

work as Director of the Peabody Museum, worked indefatigably as chairman of the Monuments Commission of UNESCO and as chairman of the U.S. National Committee for the Preservation of the Nubian Monuments to raise the monumental sums of, first, ten million dollars and, further, an allocation of twelve million for the protection of Abu Simbel.

This is a most significant victory in a world which views materialistic values through a different prism from that with which it inspects cultural values. The Nubian campaign constitutes a permanent landmark in the history of intellectual coöperation. This is not the first time that the United States has reacted generously to a noble cause; but this is the first time the United States has joined freely in international cultural fellowship. It is also the first time that this same fellowship has invoked the principle that certain religious, historical and artistic monuments, in which mankind has expressed its deepest faith and highest aspirations, belong not only to the nation where they might happen to exist, but to the whole human race and are part of our common patrimony, regardless of when they came into existence or the place where they happen to be.

To John Otis Brew we owe, through his work in the Nubian campaign, a definition that culture as essential element of the intellectual and moral solidarity of mankind has been recognized by the United States for all the world to see, as an important factor for the promotion of peace by the spirit. This is the guidance which Dr. Brew gave us in his work for the Nubian campaign; his success is simply a demonstration of the right of his cause.

On 26 March 1965, H.I.H. The Crown Prince of Ethiopia appealed personally to Dr. Brew requesting aid for the safeguard of the Coptic Christian churches of Lalibela. Dr. Brew enlisted the support of his own organization, the International Fund for Monuments, and the first phase of the work to restore these extraordinary rupestrian temples has been completed. The second and final phase is already under way.

As a footnote to the Nubian campaign, Dr. Lassalle remarks that it was an amusing feature that "Jo had not only my coöperation (an old Maya as I am from Chiapas in Mexico) but also that of H.S.H. Prince Sadruddin Aga Khan (an old Persian)."

Robert R. Garvey, Jr., secretary of the Advisory Council on Historic Preservation in the United States Department of the Interior, comments thus on Dr. Brew's part in the establishment of the International Council on Monuments and Sites (ICOMOS):

> In 1957, as Chairman of the International Committee for Monuments, Artistic and Historical Sites, and Archaeological Excavations, he sponsored the recommendation that UNESCO undertake a year-long international campaign for the recognition of monuments. International Monuments Year was scheduled for 1964. One of its objectives was the establishment of the International Council on Monuments and Sites.
>
> Dr. Brew's International Monuments Committee accepted the responsibility of preparing draft statutes, program proposals and other basic documents necessary for the establishment of such an international, nongovernmental body. Under his leadership this work was accomplished. In 1964, at the Second International Congress of the Architects and Technicians of Historical Monuments, Dr. Brew headed an *ad hoc* committee that studied and revised the draft documents establishing provisional organization for ICOMOS. Thus, during International Monuments Year of 1964, the first steps were taken to organize the Council. In 1965 the provisional establishment called the first congress and invited member states of UNESCO to organize national committees and provide delegates to a meeting in Warsaw, Poland, where the International Council on Monuments and Sites would be formally created and its first general assembly conducted. Dr. Brew served as a member of the Provisional United States National Committee, advising and assisting the delegation that was to represent the United States at the first congress.
>
> Following the organization of ICOMOS, Dr. Brew served as the first president of the United States National Committee and led this group through a successful year. Since that time he has remained active on the committee, always guiding its deliberations, especially as they relate to international activities.

Throughout this active period, UNESCO's International Committee has had the additional responsibility of preparing a Draft Recommendation Concerning the Preservation of Cultural Property Endangered by Public or Private Works. Dr. Brew was the author of the original draft. When presented to the General Assembly of UNESCO in 1968, it will have undergone three revisions. During each stage of development, the United States officials responsible for making suggestions have profited from the wise counsel of Dr. Brew. When this important international recommendation is finally approved, his contribution will have been more important than that of any other single person.

Such a recital of governmental and international activity should not obscure the detailed work that J. O. Brew has done over the years for local and regional organizations. In the Southwest, as president of the Museum of Navajo Ceremonial Art in Santa Fé, he has given invaluable help to a small privately supported institution, founded by the late Mary Cabot Wheelwright. In New England he has long been a trustee of the Fruitlands Museum in Harvard, Massachusetts, a member of the advisory board of Plimoth Plantation, and an officer of the Trustees of Donations for Education in Liberia (vice-president, 1958–68, now president). As a member of the Massachusetts Historical Commission since its creation in 1963, he has been uniquely helpful because of his long association with the National Park Service.

Dr. Danson has already commented upon the way in which the excavations at Awatovi "tied the historic period into the prehistoric and thus pushed the history of the Hopi back in time." Thus it is no surprise that J. O. Brew has ever been ready to put the techniques of archaeologists at the disposal of historians whenever, even within the recent centuries of documented history, they can prove helpful. In 1957, for example, he arranged for Mr. Oriol Pi-Sunyer, then a graduate student at the Peabody Museum, to go to Monticello to excavate the Mulberry Row industrial area for the Thomas Jefferson Memorial Foundation. In an essay titled "Historic Sites Archaeology in the Study of Early American History" in *The Reinterpretation of Early American History* (San Marino: The Huntington Library, 1966) I drew attention to the Awatovi report as a singularly felicitous example of the blending of archaeology and history. While J. O. Brew became a Fellow of the American Academy of Arts and Sciences in 1952 on the basis of his archaeological accomplishment, it should be noted that he has also been elected to the limited, semihonorary ranks of three learned bodies in Massachusetts that are chiefly the stamping ground of historians—the Colonial Society of Massachusetts (1949), the Massachusetts Historical Society (1959), the American Antiquarian Society (1965)—and that in all three he has proved a very welcome and stimulating colleague. In 1967 he was a valued working member of a committee of the National Trust for Historic Preservation, (of which I was chairman) that, at the instigation of the Ford Foundation, was considering means of improving the professional training of architects and craftsmen currently needed for work in historic preservation. Since its creation in October 1967, he has been a member of the National Trust's Standing Committee of Professional Consultants.

Mrs. Lambert has pointed out the breadth of J. O. Brew's interests in the field of anthropology, and Dr. Haury has remarked on the consummate skill with which he can inspire previously indifferent government officials with an enthusiasm for archaeology. These are natural enough aspects of a man who combines a taste for good food, wine, company, and conversation with the highest standards of detailed and accurate learning, who can organize and administer complex projects without losing an incurably humorous detachment, who has an eye for landscape, an ear for words, and an inquiring interest in and sympathy for all kinds of people. So he has been a valued syndic of the Harvard University Press, president of the Harvard Faculty Club from 1951 to 1955, and for fifteen years an Associate of Lowell House, frequently present at gatherings of the Senior Common Room. So too he became a member of the Club of Odd Volumes in Boston in 1953 and, since 1965, has been its genial and much-loved president.

Some men when they retire from administrative posts do not know what to do with themselves. That will not be the case with J. O. Brew. His many friends throughout the world hope that as Peabody Professor of American Archaeology and Ethnology he will again have the leisure to return to writing books in which he will share with them his broad knowledge and wisdom. He has an uncommonly good literary style, which is more than can be said for many eminent scholars in the United States.

CHAPTER XVIII

Samuel Eliot Morison

IN THE SPRING OF 1964 an elderly Cambridge lady rushed into Leavitt and Peirce's tobacconist shop in Cambridge in a state of extreme agitation. Calling for a chair to collapse in, she moaned: "I didn't know he was dead." The cause of her distress was an exhibition in the left-hand display window of some of the works of Samuel Eliot Morison, with a selection of the numerous honors bestowed upon him. Had the lady not given way to grief before reading the broadside that I had composed, at Richard Ehrlich's request, to explain the exhibition, she would have seen that the subject was still very much with us. It stated:

SAMUEL ELIOT MORISON

JONATHAN TRUMBULL PROFESSOR OF AMERICAN
HISTORY, EMERITUS · REAR ADMIRAL, UNITED STATES
NAVAL RESERVE, RETIRED · STILL A MOST ACTIVE
HISTORIAN AND SAILOR

FEW BOSTONIANS live today in the house where they were born seventy-six years ago, or have sailed so far between then and now. Few men anywhere have advanced from private of infantry to rear admiral in the service of their country, and even fewer professors of history have reached the latter rank from civilian life. One Boy's Boston carries Samuel Eliot Morison's autobiography only from 1887 to 1901, yet the tastes and enthusiasms of his last sixty-three years can be deduced from the formidable list of his other writings. In his twenties he transformed the papers of his Federalist ancestor, Harrison Gray Otis, into a brilliant biography. His passion for the sea, first revealed in The Maritime History of Massachusetts, *led him to become the biographer of Christopher Columbus and the Historian of United States Naval Operations in World War II. His devotion to Harvard, where he taught for forty years, with time out only for two wars, an Oxford interlude, and cruising in the wake of Columbus, caused him to become its Tercentenary Historian. Three years as Harold Vyvyan Harmsworth Professor of American History in the University of Oxford in the Twenties inspired the* Oxford History of the United States, *the most readable work of its kind yet written. He deals with equal mastery with William Bradford, John Paul Jones, and Francis Parkman; with Portuguese voyages in the fifteenth century, Boston Puritans in the seventeenth, Plymouth ropemakers in the nineteenth, and naval strategy in the twentieth, in a literary style that is unrivaled. It is small wonder that the Balzan Foundation, when it wished to award in history something comparable in distinction to a Nobel Prize in the sciences, chose from the entire world Samuel Eliot Morison as the first recipient.*

   The following year Thomas N. Bethell, then managing editor of Boston, *the monthly magazine published by the Greater Boston Chamber of Commerce, asked me to write a profile of Sam Morison for them. Chambers of commerce so seldom think of great historians as municipal assets, to be considered on equal terms with electronic plants and banks, that I promptly complied with Tom Bethell's request. Thus "Portrait of the Admiral as a Renaissance Man"—the title was* not *mine—appeared in the September 1965 issue of* Boston (LVII, 9, 18–24, 52–58). *Having been published three years ago, it is, of course, now incomplete, for the subject, although retired from the Harvard faculty and the Navy, actively continues the writing of history.* "Old Bruin": Commodore Matthew C. Perry 1794–1858 *appeared in 1967. A revision of the 1913* Life and Letters of Harrison Gray Otis, *which in the process turned into practically a new book, is now in press. Like Rudolph Ruzicka, Samuel Eliot Morison never flags or slackens. They are a difficult pair to keep up with.*

The photograph shows Rear Admiral and Mrs. Morison with Capitaine de Vaisseau Rostand, chief of the Service Historique de la Marine, during a visit to the landing beaches of France in the summer of 1955 while he was completing the final draft of the eighth volume of his series on World War II naval operations.

W HEN in July 1965 various acquaintances remarked on a life of Admiral Morison that I was said to be writing, this was news to me. I puzzled over it until someone sent me a clipping that explained the confusion. In the spring of 1964 the tobacconists Leavitt and Peirce in Cambridge, who have a fondness for Harvard history, wished to devote one of their windows to a display of Samuel Eliot Morison's numerous and remarkable writings. For this purpose I prepared a broadside describing his *curriculum vitae*. A year later Houghton Mifflin Company asked permission to reprint this on the dust jacket of Admiral Morison's latest book, *Spring Tides*. During the Fourth of July weekend a Boston newspaper in a note about this book said "Walter Muir Whitehill, writing about another historian, Samuel Eliot Morison, is just one of the many delights that await not only Adm. Morison's legion of friends and admirers but all those who love the sea." Then, in the flurry of going to press, somebody who had not read beyond that sentence, and knew nothing of the nature of *Spring Tides*, supplied a photograph of the author and his wife with the caption: "Adm. Morison and his wife are the subject of Walter Muir Whitehill's *Spring Tides*," affixed a headline: "Boston Awaits Book About Adm. Morison," and I had inadvertently become the author.

I wish books were as easily written as that! I have known Samuel Eliot Morison long enough to bear competent witness that he writes his own books, and does so laboriously by hand. He has always done the greater part of his own digging. Even massive undertakings like the fifteen-volume *History of United States Naval Operations in World War II* he has accomplished with a smaller staff than one would think possible; whatever facts his assistants dredged up for him were transmuted into ideas and prose that were pure and unmistakable Morison.

As I pointed out in the Leavitt and Peirce broadside, few Bostonians live today in the house where they were born, or have sailed so far between then and now. Number 44 Brimmer Street, a four-story red brick house at the corner of Mount Vernon Street, looks from the outside much as it did on 9 July 1887, when Samuel Eliot Morison was born there, or in the previous decade when his grandfather built it. Although the interior has been titivated at various times, it has never lost the character of a comfortable, high-studded Boston house of the years immediately following the Civil War, filled with books and with portraits and furniture inherited from two or three earlier generations. Indeed, the photographs of grandfather and grandson, the builder and the present occupant of 44 Brimmer Street, taken in the second-floor library sixty-four years apart, show startling similarities not only in furnishings but in the physical appearance of the men themselves.

One Boy's Boston 1887–1901, published in 1962, recalls the memories and impressions of Samuel Eliot Morison's first fourteen years, beginning with an unforgettable scene.

> One autumn day in 1887, Dr. Charles Montraville Green, "with his little round hat and his walking stick and his beard of pubic hair" (as the famous "Ballad of Chambers Street" describes him), was walking along Brimmer Street, at the foot of Beacon Hill in Boston. As he approached No. 44, his astonished gaze beheld a baby carriage, unattended, bouncing down the stone steps. Upon

hitting the sidewalk it pitchpoled, hurling the contents—one mattress, one pillow and one baby—into Brimmer Street. By a strange quirk of fate the mattress landed first, with baby on top, and the pillow on top of him. Dr. Green rushed forward, expecting to administer first aid to the howling infant, but found him unhurt, and identified him as Samuel Eliot Morison, whom he had brought into the world at the same house on the previous 9th of July.

What had happened was simply this: nurse Lizzie Doyle, pausing at the top of the steps to gossip with the parlormaid, momentarily released the perambulator's handle. Since no harm ensued, Lizzie was forgiven, and she continued as my nurse long enough to be remembered with deep affection.

The remaining eighty pages of this slim little book are equally lively and instructive, but they stop almost with the turn of the century. The author's biography for the next sixty-four years has to be pieced together from casual remarks in the fifty-some volumes that he has published in approximately the same number of years.

Only from the late 1930's onward can I write from personal knowledge, for in the autumn of 1922, when I entered Harvard College as a freshman, Samuel Eliot Morison had just gone to Oxford as the first Harold Vyvyan Harmsworth Professor of American History. When he returned to Harvard in 1925, I as a senior was too immersed in the Spanish Middle Ages even to think of taking a course in American colonial history. It was only when I had come back from Spain in 1936 and had gone to work at the Peabody Museum of Salem that I came to know him. Since the collections of that ancient museum, established in 1799 by the Salem East India Marine Society, were rich sources of the maritime history of New England, I immediately turned to Sam Morison's writings for guidance in my ignorance. Soon I made his acquaintance. Thus, although we never met in a classroom, I have regarded him for most of the past thirty years as a uniquely valued teacher, friend, and ally.

Both of Samuel Eliot Morison's grandfathers were members of the Harvard class of 1839, although they were of quite different origins and do not seem to have been friends. Samuel Eliot (1821–1898) was the grandson of the Federalist merchant of the same name who in 1810 had established the first professorship of Greek literature at Harvard College. His wife, Emily

Marshall Otis, named for her mother, the greatest Boston beauty of the 1820's and '30's, was the granddaughter of Harrison Gray Otis, Federalist lawyer and statesman. Nathaniel Holmes Morison (1815–1890) hailed from Peterborough, New Hampshire, where his family were farmers, and reached Harvard by his own efforts after working in a woolen mill and a machine shop. Grandfather Eliot was a schoolmaster, and for a time president of Trinity College, Hartford. Grandfather Morison also became a schoolmaster, but in Baltimore, where he was the first provost of the Peabody Institute. Between Otises, Eliots, and Morisons there was an extraordinary brew of geniality and worldliness, asceticism and frugality, inherited wealth and country enterprise, with Harvard College entering the picture in various generations. After John Holmes Morison, Nathaniel's son from Baltimore, had been graduated from Harvard College in the class of 1878, he stayed in Boston to practice law. In 1886, when he married Samuel Eliot's daughter, the young couple were persuaded to live on the third floor of her parents' house at 44 Brimmer Street; hence the incident of Lizzie Doyle and the perambulator which bounced Samuel Eliot Morison at the feet of Dr. Green.

Sam Morison grew up on Brimmer Street, and at appropriate times was sent to Mrs. Shaw's School and to Noble and Greenough's. Each summer the Morisons spent July and August in Northeast Harbor, Maine, where their son acquired what he describes as his "almost passionate love for the sea and Mount Desert Island," as well as staying for a few weeks with the Eliots in their summer home at Beverly Farms. It was at Northeast Harbor that he began his seafaring career, cruising around Mount Desert Island in the summer of 1901 with Samuel Vaughan in the sixteen-foot open North Haven dinghy *Leda*. During that cruise he met, at Bartletts Island, Augustus Peabody Loring (1885–1951), who was to be his valued friend for the next fifty years.

That autumn Sam Morison entered St. Paul's School at Concord, New Hampshire, and in September 1904 Harvard College, with Gus Loring rooming near him. Midway in his undergraduate career his parents took title to Bleakhouse in Peterborough, New Hampshire, a place purchased in 1857 by Nathaniel Holmes Morison, "who was never quite happy—as no Morison has a right to be—beyond the view of Monadnock." Thus he supplemented his early passion for the Mount Desert Island with a love for the hills of southern New Hampshire.

After receiving his Harvard A.B. in 1908, Morison spent a year in Paris at the École des Sciences Politiques before returning to Harvard as a graduate student in history. On 28 May 1910 he married Elizabeth Amory Shaw Greene, who (although of Boston origin) had been born in Paris and had lived there during her girlhood. After spending the summer in a newly built bungalow on Sawyers Cove, Blue Hill Bay, in a remote western corner of Mount Desert Island, far from the amenities of Northeast and Bar harbors, the Morisons settled in Otis Place in Boston. For the next half-dozen years they lived there or in lower Mount Vernon Street, within a stone's throw of 44 Brimmer Street.

Readable history is only written by men who have some strong personal enthusiasm for their subjects. Furthermore, firsthand acquaintance with the scene and people, or their latter-day successors, never does any harm. Thus Morison's first book, a biography of his great-grandfather, Harrison Gray Otis, written because the subject interested him, is many times more readable than the run of doctors' theses. The chief source for the biography was a mass of Otis papers then in the 44 Brimmer Street house, which Morison was encouraged by Professor Albert Bushnell Hart to explore as a thesis subject. He received his Ph.D. in 1912; the book was published the following year by Houghton Mifflin in two volumes.

His second book, which followed in 1921, sprang also from personal enthusiasm. Of the circumstances, he wrote thirty years later in *By Land and By Sea*:

> Fortunately I have been able to combine the profession of historian with my hobby of sailing. From childhood I have sailed the sheltered waters of Mount Desert and ranged the coasts of New England and Nova Scotia in all manner of sailing craft; and from childhood, too, I have been an avid reader of old voyages, naval battles, and every sort of maritime history. A book that particularly delighted me was *The Clipper Ship Era* by Captain Arthur H. Clark, which came out in 1910. I read it, enthralled, when sailing from Northeast Harbor to Marblehead that summer; then and there I determined some day to write the story of the merchant marine of my native state. The opportunity came after World War I, and *The Maritime History of Massachusetts* was the result.

But there were interruptions along the way before the opportunity arrived. In the autumn of 1914 Morison substituted at Berkeley for a University of California history professor on leave. Toward the end of the academic year 1915–1916, which he spent as an underpaid tutor in history at Harvard, Morison was asked by Professor Edward Channing to take over his course in colonial history in the autumn. That summer he and his family—eventually three daughters and one son—moved to Concord in order to bring up the children in the country. After the United States entered World War I, he bacame a private of infantry, with service as disparate as the Depot Brigade at Camp Devens and the American Commission to Negotiate Peace in Paris. Returning to Harvard and Concord in the late summer of 1919, he found little that was congenial in the current state of the world, which was slipping either into high-finance capitalism or into communism, neither of which suited his essentially liberal turn of mind. So he immersed himself in aspects of the Massachusetts past which were sympathetic to his seagoing temperament, and in eleven months from the beginning of research—during half of which he was actively teaching—produced the finished copy of *The Maritime History of Massachusetts*.

The book became a classic almost as soon as it was published in 1921. The Otis biography had been good, sound, readable work, far above average, but the *Maritime History* had a flair, a sweep that, combined with remarkable literary craftsmanship, put it in a class by itself. Moreover, after more than forty years, its contents remain as valid and as useful as the day the book was finished. The fire and enthusiasm with which it had been written gave it a character very different from books worried over intermittently for years, in the manner of dogs gnawing bones. Years later, when Morison told Bernard Berenson that he was about to attempt a one-volume history of the United States, Berenson advised: "Write it in one swoop; then it may have literary value." The *Maritime History* was, indeed, a one-swoop book, which achieved a standard of literary distinction seldom equaled and never surpassed in American historical writing. Too few statesmen speak like Winston Churchill and John F. Kennedy; too few historians write like Samuel Eliot Morison. For readers unfamiliar with the book, it is worth quoting its concluding paragraphs, describing a California clipper ship making port in Boston after a voyage around the world.

A summer day with a sea-turn in the wind. The Grand Banks

fog, rolling in wave after wave, is dissolved by the perfumed breath of New England hayfields into a gentle haze, that turns the State House dome to old gold, films brick walls with a soft patina, and sifts blue shadows among the foliage of the Common elms. Out of the mist in Massachusetts Bay comes riding a clipper ship, with the effortless speed of an albatross. Her proud commander keeps sky-sails and studdingsails set past Boston light. After the long voyage she is in the pink of condition. Paintwork is spotless, decks holy-stoned cream-white, shrouds freshly tarred, ratlines square. Viewed through a powerful glass, her seizings, flemish-eyes, splices, and pointings are the perfection of the old-time art of rig-ging. The chafing-gear has just been removed, leaving spars and shrouds immaculate. The boys touched up her skysail poles with white paint, as she crossed the Bay. Boom-ending her studding-sails and hauling a few points on the wind to shoot the Narrows, between Georges and Gallups and Lovells islands, she pays off again through President Road, and comes booming up the stream, a sight so beautiful that even the lounging soldiers at the Castle, persistent baiters of passing crews, are dumb with wonder and admiration.

Colored pennants on Telegraph Hill have announced her coming to all who know the code. Topliff's News Room breaks into a buzz of conversation, comparing records and guessing at freight money; owners and agents walk briskly down State Street; countingroom clerks hang out of windows to watch her strike skysails and royals; the crimps and hussies of Ann Street fore-gather, to offer Jack a few days' scabrous pleasure before selling him to a new master. By the time the ship has reached the inner har-bor, thousands of critical eyes are watching her every movement, quick to note if in any respect the mate has failed to make sailor-men out of her crew of broken Argonauts, beachcombers, Kanakas, and Lascars.

The "old man" stalks the quarter-deck in top hat and frock coat, with the proper air of detachment; but the first mate is as busy as the devil in a gale of wind. Off India Wharf the ship rounds into the wind with a graceful curve, crew leaping into the rigging to furl topgallant sails as if shot upward by the blast of profanity from the mate's bull-like throat. With backed topsails her way is checked, and the cable rattles out of the chain lockers for the first time since Shanghai. Sails are clewed up. Yards are braced to a perfect parallel, and running gear neatly coiled down. A warp is passed from capstan to stringer, and all hands on the capstan-bars walk her up to the wharf with the closing of a deep-sea voyage:

> O, the times are hard and the wages low,
> *Leave her, Johnny, leave her;*
> I'll pack my bag and go below;
> *It's time for us to leave her.*

In the spring of 1922 Morison went to Oxford as the first holder of the professorship of American history endowed by Lord Rothermere in memory of his son, Harold Vyvyan Harmsworth, who had been killed in the war. There he remained for three years as a member of the senior common room of Christ Church, and there he wrote *The Oxford History of the United States, 1783–1917*, which was published in 1927 after his return to Harvard. In the Twenties American history was regarded as quite extraneous to the Honour School of Modern History at Oxford. This two-volume work was consequently addressed to literate readers who knew a good deal about history in general but nothing to speak of about the United States. Three years later, in collaboration with Henry Steele Commager, he produced a different treatment of the same matter in *The Growth of the American Republic*, designed as a textbook for use in this country. Although the 1927 *Oxford History* remains a special favorite of mine, the textbook too has literary value; that it has gone through five editions in the course of thirty years and has been translated into Italian, German, Spanish, and Portuguese is sufficient evidence of its usefulness.

On returning to Harvard in 1925, Morison was promoted to a professorship of history. Although the family was happily settled in Concord, with fields and horses within easy reach, when 44 Brimmer Street became vacant on the death of his mother the following December they regretfully left Concord and moved into Boston. As Bleakhouse in Peterborough, kept open the year round, was available for spring and fall weekends, frequent visits there, with horses at hand, and summers at the Sawyers Cove bungalow, with boats, reconciled the Morisons to academic years spent in Boston. In 1934, after Bleakhouse had been given to the Society for the Preservation of New England Antiquities, the Morisons built Pleasance in Canton, near the Great Blue Hill, to have a place for country week-ends nearer at hand.

In 1926 Morison was appointed historian for the Three-hundredth Anniversary of Harvard College, which was to be celebrated a decade later. A visit to Toledo on the way home from Oxford, during which he surveyed the remarkable series of portraits of archbishops in the chapter house of the cathedral, led him to wonder where a comparable sequence could be found in North America:

> It suddenly dawned on me that my own alma mater, Harvard College, was about the oldest institution and certainly the oldest corporation in the United States. And as I had recently been steeped in the history of the universities from which Harvard stems —Oxford and Cambridge—why not write the history of my university?

President A. Lawrence Lowell promptly told him to go ahead. On the reasonable theory that the latest period in the history of a country or a university is the most neglected, Morison started with a collaborative volume, *The Development of Harvard University since the Inauguration of President Eliot, 1869–1929*, which appeared in 1930 while he was at work on *The Founding of Harvard College*, published in 1935. As the tercentenary of the Massachusetts Bay Colony obviously preceded the tercentenary of Harvard College, he fitted in *Builders of the Bay Colony* in 1930—biographical portraits of nine men and one woman who "would have led obscure lives but for a dynamic force called puritanism which drove them to start life anew in a wilderness." In 1936, the year of the Harvard Tercentenary, he followed *The Founding of Harvard College* with two volumes on *Harvard in the Seventeenth Century* and the single volume *Three Centuries of Harvard, 1636–1936*, designed for the reader who required less profusion of detail. *The Puritan Pronaos: Studies in the Intellectual Life of New England in the Seventeenth Century*, delivered as the Stokes Lectures at New York University in 1934 and published two years later, were closely associated in mood with *Builders of the Bay Colony* and the Harvard history.

In some hands the Harvard history might have been a pedestrian and bureaucratic effort, hardly more interesting than a telephone directory. In Morison's it was very different, for as he saw it, it opened an opportunity to study the history of ideas as expressed through academic institutions. It carried me back to medieval universities, Paris, Bologna, Oxford and Cambridge, and to the Netherlands universities, which the founders of Harvard imitated so far as their slender means would permit. It gave me an opportunity to study the lives and the ideas of English Puritans who founded New England and Harvard.

But before the volume on the eighteenth century was undertaken, the sea called him back, for fifteen years had passed since the publication of *The Maritime History of Massachusetts*.

Nine years ago I sat near Sam Morison in Trinity Church, Boston, during the consecration of Bishop Stokes. During a lull in the proceedings, he whispered to me that his family's pew had been near where we were sitting and that as a boy he liked to imagine that a stained-glass window of the Last Supper that one could see only indistinctly from this spot had depicted not Our Lord and his disciples but Columbus and the egg! With so precocious an enthusiasm for Christopher Columbus, it is not surprising that Morison wished to write his biography. Moreover, as he embraced the theory of his model, Francis Parkman, that the historian should visit the scene of the actions that he describes, such a project would provide an unassailable excuse for going to sea.

In 1916, when preparing to take over Edward Channing's History 10, Morison had become fascinated with the vast literature on the discovery of America and had vowed that some day he would sail at least to the West Indies to examine Columbus's landfalls and coastlines, for that seemed "the only way to find what kind of seaman and navigator he was; or, indeed, exactly where he sailed." Twenty years later, with the Harvard Tercentenary over, he "decided that it was now or never," took leave from Harvard, chartered a yawl, and sailed to the Windward and Leeward islands with a party of friends that included the sea-born Lincoln Colcord, whom he always referred to as the "Sage of Searsport." This brief excursion, combined with further documentary investigation in Lisbon, Paris, and London, convinced Morison that he must undertake a definitive biography of his hero as a seaman, explorer, and navigator. Thus armed with proof "that Parkman's outdoor methods could profitably be applied at sea," the Harvard Columbus Expedition was organized. Morison, Paul Hammond, and other friends purchased and fitted out the barkentine *Capitana* to cross the ocean in Columbus's wake and view islands and coasts as he had seen them. William D. Stevens provided his ketch *Mary Otis* as the *Nina* of the expedition. Sailing in August 1939, into what soon became a war zone, the expedition visited the Azores, Lisbon, Huelva, Cadiz, Madeira, before returning along the route of Columbus's third voyage from Gomera in the Canary Islands to Trinidad in the West Indies, with detailed reconnaissance in the Caribbean following. In the summer of 1940 further exploration through the Bahamas and around Cuba was carried out in *Mary Otis*.

As preliminary studies for his larger work, Morison published two small books, *The Second Voyage of Columbus* (1939) and *Portuguese Voyages to America in the Fifteenth Century*. The biography that was the motive of the expedition, *Admiral of the Ocean Sea, A Life of Christopher Columbus*, appeared in 1942 in two forms: in two volumes with full notes and documentation, and in a condensed single volume that was widely distributed by the Book of the Month Club. The way was now clear for another seagoing project that was to become the most extensive and difficult of any in Morison's career—the *History of United States Naval Operations in World War II*. President Franklin D. Roosevelt, who had a lifelong taste for naval history, after reading some of *Admiral of the Ocean Sea*, accepted Morison's proposal to be the Navy's historian, based on actual participation. Thus in May 1942 the professor was commissioned a lieutenant commander in the Naval Reserve and given a set of orders which permitted him to move about the world at will. But having such a set of orders is one thing, and getting to a good vantage point to observe an action whose planning has been cloaked in deep secrecy is another. That he was invariably in the right place at the right time for the next three and a half years was due more to his qualities as a man and a sailor than to his formal credentials. He recently recalled the problem thus:

> As my position in the Navy was unprecedented, I had to move warily and gingerly in order to obtain co-operation from those who were doing the fighting. Amusingly enough, their initial suspicions of a "long-haired professor in uniform" were dissolved by perusal of my *Admiral of the Ocean Sea*, which told them that I was a sailor before I became a professor, and thus exorcised the academic curse. So, thanks to Columbus, the Navy accepted me;

and with many of its members I made warm friendships, which even survived what I felt obliged to write about some of their mistakes.

From November 1942 until July 1946 I was on duty in the Office of Naval Records and Library at the Navy Department, attempting to arrange and salt down records of current operations for future professional and historical use. Thus at various periods during the war I saw a good deal of Sam Morison between operations. As he worked for the Secretary of the Navy and I for the Commander in Chief, United States Fleet and Chief of Naval Operations, it would have been necessary for us to send memoranda up and down through extended and exalted channels had we desired to communicate with each other officially through the standard forms of Navy correspondence. But that did not prevent us from working in our shirtsleeves in opposite corners of an overcrowded room, whenever he was in Washington, in terms of informal scholarly harmony. Shortly after I reported for duty, he returned from the invasion of North Africa, but he was soon off to the Pacific to see the last phases of the Guadalcanal campaign; and so it went, until the surrender of Japan. He would return with firsthand observations and memoranda, filling longhand notebooks; plunge into any official reports that had reached Washington, and begin a first draft of a chapter. All too soon, an oblique word would reach him that Admiral Ainsworth, or some other friend, would be glad to see him if he turned up at Pearl Harbor at such and such a moment, and off he would go, soon to find himself on the bridge of a flagship in action.

As the war progressed, and amphibious operations multiplied in size and complexity, one often wondered how even Sam Morison could ever filter these events through his mind and reduce them to ordered volumes. And when the war was over, there remained the equally portentous task of discovering and digesting the naval records of the enemy side, with the additional barrier of the Japanese language. Yet between 1947 and 1962 he completed the history in fifteen volumes, publishing in addition in 1963 a single volume, *The Two-Ocean War, A Short History of the United States Navy in the Second World War*, that, far from being a scissors-and-paste condensation, is an original work that could be read with fascination and delight even by those already familiar with the fifteen volumes that had preceded it. Few other men, if any, could have done it. That one individual could produce a work of this quality is owing to his long experience in reducing complex sources to order, unremitting industry, and a lifelong concern for niceties of literary style.

On 19 November 1947 he and I took the morning train from Boston to Rockland, Maine, to attend the funeral of our friend Lincoln Colcord. The sun was low over Penobscot Bay as we drove up to the church in Searsport for the late afternoon service. Yet after a brief visit with Link's family, and the consumption of a piece of pie in the kitchen, Morison entered a waiting cab that drove him to the Bangor airport where he took a plane to Boston, so as to spend the last hours of the evening in the library of 44 Brimmer Street working on the naval history. I, who was eighteen years younger, happily spent the night in Searsport and returned only the next day. But I had that day the clue as to how he often accomplished the seemingly impossible. At this moment, work was a salvation, for the sudden death of his beloved wife, Elizabeth Greene Morison, in 1945— a year before he returned to Harvard from the Navy—had left him alone in 44 Brimmer Street. Four years later, on 29 December 1949—he married in Baltimore the beautiful singer, Priscilla Barton, who has proved, as the dedications of his later books attest, the ideal companion of his work and play. For a time many of his Boston friends feared that the newlyweds might be tempted to live in a pleasant house of Priscilla's near Baltimore, but after nearly sixteen years of married life they are still wintering in 44 Brimmer Street. The chief change in the pattern consisted of turning over to the children Pleasance and the Sawyers Cove bungalow, and building on the wooded headland at the eastern entrance to Northeast Harbor a new house, called Good Hope, convenient and accessible, and adapted for longer stays in Maine. Here Priscilla Morison's genius for horticulture has enhanced the natural beauty of the evergreen forest by creating intimate terraces and bosques on a variety of levels where flowering beds, in which delphinium reflect the blue of the sea, enliven the green of the woods. But her talents are by no means confined to music or to horticulture. Priscilla Morison constantly helps her husband, not only "running interference" (or as he prefers to call it, "repelling boarders") socially, but listening as he reads his manuscripts aloud and helping him to find the correct phrase and *le mot juste*.

Samuel Eliot Morison taught at Harvard for forty years—with time out only for two wars and the Harmsworth professorship at Oxford—until his retirement in 1955 as Jonathan Trumbull Professor of American History,

Emeritus. In the United States Naval Reserve he progressed on active duty from lieutenant commander to captain, retiring, on reaching the age limit in 1951, with the rank of rear admiral. But formal retirement either from history or the Navy was only a technicality, for he worked even harder for both afterward. Although he resumed teaching at Harvard soon after the war, he maintained offices at the Navy Department and the Naval War College in Newport, where staffs so small as to contradict Parkinson's Law assisted him in organizing enemy documents and other tasks essential for the completion of the naval history. The fifteen volumes of that work, published in as many years, were by no means his sole occupation.

The variety of other books that appeared between volumes of the naval history has been extraordinary. Like the winetaster who can move from glass to glass without confusing or muddling bouquets, Morison enjoys varying the taste of ideas. He once remarked that he liked to keep a major work and a minor one going at the same time. While the naval history was in progress a dozen "minor" works appeared. *The Ropemakers of Plymouth*, a history of the Plymouth Cordage Company, which had since 1824 been an enterprise of the family of his boyhood friend Augustus P. Loring, appeared in 1950, followed by a new edition of William Bradford's *Of Plymouth Plantation* in 1952, and *The Story of the "Old Colony" of New Plymouth, 1620–1692* in 1956. For a volume of collected essays and addresses that Alfred A. Knopf issued in 1953 under the title *By Land and By Sea*, Morison wrote introductory headnotes that agreeably enhance the book's quality. *The Story of Mount Desert Island, Maine* and *One Boy's Boston* similarly drew upon his own past, but *Freedom in Contemporary Society* (translated into Portuguese and Korean) and *Strategy and Compromise* deal with global matters. *The Parkman Reader* (1955) and a Limited Editions Club edition of Prescott's *History of the Conquest of Peru* (1957) were editorial efforts to bring the writings of two of his historical heroes to a wide modern audience, while *John Paul Jones: A Sailor's Biography* (1955) gave him an opportunity to change the taste of World War II by a deep draught of the American Revolution. Nor was Columbus forgotten, for in 1955 he wrote a wholly new book, *Christopher Columbus, Mariner*, "in the hope of reaching a wider public." The success of that hope is indicated by translations into Japanese, Italian, Dutch, Hungarian, Polish, Russian, Persian, Arabic, and Marathi. Furthermore, in 1963 he edited *Journals and Other Documents on the Life and Voyages of Christopher Columbus*, a long-projected documentary companion to *Admiral of the Ocean Sea* that had been delayed by the war.

It is therefore small wonder, as I suggested in concluding the Leavitt and Peirce broadside, that the Balzan Foundation, when it wished to award in history something comparable in distinction to a Nobel Prize in the sciences, chose from the entire world Samuel Eliot Morison as the first recipient. As the late Pope John XXIII was to receive a Balzan peace prize, the presentation ceremonies were held in Rome in May 1963 under circumstances of great splendor. *Vistas of History*, published in 1964, contains an account of the occasion, as well as the address "The Experiences and Principles of an Historian" that Admiral Morison gave after receiving the award. This address, taken with "History as a Literary Art"—which he originally allowed me to publish in 1946 as an Old South Leaflet but is reprinted in *By Land and By Sea*—gives the essence of his approach to the writing of history.

The story does not stop with the Balzan Prize, for in 1964 Admiral Morison received the Medal of Freedom, the highest civilian award that the President of the United States can bestow, which helps keep in balance the Legion of Merit received from the Navy, and honorary doctorates from Harvard, Yale, Oxford, Trinity, Amherst, Union, Bucknell, Notre Dame, Holy Cross, and Boston College. There is a nice ecumenical quality in a Harvard professor's being honored by Yale, and a devout Episcopalian— long a parishioner of the Church of the Advent, across Mount Vernon Street from his house—receiving degrees from three Catholic institutions.

The next twelve months saw the publication of three very different books. *The Caribbean As Columbus Saw It*, written in collaboration with his Colombian friend, Mauricio Obregón, illustrates Columbus's landfalls as observed from the cockpit of Obregón's Cessna 310 airplane. *Spring Tides* is a prose-poem on the sea that evokes cruising both in Maine waters and the Aegean, while the *Oxford History of the American People* is an 1150-page retelling of the subject from the origin of man in America to the death of John Fitzgerald Kennedy.

This third history of the United States which Morison has written in the past forty years is a wholly new work. It is "in a sense," as he states in his preface. "a legacy to my countrymen after teaching and writing the history of the United States for over half a century." It is a huge single volume, heavy to hold in the hand, but far from heavy in its approach. As it is designed for popular reading, it eschews the scholarly apparatus of footnotes and references. "Readers may take a certain amount of erudition for granted," he notes. Through the literary artistry of which Morison is a master, this distillation of a lifetime of thought and research has become a series of vivid characterizations that can be read with delight, and will long stick in the mind of the reader. The American people are indeed reading it, for *The New York Times* of 25 July 1965 notes that after eleven weeks on the best-seller list, 60,000 copies (out of an initial printing of 122,000) have already been sold, in addition to a quarter of a million distributed by the Book of the Month Club.

What now? Most men would rest on their oars, but not SEM. He and Mauricio Obregón are thinking of flying around the Mediterranean, following in the wake of Ulysses. He is already deep in research for a biography of Commodore Matthew C. Perry and will in 1966 go to Japan in his footsteps. This at seventy-eight is New England seafaring vigor at its best.

Ovid would have enjoyed describing the metamorphoses of Samuel Eliot Morison. What other man ever has been, or is likely to be, a professor both at Oxford and Harvard, a private of infantry and a rear admiral? Like Proteus, another "Old One of the Sea," who was the source of much indispensable information to mariners, his aspect changes frequently, with disconcerting rapidity. I remember him resplendent in academic costume or blue naval uniform, as well as in oilskins at the wheel of the *Emily Marshall*. I recall his enjoying a clam chowder at Mount Desert made by the late Enos Verge of Thomaston, picnicking on Gus Loring's beach at Prides Crossing, carving with easy grace a roast suckling pig at a council lunch of the Colonial Society of Massachusetts, against the background of an Empire gold mirror, presiding at his own table in Brimmer Street, or leaving 20 Louisburg Square at midnight, after one of Sohier Welch's great dinners, wearing an opera hat and cape that gave him the aspect of the *noctambule* in *Louise*. I see him perhaps most often on a midday route between 44 Brimmer Street, the Somerset Club, and the Boston Athenæum, dressed with the restrained elegance of a conservative householder, but I recall occasions when clams were being dug at Sawyers Cove, when we were at Searsport, sitting on Lincoln Colcord's back porch, looking out on Penobscot Bay, or exchanging pleasantries with Waldo Peirce—*W. Peirsius Barbatus*, as he recently described that painter to me on an illegible postcard. I think of him presiding over the meetings of the American Antiquarian Society at Worcester, enlivening those of the Massachusetts Historical Society, and striding purposefully into Widener Library in well-cut riding costume, carrying green baize bags full of books. In all his manifestations there is the underlying basis of style and quality, whether in wine, food, company, conversation, or the writing of history. There is also limitless energy, and certainly in my friendship with him a great deal of human kindness. Like many New Englanders, he can have moments of shyness, which may lead to an occasional awkward remark, or none at all, but that is part of the breed. And at other times he can speak as he writes, mingling the periods of an Edward Gibbon or a Winston Churchill with the pithy homeliness of a New England general store.

Two quotations from the ancients, prefixed to books of Morison's, do much to explain the character and quality of his writing. At the beginning of *Operations in North African Waters*, the first of the naval history to be published, was set this extract from Thucydides:

> Of the events of the war, I have not ventured to speak from any chance information, nor according to any notion of my own; I have described nothing but what I either saw myself, or learned from others of whom I made the most careful and particular inquiry. The task was a laborious one because eyewitnesses of the same occurrence gave different accounts of them as they remembered, or were interested in the actions of one side or the other. And very likely the strictly historical character of my narrative may be disappointing to the ear. But if he who desires to have before his eyes a true picture of the events which have happened, and of the like events which may be expected to happen hereafter in the order of human beings, shall pronounce what I have written to be useful, then I shall be satisfied.

And some years earlier appeared on the title page of *Builders of the Bay Colony* this significant "tag" of Horace:

Quamquam ridentem dicere verum
quid vetat?

Samuel Eliot Morison

Why, indeed, may one not be telling the truth while one laughs? Samuel Eliot Morison combines, with diligence for the truth, a lively sense of humor. Our good friend and former neighbor, Bishop Wright of Pittsburgh, not long ago commented on "the deadly earnestness surrounding the discussion of the current problem of the intellectual life of America" and feared that this earnestness "suggests that knowledge and information may be on the increase and wisdom and understanding on the way out." He asked: "What has become of the humanistic touch that used to betray a humane preoccupation and that revealed itself in an occasional trace of a sense of humor?" It is this humanistic touch, revealed in more than occasional traces of wit and humor, that makes Morison's fifty volumes so uniquely delightful.

In appraising the work of his great predecessor, Francis Parkman, Morison recently wrote:

> His unusual combination of superlative skill in the three qualities that make good historical literature—research, evaluation, and literary presentation—besides the fascination of his chosen field, have caused the works of Parkman to endure longer than those of any other American historian of his era . . . Parkman's work is forever young, "with the immortal youth of art"; his men and women are alive; they feel, think, and act within the framework of a living nature. Documents are, to be sure, the basis of his History; but to him documents were not facts; rather, the symbols of events, which the historian must re-create for his readers. In Parkman's prose the forests ever murmur; the rapids perpetually foam and roar; the people have parts and passions. Like that "sylvan historian" of Keats's "Ode on a Grecian Urn," he caught the spirit of an age and fixed it for all time, "for ever panting and for ever young."

And so, in Morison's prose the California clipper still comes into India Wharf, long after the ships and the wharf itself have disappeared. Normally one takes stock of the memories of one's friends when writing obituaries. In this instance I am glad that the shoes of Francis Parkman are still filled by Samuel Eliot Morison, and that, guided by Thucydides and Horace, he is still going to cover a lot of territory in them.

This book has been designed
by R. L. Dothard Associates and printed
by The Lane Press in Burlington, Vermont.
It is set in Monotype Janson and printed
from the type on Ticonderoga Text paper.
The illustrations have been struck in
by offset lithography. It has been bound
in Bancroft's Linen Finish cloth at The
Book Press in Brattleboro, Vermont.